"IS TWO OVER ONE RAILROAD FARE?" 16TH AND DOCK—RICHMOND, VA.

MORE
CLASSIC AMERICAN RAILROADS

MIKE SCHAFER

MBI Publishing Company

KANSAS CITY SOUTHERN RAILWAY
LOUISIANA & ARKANSAS RAILWAY

KCS Lines L&A

KCS Lines L&A

The ALTON GM&O Route

CHICAGO

KANSAS CITY

SPRINGFIELD

THE DIRECT ROUTE
Between the Midwest
and Gulf Ports

ST. LOUIS

JACKSON, Tenn.

JACKSON, Miss.

MERIDIAN

MONTGOMERY

MOBILE

NEW ORLEANS

OCTOBER 1948

Gulf, Mobile & Ohio
RAILROAD
The Alton Route

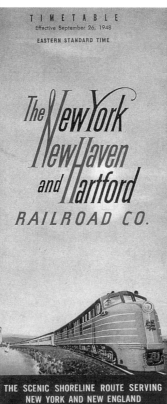

TIMETABLE
Effective September 26, 1948
EASTERN STANDARD TIME

The New York
New Haven
and Hartford
RAILROAD CO.

THE SCENIC SHORELINE ROUTE SERVING
NEW YORK AND NEW ENGLAND

SOUTHERN
RAILWAY SYSTEM

THE SOUTHERN SERVES THE SOUTH
SR

PASSENGER TRAIN SCHEDULES

APRIL 29, 1962

CHESAPEAKE
AND OHIO
RAILWAY

Passenger Schedules
ALONG THE CHESSIE ROUTE

Issued
April 28, 1957

4013

NICKEL PLATE ROAD

PASSENGER
SCHEDULES

FEBRU

B W BO

Acknowledgments

This book really has several authors—not just me—and I would like to introduce them. For a couple, this is their first crack at book writing; I think all of them did a splendid job.

First of all I am indebted to Kevin EuDaly of White River Productions. Kevin authored three chapters in this book: Chesapeake & Ohio, Kansas City Southern, and—Kevin's personal favorite—Missouri Pacific.

Next in line I would like to thank longtime (more than 35 years!) friend Jim Boyd, former editor of *Railfan & Railroad* magazine, for his authorship of the Bangor & Aroostook and Wabash chapters. Several other folks helped by authoring a number of the other chapters, and I am indebted to their promptness, thoroughness, and expertise on the various subjects they chose to tackle. Will the following please stand up and take a bow for their authorship of the chapters so noted: Tracy N. Antz (Lehigh Valley); Ed De Rouin (Chicago Great Western); Ron Flanary (Southern Railway); Kevin Holland (New York, Chicago & St. Louis); John Phillips (Northern Pacific); and Sean Zwagerman (Western Pacific). Also, a thanks to Scott Hartley for his "New Haven Survives" sidebar in the New York, New Haven & Hartford chapter.

I also called upon the help of several other people regarding some of the factual proofreading respective to their specialty railroads. So, more applause is in order for: Warren Calloway, for his assistance with the Seaboard Air Line chapter; Scott "Mr. New Haven Railroad" Hartley for untangling the rather convoluted history of the NYNH&H; my former junior high English instructor and fellow Chicago Great Western afficionado, Chet Hollister; and Jim Shaughnessy—a name and person forever closely associated with Delaware & Hudson (and who has written a wonderful book on same).

Garnering photos is perhaps one of the most challenging aspects of preparing a book of such historical nature. I've been taking railroad photos religiously since the early 1960s, but I've hardly covered every railroad during the ensuing decades and must rely on the work of many colleagues. Locating photos depicting the American railroad scene is particularly tricky prior to the 1970s, before interest in railroading and railroad photography suddenly seemed to explode. Although it's pretty easy these days to obtain great photos of new General Electric diesels on Burlington Northern Santa Fe's busy Chicago–Twin Cities main line, locating a shot of a Bangor & Aroostook passenger train that was discontinued in the 1950s is quite another matter (and, thank you Jerry Angier for helping with *that*). In any event, many people came through with some truly wonderful illustrative material for *More Classic American Railroads*, and I am particularly indebted to Jim Boyd, Jim Shaughnessy, Kevin and James EuDaly, Dave Ingles, and Kevin Holland as well as the many other photographers noted in the caption credits. I would also like to thank Carstens Publications of Newton, New Jersey, for the loan of selected early black & white material from their *Railfan & Railroad* collection. Readers of this book who wish to expand their knowledge of American railroading are urged to check out Carsten's *Railfan & Railroad* magazine.

And in closing, I'd be remiss not to thank several other folks for their assistance in this book's preparation in one way or another: Anthony and Lynne Miranda of Rochelle (Illinois) Railroad Park; Mike Blaszak; Jim Popson, Andover Junction Publications' Macintosh expert and scanning technician; Andover's Steve Esposito and Tanya Anderson; and Keith Mathiowetz and Zack Miller at MBI Publishing.

—*Mike Schafer*

First published in 2000 by MBI Publishing, 729 Prospect Avenue, PO Box 1, Osceola, WI 54020 USA

© Andover Junction Publications, 2000

Book design and layout by Mike Schafer, Andover Junction Publications, Lee, Illinois, and Blairstown, New Jersey.

Cover design by Tom Heffron

Map reproduction by permission of *The Official Railway Guide* and Primedia Information, Inc.

MBI Publishing books are also available at discounts in bulk quantity for industrial or sales-promotional use. For details, write to Special Sales Manager at Motorbooks International Wholesalers & Distributors, PO Box 1, Osceola, WI 54020-0001 USA.

Library of Congress Cataloging-in-Publication data available

ISBN 0-7603-0758-X

On the front cover: Linking the North and South, maverick carrier Gulf, Mobile & Ohio shows off its new Electro-Motive SD-series diesels running on Chicago-Bloomington, Illinois, train No. 97 at Odell, Illinois, in 1972. *Doug Steurer*

On the frontispiece: Three of the classic railroads featured in this book—Chesapeake & Ohio, Seaboard Air Line, and Southern Railway—pose for a postcard view of the famous triple overpass in Richmond, Virginia, during the early twentieth century. C&O trains rode the highest level of the famous railroad landmark, which still stands, and under C&O the Seaboard's main line cut south from Main Street Station while Southern occupied the ground-level trackage. *Mike Schafer collection*

On the title page: At famed Starrucca Viaduct—an architectural legacy of the Erie Railroad in northeastern Pennsylvania—an eastbound Erie Lackawanna freight soars high above the valley of Starrucca Creek as a Delaware & Hudson freight out of Canada rolls southward for Wilkes-Barre, Pennsylvania. The date is May 13, 1972, and Erie successor Erie Lackawanna is a dozen years old, but venerable D&H is nearly halfway through its *second* century of service. *Jim Shaughnessy*

On the back cover, top: A set of Western Pacific Electro-Motive F-unit diesels stand ready at Salt Lake City to take the westbound *California Zephyr* into the Utah night in July 1969. *Mike Schafer*

On the back cover, lower: Chesapeake & Ohio's steam era came back to life when it hosted a restored C&O 4-8-4 Northern, No. 614, on its Cincinnati–Washington main line at Thurmond, West Virginia, in the fall of 1981. Shortly thereafter, C&O disappeared into the growing CSX Transportation system, and America lost another classic railroad. *Jim Boyd*

End Paper: Jim Shaughnessy

Printed in Hong Kong

Contents

Kansas City Southern was one of only three railroads in this volume that was still in existence when this book was being prepared. In a gesture to the railroad's rich heritage, KCS management assembled a business train that was pulled by historical Electro-Motive F-type diesels, and the whole train was painted in the railroad's eye-catching passenger-train livery of black, yellow, and red, popularized on the railroad's *Southern Belle* streamliner. The business train is shown near Kansas City on a shake-down run in April 1996. *Dan Munson*

Foreword

A great philosopher once said, "May you live long enough to see your ordinary, everyday stuff turn into timeless classics." (Actually, I said that during a pizza session after a railroad club slide show in New Jersey.) Plowing through my slide collection for this book certainly reinforced that feeling as I began unearthing images of departed locomotives and railroad names and liveries that have vanished with sobering finality. It is still hard to consider all of this once-ordinary, everyday stuff as the fodder for another *Classic American Railroads* book.

I suspect that author Mike Schafer feels the same way. He and I have been friends since he was in high school, and we spent much of the 1960s discovering the wonderful world of railroading together before our respective careers took us in different directions.

Railroading is pure geography mixed with a generous dose of hardware and humanity that all blends into an intense experience in Americana. Mike and I shared much of this. We were together to see not only the railroads of our northern Illinois homeland but to experience the grandeur of the *California Zephyr* in the Feather River Canyon on the Western Pacific and hear our first rich "Down East" accent from a Bangor & Aroostook roundhouse foreman at Northern Maine Junction. We both equate the Wabash with Decatur, Illinois, and its penetrating aroma of the Staley feed mills and have a vivid memory of the New Haven's *Owl* at Bridgeport, Connecticut, in the middle of the night.

We were lucky enough to be born at the right time to be in the right place to observe and photograph this richly colorful era in American railroading. Back then it was everyday stuff that was gathered on weekend trips in a Volkswagen Beetle or cross-country vacations that were paid for by long hours in workaday jobs, but we seem to have lived long enough to have our work put between hard covers bearing the word "classic."

I hope you enjoy the journey as much as we did.

—Jim Boyd
Crandon Lakes, New Jersey

Introduction

It seems like only yesterday I was writing an Introduction for *Classic American Railroads*. Almost four years later, I'm doing it again, only this book is called *More Classic American Railroads*. The emphasis is, of course, on "more."

In that first volume, we selected several of the most well-known of America's multitude of "classic" railroads. However, for every railroad company we chose to feature in that book, we had to leave out at least two others. Furthermore, at that time, the publisher and I weren't even sure there would be a follow-up volume. Well, the response to the first volume was overwhelming. The audience loved it, and they told us so through letters, phone calls, and even face to face. So, here we go again!

As with the first book, choosing which railroads to feature was one of the trickier aspects of the project. About the only thing more agonizing was editing down the hundreds of superb illustrations sent to us by contributors to those you see within. As with the first book, for every railroad we chose, we had to leave out one or two others. (Let's hope for a third volume!) My criteria for selection in this book remains the same:

Longevity: I arbitrarily required a railroad to have existed for at least a half century. It takes time for a railroad to "age" into a classic, you know. Oh, there is an exception. In this volume, you'll find a railroad that existed for only 32 years: the Gulf, Mobile & Ohio. But the "Gee-Mo" was one of those extra-cool railroads that seem to have a disproportionately higher number of devotees relative to its size. The GM&O Historical Society, after all, has nearly a thousand members!

Public recognition: I selected railroads that, at least within the region they served, enjoyed at least a modicum of recognition by the general public.

Accomplishments and charisma: I included railroads that had made notable contributions to the railroad industry. But I also included railroads simply for their charm and charisma, even if they didn't pioneer piggybacking, dieselization, or streamliners.

Location: I wanted every major region of the U.S. represented. This is getting a bit problematic for the West, which historically has had many fewer railroads than, say, the Northeast, but the little Western Pacific puts on a big show in this book.

As with the first book, the histories herein are written to provide an overview and are not meant to be comprehensive. Should one or more of the railroads herein strike a particular fancy with you, you can find out more about that railroad through any number of books written on specific railroads, available at hobby shops, railroadiana shows, or through advertising in magazines such as *Trains* and *Railfan & Railroad*. Not only are the histories of these railroads fascinating in their own right, they'll provide provide a better understanding of existing contemporary companies.

And now, on with the show.

Mike Schafer
Lee, Illinois
March 2000

FACING PAGE: We're at Jacksonville, Illinois, as the fireman on the Wabash Railroad's "west local" snags train orders held up by the operator while the train rolls past the interlocking tower guarding the Wabash-Gulf, Mobile & Ohio crossing. The date is June 19, 1962, and the Wabash Railroad is in twilight. This venerable carrier was among the first modern, post-World War II classic railroads to be merged out of existence. Although the Erie and Delaware, Lackawanna & Western had quietly merged in 1960, the personalities of those two carriers seem to carry on in the resulting new railroad known as Erie Lackawanna. However, when the Wabash was merged along with the Nickel Plate into the Norfolk & Western, its identity was completely wiped out. For the first time, there seemed to be a true sense of loss in terms of a vanished entity. Inspired by Wabash's memorable banner emblem, the term "fallen flag" soon became popularized in reference to classic railroads that were being swallowed up in an intensifying merger mania out of which four major systems emerged from the Wabashes, Nickel Plates, Seaboards, and Eries of yore. Dave Ingles

Bangor & Aroostook

The state of Maine really is as remote and isolated as it appears on a map. The Boston & Maine reached from Boston to Portland in 1844, and there was a link to Bangor with the creation of the Maine Central in 1862, but the state's vast northern regions remained untouched even after the European & North American extended from Bangor to Vanceboro in 1871 on its way to the Canadian seaport of St. John, New Brunswick.

Maine's northernmost county, Aroostook, is bigger than the entire states of Connecticut and Rhode Island combined, and its mountainous terrain is covered with valuable timber. It also has an ideal climate for growing potatoes. Aside from crude wagon roads, the only link to the outside in the 1880s was a narrow-gauge Canadian line from St. John that came down into Houlton and Caribou, Maine. Rail transportation to the lower states required reloading into standard-gauge cars, and the sailing ships from St. John favored markets in Great Britain rather than the U.S. This worked reasonably well for timber, but the perishable potatoes did not travel well via such a slow routing.

In 1889 the Canadian Pacific built a line laterally across Maine as a shortcut between Montreal and St. John, but Aroostook County remained isolated. It was Albert A. Burleigh, a Civil War veteran and Houlton businessman, who successfully put together a plan to finance and construct a railroad into the northernmost regions of Aroostook County.

Under the "Burleigh Scheme," Aroostook County would finance its own railroad, and the new 200-mile Bangor & Aroostook Railroad Company was chartered on February 13, 1891, to build from Brownville northward to Caribou, with branches to Fort Fairfield and Ashland. Further legislation authorized the company to lease the existing Bangor & Piscataquis Railroad and Bangor & Katahdin Iron Works Railway, which reached up from Old Town (just north of Bangor) to Greenville and Brownville. The new railroad was completed from Brownville to Caribou in 1895,

BANGOR and AROOSTOOK *Railroad* *Serving Northern Maine*

MAINE

PASSENGER TRAIN SCHEDULES

Effective April 30, 195

Eastern Daylight Saving Time

with the branch from Oakfield to Ashland finished a year later. Although the logical initials for the Bangor & Aroostook were "B&A," the railroad's reporting marks became "BAR" to avoid confusion with the Boston & Albany.

Ironically, the BAR, which was conceived to avoid the problems of the 3-foot 6-inch narrow-gauge New Brunswick Railway, had at its southern end the Bangor & Piscataquis, which had been built in 1869 to 5-foot 6-inch broad gauge—and that line, in turn, connected with the two-foot-gauge Monson Railroad! However, the B&P had been converted to standard gauge by 1879, well before it was taken over by the BAR, but the diminutive, six-mile-long Monson remained a two-footer for its entire history until it was abandoned in 1943.

With the arrival of the BAR, the timber and potato businesses boomed, and adding to the region's economy was a big new Great Northern Paper Company mill at Millinocket in 1899. In the first decade of the new century, the BAR continued to extend its track to lace together the communities in the northernmost reaches of Aroostook County.

On the south end, however, the BAR had to use the Maine Central (whose initials were MEC so as not to be confused with the Michigan Central) south of Old Town to reach the Penobscot River seaport of Bangor. The BAR would always be dependent on the MEC for rail access to Portland and Boston, but it knew that it needed its own seaport to truly prosper. Great Northern Paper was already planning to expand its operations and needed power plant coal. The BAR knew that having its own seaport would guarantee the business and give the railroad full control of its own rate-making to keep its best customer happy. In December 1904 the Northern Maine Seaport Railroad was incorporated by BAR interests to build south from South Lagrange to Searsport and Cape Jellison, on Penobscot Bay.

The new line crossed the MEC at Hermon, six miles west of Bangor, and there BAR would build its big Northern Maine Junction freight yard and locomotive roundhouse. The railroad's major

FACING PAGE: Yard switchers team up at Oakfield, Maine, to switch up the daily Bangor & Aroostook freight scheduled to head south to Bangor later in the day. *Mike Schafer*

FACING PAGE, INSET: For many years, BAR locomotives, rolling stock, and other selected physical plant wore patriotic colors, as proudly displayed on this water tank at Northern Maine Junction. *Mike Schafer*

LEFT: For a relatively brief time, BAR sported streamlined trains. The *Aroostook Flyer* and the *Potatoland Special* were prominently promoted in this public timetable from 1951. All rail passenger service would be gone from the BAR a decade later.

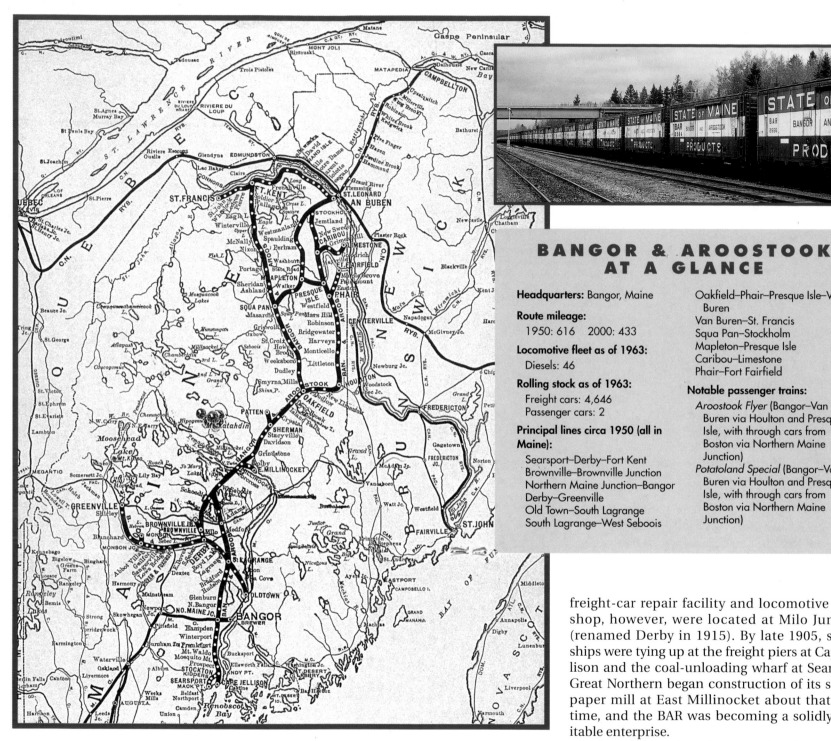

This map from a 1926 public timetable shows the Bangor & Aroostook's reach in its "classic" period. By the 1980s, a number of changes had taken place, perhaps the most notable being the abandonment of significant chunks of the main passenger route, between Houlton and Phair and between Caribou and Van Buren. In the case of the latter, Van Buren became the terminus of a branch out of Fort Kent. In addition, the alternate line between South Lagrange and Schoodic via Adams as well as the whole Greenville branch had been abandoned along with the branches to Oldtown and Cape Jellison. On the other hand, BAR's acquisition by Iron Road Railways in 1995 resulted in an expansion when Iron Road Railways added the former Canadian Pacific trans-Maine line between Brownville Junction and Montreal to the BAR system. *Map courtesy Jerry Angier; inset photo of boxcars, Jim Boyd*

BANGOR & AROOSTOOK AT A GLANCE

Headquarters: Bangor, Maine

Route mileage:
1950: 616   2000: 433

Locomotive fleet as of 1963:
Diesels: 46

Rolling stock as of 1963:
Freight cars: 4,646
Passenger cars: 2

Principal lines circa 1950 (all in Maine):

Searsport–Derby–Fort Kent
Brownville–Brownville Junction
Northern Maine Junction–Bangor
Derby–Greenville
Old Town–South Lagrange
South Lagrange–West Seboois

Oakfield–Phair–Presque Isle–Van Buren
Van Buren–St. Francis
Squa Pan–Stockholm
Mapleton–Presque Isle
Caribou–Limestone
Phair–Fort Fairfield

Notable passenger trains:

Aroostook Flyer (Bangor–Van Buren via Houlton and Presque Isle, with through cars from Boston via Northern Maine Junction)

Potatoland Special (Bangor–Van Buren via Houlton and Presque Isle, with through cars from Boston via Northern Maine Junction)

freight-car repair facility and locomotive back-shop, however, were located at Milo Junction (renamed Derby in 1915). By late 1905, sailing ships were tying up at the freight piers at Cape Jellison and the coal-unloading wharf at Searsport. Great Northern began construction of its second paper mill at East Millinocket about that same time, and the BAR was becoming a solidly profitable enterprise.

The BAR continued to extend and connect its lines, and in 1915 its final physical expansion was a bridge over the St. John River at Van Buren to connect with the National Transcontinental Railway of Canada (later, Canadian National) at St. Leonard, New Brunswick. This opened up a whole new source of year-around timber for the lumber mills. With the completion of the bridge, the BAR was operating 858 miles of railroad between Searsport and the upper tip of Aroostook County.

During World War I, control of the BAR—and most other U.S. roads—was assumed by the federal government under the United States Railroad Administration; BAR control resumed in 1920. On November 8, 1924, a fire destroyed the entire dock facility at Port Jellison, and the BAR decided to move all operations to Searsport, which had better deep-water access. A new merchandise pier was built near the coal-transloading wharf. At the same time, the Fraiser Paper Company began building a large new paper mill at Madawaska, which would keep the railroad and seaport even busier. By the end of 1927, the railroad had earned over $1 million in profits on a gross of more than $6 million.

The Great Depression of the 1930s hit the north country hard, but while the price for potatoes was dropping, the harvest volume was nearly normal, and the coastal ships which were idled elsewhere offered very low rates to move the spuds from Searsport to market in the lower states. A few branch lines were abandoned, and the railroad had to fight a fierce winter storm in December 1933, but the BAR emerged from the Depression in reasonably good shape.

Since the BAR was not even created until the 1890s, its locomotives had always been relatively modern, if generally small. American-type 4-4-0s initially handled passenger service, while freight was in the charge of 2 6-0s and 4-6-0s. Modern freight 2-8-0s came along in 1914 and 1921. The railroad got its first "big" engines with five Alco

light 4-6-2s in 1927 and seven husky 4-8-2s in 1929 and 1930. Three more 4-8-2s followed in 1935, along with five heavy 2-8-0s in 1937.

In the late 1930s the BAR was running morning and evening passenger trains in each direction between Bangor and Aroostook County and covering most of its other lines with passenger locals or mixed trains. On October 15, 1936, the railroad made a bold move to replace much of the local train service with buses and created its "Highway Division," the Bangor & Aroostook Transportation

BAR is no stranger to snow and, like other New England carriers, keeps plows at the ready for howling northern Maine blizzards. In 1981, an Electro-Motive GP7 shoves a wedge plow along near Brownville. *Don Marson*

The southbound *Aroostook Flyer* eases into Derby in 1947. The *Flyer*'s locomotive will pick up the baggage car positioned on the Greenville main to be forwarded to points south. *Howard Moulton, courtesy Jerry Angier*

ABOVE: The Bangor & Aroostook dieselized with locomotives from General Motors' Electro-Motive Division, largely F- and GP-series models. In this 1955 scene at Brownville Junction, an F3, a GP7, and a GP9 head an inbound train about to stop to switch the Canadian Pacific interchange. *Jim Shaughnessy*

TOP RIGHT: The road-freight diesels displaced large steam power such as this white-tired 4-8-2 wheeling a freight through the Maine countryside in the late 1950s. *Railfan & Railroad collection*

RIGHT: The Bangor-bound *Potatoland Special* shows off its new Electro-Motive E7 passenger diesel at Oakfield on July 27, 1950. Like numerous other railroads during the years immediately following World War II, BAR sought to upgrade its passenger services, not realizing the full implications of the automobile boom that would also follow the war. In 1954, the *Potatoland Special* would also receive new, streamlined sleeping cars that would operate through between Van Buren and Boston via the Maine Central at Northern Maine Junction and the Boston & Maine at Portland. *Bruce Owen Nett, courtesy Jerry Angier*

Company. This let the railroad drop the expensive small passenger trains while concentrating on its two remaining mainline runs, the old "Aroostook Accommodation" between Bangor and Fort Kent that carried sleepers up from Boston, and the *Aroostook Flyer*, which made a daytime round trip between Van Buren and Bangor.

World War II found the BAR able to handle the heavy wartime traffic, as ammunition moved through Searsport, and Army Air Corps B-17 bombers took off out of Presque Isle for their trans-Atlantic journey to combat. In June 1945 the

BAR got its last and biggest steam locomotives in the form of five heavy 4-8-2s acquired second-hand from the New York, Ontario & Western.

In July 1946 the BAR hosted General Motors road freight diesel demonstrators. The A-B-A (cab-booster-cab) set of Electro-Motive Division F3s dramatically outperformed steam in both freight and passenger service, and the railroad was sold on the idea of dieselization. In April 1947 it ordered two A-B-A F3 sets from EMD, and two more A-B-A sets were delivered in May 1948. The last two cab units were equipped with steam boilers for passenger service, and they immediately replaced the 4-6-2s on the *Aroostook Flyer*.

In 1948 the BAR accelerated its diesel program by ordering eight of EMD's short-lived BL2 freight locomotives that were an odd hybrid between a freight cab unit and the rapidly developing road-switcher format. Internally, the BL2s were identical to the solid and reliable 1500-hp. F3s, but their unique carbody design, designed for switching visibility, would be obsolete within a year.

The BL2s were delivered in March 1949 and were followed a month later by four 1000-hp. EMD switchers and a pair of impressive 2000-hp. E7 passenger cab units, also from EMD. All three types came painted in a handsome dark blue and gray livery trimmed in rich yellow.

To go along with the new passenger diesels, in 1949 the BAR acquired three new stainless-steel coaches and a buffet-lounge that had been modernized in the Derby Shops to transform the *Aroostook Flyer* into a modern streamliner. Equipment on the old accommodation was upgraded, and that service became the *Potatoland Special*.

While the passenger cars got the public's attention, it was BAR's approach to freight cars that provided the real revenue. Since 1896 it had been acquiring a fleet of special potato boxcars, which were replaced by refrigerator cars in the 1920s. Since potatoes travel best at a temperature of 40 degrees, the refrigerator cars were cooled by ice in the summer and warmed by charcoal heaters in their ice bunkers in the winter. Maintaining a fleet of reefers big enough to handle the winter traffic peaks was a constant problem. In 1950 the BAR began building a fleet of 500 insulated boxcars that could be heated for potatoes in the winter and used as lumber cars in the summer. The boxcars were painted in a dramatic red, white, and blue livery with huge STATE OF MAINE PRODUCTS lettering that brought the railroad nationwide attention.

The railroad also began an extensive program of acquiring and building refrigerator cars. An arrangement was made with the Pacific Fruit Express Company to use the BAR's refrigerator cars in the summer to handle produce out of California and then be returned to Maine for the winter potato season.

The locomotives that dieselized the BAR in the late 1940s and early 1950s still moved BAR freight in the 1970s. A string of F-units and Geeps in charge of the daily southbound through freight out of Oakfield thunder over the Mattawamkeag River in October 1976. *Mike Schafer*

Although its diesel roster was pretty straightforward, the BAR was one of only a few railroads to embrace EMD's short-lived BL-series (for "Branch Line") locomotive, which was an evolutionary link between the F-series cab-type locomotives and the GP-series road-switcher-type units. Long after BL fleets had vanished from other owning railroads, BAR's soldiered on and became so closely associated with the BAR that during the 1980s the railroad operated a series of BL2-powered excursion runs for railroad fans. Always public-minded, the BAR even repainted one of the units back into its 1949 gray, blue, and yellow colors and named it *The American Railfan*. In this special lineup sponsored by the railroad in 1981, three of its BL2s, including *The American Railfan* at far left, display three of BAR's diesel paint schemes. *Jim Boyd*

Without a direct link to an ocean port, it is doubtful the BAR would have prospered as much as it did. Searsport was thus a key point on the railroad. At Searsport in 1981, the "Searsport job" out of Northern Maine Junction works the piers. Inbound oil in tank cars instead of outbound potatoes in refrigerator cars had become the primary traffic moving through this ocean port. *Mike Schafer*

By 1950 the BAR had enough diesels to replace steam in the slack season and came up with a novel way to dieselize completely. In November 1950 it took delivery of a dozen EMD GP7s—the new "Geep" (pronounced "jeep") road-switcher that superceded the BL2 model—and worked out a deal to lease ten of them to the Pennsylvania Railroad between May and November. The PRR needed the power to handle iron-ore trains between Lake Erie and Pittsburgh, but that traffic came to a halt every winter when the lakes froze over—which was precisely when the BAR needed the extra power. The last steam run on the BAR was 4-6-2 No. 251 on the Greenville mixed (freight and passenger) train in June 1951. The railroad had replaced 71 steam locomotives with 43 diesels to handle essentially the same tonnage.

BAR passenger service, unfortunately, was experiencing a serious drop in ridership as highways improved and airline service was begun between Aroostook County and Boston. The *Aroostook Flyer* was the first to perish, being replaced by BAR bus service in late 1957. The *Potatoland Special*, which included through cars from Boston, lasted until the Maine Central and Boston & Maine dropped their Boston–Bangor connection in 1960, and the BAR finally terminated the *Potatoland* on September 4, 1961.

Throughout the 1960s, trucks began to make serious inroads into the potato business as Interstate 95 was being completed ever farther into Maine. By 1968 the BAR, MEC, and B&M were almost powerless to fight for the traffic because the recently created Penn Central below Boston was rendering such poor service that the potatoes were often rotting before they got to market. PC almost singlehandedly killed the potato business in the winter of 1969 when hundreds of BAR cars froze up in Selkirk Yard near Albany, New York, wiping out an entire season's crop. Maine farmers, deeply in debt and unable to sell their damaged crop, were unable to collect any damages from the bankrupt PC, and many went out of business. Most who survived would never ship by rail again.

In 1969 the now-struggling BAR was purchased by the Amoskeag Corporation, which brought in the dynamic Frederick C. Dumaine Jr. as president. "Buck" Dumaine, who had just revitalized the Delaware & Hudson, began to trim excess BAR trackage and refocus operations on the remaining profitable paper mill business. The paper mills had converted from coal power to fuel oil, and the coal wharf at Searsport now hosted strings of tank cars instead of boxcars of potatoes. Into the mid-1970s the BAR was still gathering

some refrigerator cars from the potato houses in Aroostook County and delivering bags of spuds to ocean-going freighters at Searsport. By the end of the decade, however, the railroad gave up on the potato business for good. Fast and flexible 18-wheelers were now handling bagged spuds and frozen french fries to market on Interstate 95.

BAR had continued to buy more EMD Geeps in the early 1950s, and in the 1960s it simplified its paint scheme to a solid blue with yellow lettering. Eight 2000-hp. GP38s were purchased in 1966 and 1967. In 1972 a colorful black, gray, and vermilion paint scheme was developed and applied to nearly everything.

In 1977, Dumaine and the BAR were thwarted in an attempt to take over Maine Central—the only direct rail connection to the lower states. Throughout the 1970s and 1980s the BAR continued to prune its mileage of low-revenue branches and was surviving by adjusting to the realities of the remaining business. By 1984 most of the BL2s and F3s had been retired. For the railroad's 100th anniversary in 1991, though, F3 No. 42 was repainted into its as-delivered two-tone gray livery.

In November 1993 the BAR changed ownership when Fieldcrest Cannon (better known for Cannon-brand towels) bought controlling interest of the Amoskeag Corporation. Then on St. Patrick's Day 1995 the BAR was sold to Iron Road Railways Inc., which combined it with the former Canadian Pacific line from Brownville to Montreal. Iron Road began operating the new 853-mile regional system under the BAR banner. With CP's earlier acquisition of the D&H south out of Montreal, the BAR finally had a friendly alternative route into the lower states, albeit via Canada.

Thus the Bangor & Aroostook entered the twenty-first century as part of a new regional system, still heavily dependent upon the original three paper mills and the seaport of Searsport. Iron Road, however, honors the BAR's past by painting its locomotives in the historic blue and gray and applying the traditional "Serving Northern Maine" herald.

On Sept 30, 1997, BAR train No 904 is rounding the curve at a scenic—and lonely—outpost known as Camp 12 Maine, so-named for the trackwalkers' shack which once stood here. Due to proclivity of boulders that fell from the bluff from which this photo was taken, workers had to be camped here to carry out their track-inspection duties before the passage of any train. Camp 12 is on the former Canadian Pacific main line (or "Maine" line, if you will) between Brownville Junction and Greenville acquired by BAR owner Iron Road Railways. *George Pitarys*

GEORGE WASHINGTON'S RAILROAD
Chesapeake & Ohio

Chessie
CHESAPEAKE AND OHIO RAILWAY ®

The Chesapeake & Ohio can be traced back to 1836 when the Louisa Railroad received a charter and became the first railroad to build through central Virginia. By December 1837, tracks had been laid from Taylorsville to Frederick Hall, Virginia. The Louisa continued to expand, east to a junction with the Richmond, Fredericksburg & Potomac at Hanover Junction (today, Doswell), Virginia, and west to Gordonsville and Shadwell.

In 1850 the Louisa became the Virginia Central, and by this time the railroad extended from Richmond to the Jackson River, ten miles west of Clifton Forge, Virginia, which remained the end of the line until after the Civil War. The VC became one of the primary railroads used by Confederate troops, transporting Stonewall Jackson and his gray-uniformed soldiers until the rails—and Richmond—were destroyed. Unfortunately the VC was completely within the battle zones of the Civil War and suffered greatly. But, it served as an important artery for Gen. Robert E. Lee's army until Appomattox and was a large part of the success in delaying defeat for the Confederacy.

The VC answered postwar challenges head on. Within just 15 days of the surrender at Appomattox, trains were operating 40 miles west of Richmond. The first postwar revenues went for new rails, which were all down by November 1865. By the spring of 1866, daily service had begun over 204 miles of right-of-way. VC leaders next set their sights on the Ohio River, taking over several smaller roads and changing the name to the Chesapeake & Ohio Railroad Company in 1867. In 1869, the company came under control of railroad builder Collis P. Huntington.

During the late 1860s the road had been pushed west toward White Sulphur Springs, West Virginia, over the Allegheny Mountains. In 1871 a line from the new city of Huntington, on the Ohio river, to Charleston, West Virginia, was opened, and in 1872 it reached Kanawha Falls, West Virginia. The route through the mountains had yet to be completed, with work hampered by landslides,

weather, and other difficulties. On January 29, 1873, the last spike was driven, the gap closed, and 419.3 miles of road opened from Richmond to Huntington.

While the railroad's management was looking west, some Virginians wanted a shorter route between Richmond and Clifton Forge and proposed a "straight shoot" through Lynchburg. Though officials were interested, the matter was put to rest due to the financial panic of 1873. In 1888, C&O would acquire such a route by leasing the Richmond & Allegheny Railroad.

After having reached Huntington in 1873, C&O management set Cincinnati and Memphis as their next goals and also looked eastward for a better terminus east of Richmond. This eastward expansion led the railroad to the Hampton Roads region, and facilities were built at Newport News, Virginia, in 1874. The company failed in 1876 and was reorganized as the Chesapeake & Ohio Railway Company in 1878.

The C&O acquired several smaller roads as it built northwest along the Ohio River to Covington, Kentucky (across the river from Cincinnati), as well as down the Big Sandy River to Elkhorn City, Kentucky, and what would become a strategic connection with the Clinchfield Railroad. The bridge into Cincinnati was opened on Christmas Day 1888. That same year, however, Huntington had lost control of the railroad to the Vanderbilt empire, of New York Central fame.

C&O ENTERS THE NEW CENTURY

In 1900, the Pennsylvania Railroad and the NYC bought a controlling interest in the C&O, an arrangement that would last a decade. Lines into the coal fields were being built and acquired, and the Chesapeake & Ohio was proving to be a splendid property. In 1905, C&O began acquiring shares in the Hocking Valley, a central Ohio railroad that would give the C&O access to Toledo and the Great Lakes. Another important acquisition, in 1910, was the Chicago, Cincinnati & Louisville Railroad, which brought the C&O as far west as

FACING PAGE: Passengers aboard C&O train 3, the westbound *F. F. V. (Fast Flying Virginian)*, enjoy the bountiful West Virginia scenery as morning sun cascades into the valleys. Two sections of the train left Washington, D.C., and Newport News, Virginia, the previous night, joining during the small hours of the morning at Charlottesville, Virginia. The *F.F.V.* will be at Cincinnati by dinner time. *James EuDaly*

FACING PAGE, INSET: One of the most enduring and popular railroad logos of all time was Chessie the cat, born during the Depression and lasting until C&O successor CSX opted for more of a corporate look a half century later. Here, CHessie adorns a playing card.

LEFT: A C&O public passenger timetable from 1957 featured Chessie the cat and Electro-Motive E8s.

Hammond, Indiana, and on into Chicago via operating agreements on other roads. The CC&L was reorganized as the Chesapeake & Ohio Railway of Indiana and carried that nomenclature until it was severed in the 1980s.

Initially, a trackage-rights agreement was negotiated with the Norfolk & Western to get C&O trains to the Hocking Valley at Columbus. The initial C&O route was built to Waverly, Ohio, as the Chesapeake & Ohio Northern. In 1926, efforts to bypass the N&W trackage rights began as the C&O constructed a line into Columbus from Gregg, near

Waverly. During this era the famous Van Sweringen brothers of Cleveland gained control of the C&O, and a new era of expansion and success soon followed. During this period, the C&O became associated with the Pere Marquette, which webbed Michigan, crossed southern Ontario, and gave Chicago yet another route to Detroit and Buffalo.

Also at this time, the C&O attempted to merge the Nickel Plate into its growing empire. This was a drawn-out, embroiled affair that the Interstate Commerce Commission eventually ruled against in 1926. The Van Sweringens pressed on, obtaining

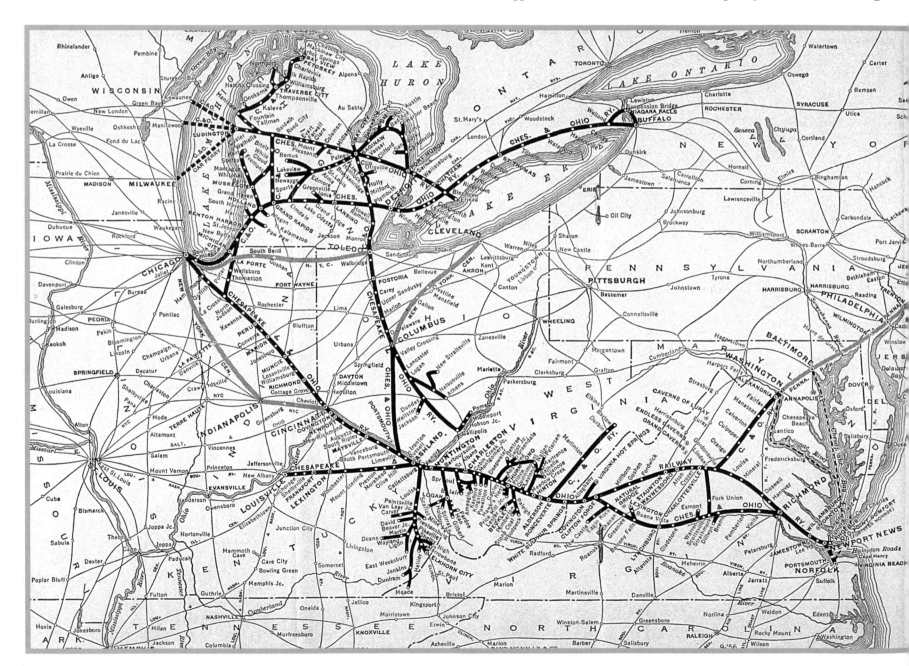

Implemented by Lionel Probert, an assistant to the president of the railroad during the Depression, Georgian-style architecture and design became a hallmark of the C&O. What could pass for a stately courthouse or college building in this 1970 scene is in reality the passenger station and regional office headquarters for C&O at Huntington, West Virginia. George Washington himself would feel right at home. *Jim Boyd*

A trio of Electro-Motive SD35s blast out of a mountain tunnel in the summer of 1968. East of Cincinnati, the C&O main line followed the Ohio River toward the Appalachian Mountains, which had to be surmounted as the railroad marched to Tidewater ports. *Jeremy Plant*

Chesapeake and Ohio Railway

▭▭▭ CONNECTING PASSENGER SERVICE—THROUGH SLEEPERS

▬ ▬ ▬ CAR FERRIES FOR PASSENGERS, AUTOS, FREIGHT

Modern streamlined coaches and room-type Sleeping cars on all C&O Mainline trains now offer The Most Passenger-Pleasing Comforts in Chessie History!

CHESAPEAKE & OHIO AT A GLANCE

Headquarters: Richmond, Va.

Route mileage circa 1950: 5,343 (includes carferry routes)

Locomotive fleet as of 1963:
Steam: 3 (fireless "cookers")
Diesel: 1,053

Rolling stock as of 1963:
Freight cars: 92,992
Passenger cars: 324

Principal lines circa 1950:
Chicago–Cincinnati, Ohio–Ashland, Ky.–Staunton, Va.—Newport News, Va.
Gordonsville, Va.–Washington, D.C.
Clifton Forge–Richmond, Va.
Ashland–Louisville, Ky.
Limeville (Ashland)–Columbus, Ohio–Toledo, Ohio
Columbus–Pomeroy, Ohio
Catlettsburg (Ashland)–Elkhorn City, Ky.
Ronceverte–Durbin/Bartow, W. Va.

Chicago–Grand Rapids, Mich.–Detroit, Mich.–St. Thomas, Ont.–Buffalo/Niagara Falls, N.Y.
Grand Rapids–Petoskey/Bay View, Mich.
Erieau, Ontario–Ludington, Mich.
Ludington–Milwaukee/Manitowoc/Kewaunee, Wis. (separate carferry routes to each city from Ludington)
Toledo–Bay City, Mich.
Port Huron–Bay City–Elmdale, Mich.
Holland–Muskegon–Hart, Mich.

Notable passenger trains (slash marks denote split points of origin or destinations):
George Washington (Washington/Newport News–Cincinnati/Louisville)
F.F.V. (Washington/Newport News–Cincinnati/Louisville)
Sportsman (Washington/Newport News–Cincinnati/Detroit)
Pere Marquettes (Detroit–Grand Rapids, Chicago–Grand Rapids/Muskegon, Detroit–Saginaw, Mich.)
Resort Special (Chicago–Petoskey; later, Washington–White Sulphur Springs, W. Va.)

control of the PM in 1928. They also tried to acquire several other roads at the time, but the stockmarket crash of 1929 and the ensuing Depression sent the Van Sweringens into bankruptcy.

DEPRESSION AND WORLD WAR— FOR C&O, SOME GOOD NEWS

For a vast majority of U.S. railroads, the Great Depression of the 1930s ushered in serious problems. Yet, for C&O the Depression had its high points. The *Sportsman* was inaugurated between the Tidewater region and Detroit and Cincinnati in 1930, exactly 40 years after the *Fast Flying Virginian* (later simply known as the *F. F. V.*)—C&O's flagship passenger train—had made its debut. In 1932, what would become C&O's new signature passenger train, the *George Washington*, made its inaugural run. The Washington–Cincinnati overnighter included a Tidewater section, a Louisville section, and through cars to Chicago. (Although C&O had its own direct line between Cincinnati and Chicago, through cars were handled over the faster, more-populated line of New York Central's Big Four Route.)

When the *George* entered service on April 24, 1932—complete with a dedication ceremony in Washington, D.C.—it was claimed to be the most wonderful train in the world and was the first long-distance run to be air-conditioned. During the first 12 months that the *George Washington* operated, passenger revenues overall were 25 percent higher than during the previous 12 months.

It was also during this era that a legendary newspaperman, Lionel Probert, had become assistant to the C&O president. It was Probert's idea to launch the *Sportsman*, which linked PM's resort areas in Michigan with those of the C&O in the Virginias, and the *George Washington*. With a flare for publicity, Probert chose the name and had the train inaugurated on the real George Washington's 200th birthday. Probert also coined the term "George Washington's Railroad" to describe the C&O, and he was behind the adoption of the colonial motif that became a C&O hallmark.

For all this work, Probert's most lasting impression was born of something he stumbled

The *Sportsman* wheels its way through glorious Virginia countryside eastbound at Ivy in October 1967 during its last full year of service. By the end of 1968, the *Sportsman* as well as the *F.F.V.* would be gone. *Jeremy Plant*

Coal moved over the C&O in seemingly endless streams, and C&O employed some hefty steam power for this task. Probably the C&O steam locomotives most closely associated with coal transport were the 2-6-6-6 "Allegheny"-type articulateds, one of which is shown eastbound—not with a coal train but with mixed freight—near Thurmond, West Virginia, in September 1955. *Gene Huddleston, Jim Boyd collection*

C&O Pacific No. 462 skims westbound through the Bluegrass State with a mixture of streamlined and heavyweight cars comprising train 23, the Louisville section of the *F.F.V.* Date: August 16, 1951. *R. D. Acton Sr.*

upon in the *New York Herald Tribune*. In 1933, while pondering a new advertising slogan, Probert saw, in the newspaper's magazine section, a lithograph of a small kitten tucked between the sheets with a paw thrust forward and one slightly open. The illustration was associated with an article on kindness to animals, but the image grabbed Probert, and he immediately sought its creator— Guido Grenewald, an artist living in Vienna. Probert moved the drawing's setting from Vienna to a C&O Pullman berth and added the slogan "Sleep Like a Kitten." This advertisement first appeared in the September 1933 issue of *Fortune* magazine and created an overnight sensation.

Within two days of the ad appearing, over 300 letters were received wanting copies of the print, and "Chessie" was born, a name Probert had decided on as part of the C&O heritage. In 1934, the C&O printed 40,000 calendars graced by Chessie, and all were snapped up immediately. In 1935, 100,000 Chessie calendars still weren't enough to meet the demand. She had become "America's Sleepheart" and soon began to adorn all manner of promotional items.

Thanks in part to strong coal traffic, C&O weathered the Depression better than many carriers. But the real boom came with World War II, which caused both passenger and freight revenues

In the heart of West Virginia coal country, two grimy Electro-Motive GP9s lumber along the C&O main line with a coal train at Quinnimont on a hazy autumn day in 1963. *James F. EuDaly*

to soar for nearly all railroads. Early in the war years, Robert R. Young—one of mid-century's more controversial railroaders—became chairman of the C&O.

POSTWAR C&O

The biggest change for C&O during the immediate postwar period was its 1947 merger with longtime affiliate Pere Marquette, thereby expanding the C&O by nearly 2,000 miles. Other ensuing changes were more subtle and not necessarily for the better.

By the late 1940s, the C&O was so closely associated with Chessie the cat that the railroad was often referred to as simply the "Chessie." The railroad and the image had become inseparable, and as a new C&O streamliner was put on the drawing board, there was no other choice than to name it *The Chessie.* The 1947 annual report announced that *The Chessie*s would be placed on daylight schedules between Washington and Cincinnati, with Newport News and Louisville sections, in mid-1948. They were to maintain a 12-hour schedule, two hours faster than the premier *George Washington*, and a brand-new type of locomotive was being developed for the main section of the train. New coaling stations to feed *The Chessie*'s monster steam turbine-electric locomotives were in place on the route, and the railroad awaited new equipment to arrive from the Budd Company.

One *Chessie* consist, including locomotive, was displayed at principal towns along the route. Among the feature cars of the stunning new stainless-steel streamliner were a dome sleeper (the rooms were to be sold as day "cabins"), "family coaches," a lounge car with a real aquarium, a twin-unit diner, and a dome-observation car.

Unfortunately, 1948 passed with no inauguration. An enormous increase in spending in 1947—while passenger revenues were declining—had sounded alarm bells. Further, *The Chessie*'s experimental steam-turbine-electrics proved unworkable just as it was becoming quickly apparent to C&O that diesels were much more efficient than the steamers of the day. By late 1948, Chairman Young was too busy fighting for his various merger proposals to spend much effort defending *The Chessie*, and it was never launched. The equipment was

The *George Washington* was C&O's principal east-west passenger train, linking Washington, D.C., and the Hampton Roads region with Cincinnati—where the westbound *George* is shown arriving in 1965—and Louisville. Through-car service was also offered to Chicago by way of New York Central trains west of Cincinnati. As part of the C&O/B&O amalgamation in the 1960s, the *George* was extended from Cincinnati to St. Louis. *Jim Boyd*

Alco RSD15 No. 6811 is at Detroit with a transfer from the Canadian Pacific in October 1961. The C&O was one of three U.S. railroads that had main lines across southern Ontario, the other two being Wabash and New York Central System. *Dave Ingles*

A classic A-B-A (cab/booster/cab) set of Electro-Motive F7s shepherd a string of coal hoppers through Fostoria, Ohio, on the Toledo–Ashland route in 1961. *Dave Ingles*

distributed to other trains, and the steam turbines scrapped. In early 1949, the C&O placed its first substantial orders for diesel locomotives. The end of steam was already apparent. Coincident to this was a crisis in the coal-producing regions that made a significant dent in revenues in 1949. The crisis of 1949 meant that the C&O's fascinating and varied roster of steam locomotives, some of which were brand new in 1949, were all destined to be scrapped by 1956.

In the 1950s a blossoming export coal market proved helpful to C&O's revenue situation, and numerous merger attempts were brought forth during the 1950s and 1960s. Talks of uniting C&O and Baltimore & Ohio began as early as 1958. In 1963, C&O took complete control of the B&O, although the two did not formally merge at that time. Through the remainder of the decade, C&O and B&O became closely aligned, with many operations—including passenger—consolidated.

During the mid-1960s, merger fever began to sweep the nation, and C&O aligned itself with one-time rival Norfolk & Western in a merger attempt that included such financially frail Northeastern

roads as Erie Lackawanna, Delaware & Hudson, and Reading. The C&O-N&W merger was fraught with complexities and seemed improbable from the beginning. First was the fact that the two roads had been in close competition for essentially their entire existence; second, they both controlled access to the great West Virginia coal fields.

On March 19, 1971, it was announced that drastic changes in the Northeast railroad picture since 1965 had made the merger less attractive. This turned everyone's attention to a formal C&O-B&O merger, which would now include the Western Maryland. The merger began in 1972, and Chessie System—complete with a modernized kitten logo—was born. The transition into one railroad was purposely slow and not completed until 1976. Chessie went on to become affiliated with the Seaboard System and finally became part of today's CSX Transportation system.

MOTIVE-POWER NOTES

Hoppers loaded with coal snaking out of the hollows of West Virginia and Kentucky remain the impression of the C&O, even with the manifest

route to Chicago and the Pere Marquette making up part of the road. But the long trains and rugged topography were the main forces in locomotive development. Primary to C&O's success in these regions was the motive-power department's thought along the lines of power. Six-wheel trailing trucks, extra large boilers, the first 4-8-2 wheel arrangement, and other achievements in steam-locomotive design and performance were achieved by necessity. Early on, the road was associated with heavy drag locomotives—engines that could take massive tonnages over the grades in the mountains—but it was also quick to recognize the possibilities of high-horsepower, high tractive-effort machines, referred to as "super-power." Engines designed with this in mind were built for one thing—speed.

The dominating philosophy on the C&O was that of single-unit power to haul heavy tonnage, and this perspective produced some of the most phenomenal locomotives in America. Though it also fielded a host of more standard power, it also produced some real monsters, including a massive 2-10-4 that weighed an impressive 566,000 pounds, a 4-6-4 Hudson that was the heaviest and most powerful in America, an ultra-modern 4-8-4 designed for passenger service in the mountains, and the most spectacular of them all, the monstrous 2-6-6-6 "Allegheny" that, with its tender, weighed more than a million pounds.

Though the C&O had an extreme array of steam power, this tendency faltered with the coming of the diesel era. Dieselization started on the Pere Marquette and swiftly moved south. C&O bought and, indeed, dieselized with an enormous quantity of F-, E-, and GP-series locomotives from the Electro-Motive Division of General Motors (EMD). By 1957 C&O had well over 500 EMD units

on the system. Though C&O sampled the likes of Baldwin, Alco, and General Electric, the EMDs were always prevalent in the roster. A scant seven years from the decision to dieselize, steam's fires were forever doused.

The C&O is many things to many people, from the steam era of classic power struggling over mountain grades with coal tonnage, to modern heavyweight trains, and finally hotshot manifest behind blue-and-yellow diesels. Much that was the C&O is gone. In the merger era, as each flag falls, it seems the railroad scene becomes much more ubiquitous. Still, a person can stand deep in the New River Gorge in West Virginia on a crystal evening and listen as a coal drag pounds its way up the valley. With the exhaust reverberating off the sandstone cliffs, the C&O of yore seems alive again. When the locomotives roar past and their CSX logos jolt you back to the present, the past seems ever more distant.

Chicago
Great Western

Stretching from Chicago west into Iowa and then southwest to Kansas City, west to Omaha, and north to the Twin Cities of Minneapolis/St. Paul, Chicago Great Western (CGW) is fondly remembered for its train operations and the appearance of property during its final decades of existence. Post-Depression CGW kept a relatively low profile. It did not participate in the diesel streamliner era like most of its peers and instead clung to its roots serving the transportation needs of the agricultural and industrial base of its hometowns.

Yet, Great Western was quite the innovator. It dieselized quickly, and it was fourth among piggyback operators in the 1950s. Modern CGW rolling stock—among them 25 auto racks and 250 refrigerated trailers—could be found on its famously long trains. The railroad was always looking for new traffic. Its Agricultural and Industrial Development people were busy seeking new customers while keeping old ones satisfied. Small wonder that when the meat-cutting industry decentralized, many offshoot companies relocated along CGW lines.

After a colorful and sometimes tumultuous history, the Chicago Great Western Railway was merged into the Chicago & North Western on July 1, 1968.

INFANT CGW

The origin of the CGW was in a land-grant railroad chartered in 1835 to build west from Chicago. For many reasons, the Chicago, St. Charles & Mississippi Airline Railroad did not build. Rights to do so were conveyed in 1854 to the Minnesota & North Western, but again, no railroad was built. When construction of the M&NW finally began, in 1884, it went south from St. Paul, not out of Chicago.

Nonetheless, railroad builder and M&NW's new leader A. B. Stickney viewed the new railway as a means to link St. Paul to Chicago and also St. Joseph, Missouri, and Kansas City. The next six years witnessed the rapid expansion of the railroad. The Chicago, St. Paul & Kansas City acquired the Wisconsin, Iowa & Nebraska, a line between Waterloo and Des Moines, Iowa. The CStP&KC

then acquired the M&NW in 1887. Through merger, acquisition, and more construction, the road reached Omaha and St. Joseph. It began construction across Illinois in 1886 and in 1888 began operating between Chicago and Dubuque, Iowa. Unable to find a suitable route the last few miles into Dubuque, the CStP&KC tunneled through a ridge to Chicago, Burlington & Quincy predecessor Chicago Burlington & Northern at Galena Junction, Illinois, and rode on that road to Portage, Illinois, where it (and Burlington) entered trackage rights on the Illinois Central Railroad for the remainder of the trip to Dubuque. To enter Chicago proper, CStP&KCC acquired rights to operate from suburban Forest Park to Chicago's Grand Central Station via the (original) Wisconsin Central.

In 1890, the railroad reached Kansas City via rights on the Rock Island and Missouri Pacific. The CStP&KC was reorganized in 1892 as the Chicago Great Western in a financial scheme that allowed it to survive the Crash of 1892.

The *Great Western Limited*, a steam-powered overnight train between Chicago and the Twin Cities via Rochester, Minnesota, entered service in 1898. Equipped with fine dining and sleeping cars, it competed with the best trains of the Milwaukee Road, Chicago & North Western, and Burlington. Other major CGW steam passenger trains included the *Tri-State Limited* and *Mills Cities Limited* between the Twin Cities and Kansas City; the *Rochester Express* and *Bob-O-Link* between Chicago and Rochester; and four trains between the Twin Cities and Omaha, the *Omaha Express, Omaha Limited, Twin City Express,* and *Twin City Limited.* The *Chicago Special* ran overnight from Des Moines to Chicago. The *Red Bird* was inaugurated in 1923 as a steam-powered luxury train serving the Minneapolis–Rochester route. The year 1925 witnessed the renaming of the *Great Western Limited* as the *Legionnaire* in honor of the veterans of the "war to end all wars" (World War I) who were American Legion members.

Steam-powered trains also served the many branch lines across Iowa and Minnesota. On low-density branches, steam trains were expensive to

Chicago
**GREAT
WESTERN**
Railway

TIME TABLES

**Chicago
Kansas City
Minneapolis
St. Paul
St. Joseph
Des Moines
Omaha
Dubuque**

EFFECTIVE OCTOBER 1, 1957

No. 155

FACING PAGE: **A westbound Chicago Great Western freight out of Chicago awaits a fresh crew at the division point yard in Stockton, Illinois, in 1967. The new crew will continue the run to Oelwein, Iowa, hub of the charismatic corn-belt carrier. Though overshadowed by much larger granger neighbors like Burlington, North Western, and Milwaukee Road, CGW had a legion of devoted followers that included employees as well as students of railroad history. The yard office shown in this view originally served as a dispatcher's office at East Stockton and was moved to Stockton proper in the 1930s.** *Mike Schafer*

FACING PAGE, INSET: **A Great Western caboose at Oelwein sports the railroad's simple yet distinctive "Lucky Strike" emblem.** *Mike Schafer*

LEFT: **Great Western's passenger timetable from October 1957 was a simple affair. The cover touted Chicago as a destination, but the Chicago passenger train had been discontinued shortly before this folder was issued.**

Pacific-type (4-6-2) No. 931 of the Chicago Great Western struts out of St. Paul Union Depot on a June morning in 1948 with the *Twin City Limited.* Eventually the train will have made a nearly 180-degree turn to the west as it heads over to Minneapolis, the last stop on its overnight journey from Omaha. Note the CGW freighthouse at upper right in the distance. *Ben F. Cutler, Railfan & Railroad collection*

operate and maintain, and as early as 1910, CGW was searching for a means to reduce the cost of branchline passenger service. The McKeen Motor Car Co. provided a product that met that need. McKeen gas-electric cars were placed in service on four routes in Iowa and Missouri in 1910.

In 1914, the Northfield–Mankato line in southern Minnesota was leased to an electric interurban company to provide freight and passenger service. The Minneapolis, St. Paul, Rochester & Dubuque Electric Traction Co., known locally as the "Dan Patch Line," provided service for many years on that branch.

Because of the inability of the nation's railroads to cope with the onslaught of traffic ushered in by World War I, CGW was, like nearly every other major U.S. road, taken over by the government though the newly formed United States Railroad Administration (USRA). Though history generally

regards USRA as a debacle, it did establish locomotive and car construction standards that would be embraced by many railroads for years following USRA's decommissioning in 1920.

After the war, CGW again took to the motorcar to reduce costs on certain passenger runs. Motorcar trains were capable of handling the mail and express business and satisfying the needs of the small town and rural passenger and shipper at considerably less cost than a conventional steam train. In 1924, gas-electric cars replaced steam trains on the 509-mile Chicago–Omaha runs of train Nos. 3 and 4. Also in the 1920s, shopworkers at Oelwein, Iowa—the hub of CGW operations— rebuilt three McKeen cars into a three-car train to also serve the Minneapolis–Rochester market. Named *Blue Bird*, the train consisted of a motor-baggage-mail car, a coach, and a parlor-club-café-lounge car. It entered service in January 1929—a year that also witnessed

ABOVE LEFT: In its twilight, train No. 8 trundles out of Oelwein for Chicago during the 1950s. Often a motorcar was assigned to the run, but on this day an Electro-Motive F-unit, baggage car, and day coach substituted. The Chicago train came off in 1956. The F-type Electro-Motive diesel pulling the train wears the railroad's celebrated maroon, red, and yellow livery. *V. A. Vaughn*

One of CGW's two Electro-Motive GP7 road-switchers works the interchange with the Illinois Central at South Freeport, Illinois, early in the 1960s. *Jim Boyd*

Electro-Motive did not have a monopoly on Great Western's dieselization. Alco and Baldwin supplied the railroad with a fleet of switchers and road-switchers for local-type duties. This Alco RS2 road-switcher is working industries at Omaha in 1954. These locomotives—still clad in Great Western colors—could be found working branch lines well into the 1970s, long after the CGW-C&NW merger of 1968. *V. A. Vaughn*

A solid string of F-units still wearing the simplified solid maroon color scheme of the 1950s roll through Illinois farmlands near Sycamore with a freight early in the 1960s. The Deramus era of the late 1950s/early 1960s would "see red" as this maroon was traded for solid red—a livery that became closely associated with railroads under the influence of Deramus. *Jim Boyd*

a negative event whose effects would be felt throughout next decade: the stockmarket crash. The growth era of the "Roaring Twenties" was over.

The Depression that followed the Crash of '29 included many lean years. Branchline trains were abandoned. The prestigious *Red Bird* became a simple motorcar run. Sleeper service vanished. The *Legionnaire* was renamed the *Minnesotan* and downgraded.

The CGW was no stranger to hardships. It endured two bankruptcies and receiverships, plus an era of mismanagement in the 1930s. It competed with strong carriers in every major center: Chicago, St. Paul, Des Moines, St. Joseph, Omaha, and Kansas City. After World War I, additional competition came from the growing system of highways across the Midwest. Shortly after the 1929 market crash, new management cut costs by closing engine terminals at East Stockton, Illinois, and Conception, Iowa. In addition, the operating divisions were

reduced from four to three. Clarion, Iowa, was downgraded from its high status as a division headquarters to merely a station. Branch lines were pared throughout the 1930s.

Financial difficulties led to CGW's second reorganization in 1941, and wholly owned companies like the Mason City & Fort Dodge, the Leavenworth Terminal Railway & Bridge Company, Independent Elevator Company, and the St. Paul

Bridge & Terminal disappeared into CGW. With the financial difficulties of the Depression not far behind, CGW had little time to prepare for World War II.

CGW: MODEST BUT INNOVATIVE

CGW was an innovative railroad from the earliest days because of intense competition from the many other railroads building across the granger states. Rather than locate its main shops and classification yard at one of its large on-line cities like Chicago or St. Paul, CGW instead opened facilities at little Oelwein, Iowa, in 1899. Oelwein was the perfect location for the main shops and yard, for here CGW's four principal routes converged. Over the years Oelwein was expanded and modernized to remain efficient and competitive.

In the early 1900s, CGW double-tracked its main line near Chicago, lengthened sidings elsewhere, and acquired new rolling stock. It saw standardized boxcar construction as a benefit and lobbied the industry to create car construction standards. It worked to bring agricultural products to the railroad. CGW was one of the first carriers to operate solid meat trains.

Unlike many steam railroads, Great Western chose not to oppose, but to work with electric interurban lines to develop interchange traffic. CGW developed engineering technologies and human resources. In the early 1910s Great Western offered employee education and safety training. In 1929 the railroad initiated the first coordinated train-air service with Universal Air Lines, although the deteriorating economy at the close of that year ended the concept. In 1936, CGW responded to increased truck competition by being one of the first railroads to offer trailer-on-flatcar (TOFC) service.

GREAT WESTERN'S POSTWAR ERA

The war effort nearly exhausted Great Western's freight steam locomotive fleet. Elderly Mikados (2-8-2s) including ten Light "Mikes" of USRA

design from 1918, were worn out. The first Mikados had been delivered in 1916 to bring a motive-power standard to CGW, replacing ten 1910-built Baldwin 2-6-6-2s referred to locally as "snakes." The Mikes provided a reliable stable in the 1920s. Thirty-six modern 2-10-4 types were purchased from Lima and Baldwin in 1929 and 1930. They were some of the largest locomotives in the Midwest and performed well on Great Western main lines; however, these "Super Power" locomotives would not see 1950.

In November 1946, General Motors F3 demonstrator set No. 291 toured the CGW. Already familiar with the economies of internal-combustion power through its numerous motorcar operations, CGW promptly embraced the diesel revolution. Orders went to the Electro-Motive Division of GM for over-the-road and switcher locomotives. American Locomotive Company (Alco) and Baldwin also received orders for road-switcher and switcher locomotives. The year 1948 found steam only in isolated yards or branches, and by 1949 the railroad was completely dieselized.

Interestingly, the Kansas City Southern played a hand in forming the character of the CGW in its final two decades, for on May 17, 1949, William N. Deramus III, son of the KCS president, was appointed as president of the CGW. He began a program to replace elderly depots and other ancil-

It's the Fourth of July weekend 1965 and the end is near for Great Western passenger service as train 14, the remnant of the old *Twin City Limited*, prepares to depart the Burlington station at Omaha for its overnight jaunt to the Twin Cities. By the end of the year, No. 14 and southbound counterpart train 13, the old *Nebraska Limited*, will have been discontinued, rendering CGW as a freight-only railroad. *Ron Lundstrom/Jim Boyd*

lary buildings, bridges, rails, and ties. New rolling stock was acquired. Signal systems were upgraded, and a consolidated dispatching office in Oelwein was opened in 1949, replacing offices in Stockton, Des Moines, and St. Paul. In the 1950s, CGW people created new traffic and customers by developing the Roseport Industrial District immediately south of St. Paul.

Deramus also introduced the long-train concept. Often six or more diesels would be assembled to haul trains of 150 cars or more (nicknamed "mortgage lifters" by crews), keeping crew and other over-the-road costs at a minimum. Records indicate that on at least one occasion a 275-car train was moved. Not as visible was the automation of accounting and consolidation of other office activities. During the Deramus tenure—and of no surprise to anyone that understood the link CGW had with Kansas City—the headquarters was moved from Chicago to K.C. In 1957, he left to bring similar change to the Katy. His successor, Edward T. Reidy, continued the Deramus tradition until merger with the North Western.

By the time of the Deramus–Reidy transition, it had become clear that the American passenger train was a troubled and endangered species. CGW's modest passenger-train fleet was especial-

When it came time to begin replacing Great Western's first-generation diesel road power—the Electro-Motive F-unit fleet—the railroad stuck with EMD and in 1963 received eight 2250-hp. GP30s. Equipped with dynamic brakes and turbocharging, these new second-generation locomotives tended to hold assignments on the Oelwein–Chicago main line. In this scene from September 1964, half of the GP30 fleet hustles toward the Windy City with train 192 west of Holcomb, Illinois. This train was an Oelwein–Chicago connection off of Kansas City–Minneapolis train 92. Note the block of piggyback cars; CGW was one of the early champions of the trailer-on-flatcar concept. *Jim Boyd*

Winston Tunnel

CGW train 192 emerges from the east portal of Winston Tunnel in 1966. *Mike Nelson*

The CGW main line between Chicago and Oewlein, Iowa, passed through not one but two tunnels: Winston Tunnel near Elizabeth, Illinois, and a short bore at East Dubuque, Illinois, which actually was on the Illinois Central, which CGW used to reach Dubuque.

Winston was Great Western's costly solution to negotiating the rugged topography of northwestern Illinois. Because of the blue clay indigenous to the area, tunnel construction was tedious and expensive. One construction worker was killed; his tombstone, located in a nearby cemetery, is inscribed KILLED AT THE WEST END OF THE TUNNEL, and his ghost reputedly haunts the area. The half-mile, brick-lined bore had tight clearances and was located on a 1 percent eastbound grade. An air-handling system had to be installed to ventilate the tunnel as engines worked hard to pull the trains out of the Mississippi River valley. Opened in 1888, Winston was rebuilt in 1902, 1918, and 1947.

Several engineering studies sought alternative routes between Elizabeth and a point west of Dubuque that would circumvent not only the tunnel, but IC trackage rights and bridge fees. The studies were done for many years but the plan was just too expensive to implement. Following CGW's 1968 merger into the C&NW, the latter closed the Chicago–Oelwein main to through traffic, and the tunnel has since fallen to ruin.

ly affected by the downturn in passenger business, as it faced considerable competition from other railroads, not to mention highways and airlines. In 1956, all passenger service ended east of Oelwein, leaving only the Twin Cities–Kansas City *Mills Cities Limited* and a Twin Cities–Omaha round trip, the *Nebraska Limited/Twin City Limited*.

Under Reidy, more new diesels were purchased. In 1963, eight Electro-Motive GP30s, clad in bright red and black, arrived on the property. Often operated in four-unit, 9000-hp. sets, they were the horsepower equivalent of six 1500-hp. F-units. Nine 3000-hp. SD40 locomotives arrived in 1966 offering the equivalent of 18 F-units—and becoming the last new CGW locomotives. By this time, all passenger service had ended.

The 1950s had been a period of prosperity for the Great Western. The ambitious plans executed by Deramus made the CGW into an efficient transportation tool. However, the 1960s were not as generous as the previous decade. Increasing labor and material costs affected the rail industry as a whole, and the transportation efficiencies and cost-control policies of the CGW could only slow the financial erosion. Competition increased dramatically as the Interstate Highway System was poured across the Midwest. The CGW was an example of ambitious railroad building in the late 1800s that—after 80 years of economic cycles, new forms of competition, and technological progress—led to a surplus of railroads in the Midwest. Merger with some railroad was inevitable.

In the post-World War II years, the CGW had become an attractive merger partner, and merger had been discussed with several other roads over a 20-year period. The first postwar merger proposal envisioned the CGW linking up with Chicago & Eastern Illinois and Missouri-Kansas-Texas (Katy). Later and independently, the St. Louis-San Francisco Railway (Frisco) and the Kansas City Southern talked merger with the Great Western, and the Chicago, Rock Island & Pacific also discussed merger with CGW for a short period. Those talks came to an abrupt halt when the companies realized that they connected at as many as 29 points and offered each other little else. The Soo Line also showed interest for a time, but ultimately the C&NW won the Great Western.

Many miss the 200-car freight trains led by large locomotive consists moving across the fertile farm fields of Illinois, Iowa, and Minnesota. CGW was a granger road that met the needs of the local farmer, while taking Wisconsin lumber to the

Kansas City gateway, and Iowa meat to Chicago. It recognized when to stop competing with the automobile for personal transportation, yet was innovative at putting trailers on flat cars. In retrospect, Chicago Great Western could not have survived another bankruptcy. The competition from railroads, waterways, and highways plus rising labor and material cost would have eventually done in the railroad. Merger into the Chicago & North Western was not a glorious fate, but it was not a bad one either.

A half-dozen F-units heads up freight 192 with 142 cars out of Dubuque on August 19, 1966. The train is grinding upgrade out of the Mississippi River valley and is approaching the west portal of Winston Tunnel, over which the photographer has found a wonderful vantage point to capture the beauty of the area. *Mike Nelson*

Delaware & Hudson

Delaware & Hudson was one of the few railroads featured in this volume that was still in existence as this book was being prepared. In fact, as of the year 2000, the D&H was the oldest surviving transportation company in the U.S. Its origins trace to 1823—four years before America's first common-carrier railroad, the Baltimore & Ohio, was born. That year, the Delaware & Hudson Canal Company was chartered to transport anthracite coal from mines around Carbondale, Pennsylvania, to New York City. The coal was moved by gravity railroad (with stationary steam engines used to hoist cars by cable on uphill portions of the route) from the mines to D&H's canal at Honesdale, Pennsylvania. The canal ended at the Hudson River at Kingston, New York.

In 1829, D&H tested the *Stourbridge Lion* steam locomotive on the 16-mile railway portion of its route between Carbondale and Honesdale, thus becoming the first railroad to operate a locomotive-hauled train in America. As railways gained favor over canals, D&H expanded its reach by acquiring nearby new railroads, constructing its own new rail lines, and setting up trackage-rights agreements with other carriers. Much of the expansion after the Civil War went south of Carbondale into the Wilkes-Barre/Scranton area in the Lackawanna and Wyoming valleys where the D&HCC tapped a tremendous amount of traffic from the area's vast anthracite beds.

A particularly important trackage-rights agreement allowed D&H trains to use the Erie-funded Jefferson Railroad between Carbondale and Lanesboro, Pennsylvania, where a direct rail connection was made with the Erie. D&H then built its own line north from Lanesboro to Nineveh, New York, where in 1871 a link was established with the Albany & Susquehanna, a railroad connecting Binghamton and Albany, New York, that D&H had leased in 1870. Eventually the D&H absorbed the A&S, and in 1955 it purchased the Carbondale–Lanesboro line from the Erie.

A lease of the Rensselaer & Saratoga in 1871 extended the D&H's reach beyond the "Capital Cities" area (Albany/Rensselaer/Schenectady/Troy) to Whitehall, New York, at the far south end of Lake Champlain. Long and deep, this body of water (which reportedly even has its own Loch Ness-type monster) became a route for D&HCC coal boats north to Rouses Point, New York, at the Canadian border. The R&S also included a line south from Balston Spa to Schenectady, a branch from Fort Edward to Lake George, and two lines to Rutland, Vermont—one from Whitehall, New York, and one from Troy via Eagle Bridge, New York, both joining at Castleton, Vermont, before heading into Rutland.

By the end of 1875, D&H had further extended its rail reach north along Lake Champlain to Plattsburg and Rouses Point through a subsidiary known as the New York & Canada. Although the Grand Trunk Railway initially provided a connection between Rouses Point and Montreal, the D&H eventually settled on the 42-mile Napierville Junction Railway as its route into the Montreal area from Rouses Point, leasing the NJ in 1888 and purchasing it in 1907.

D&H acquired its North Creek (New York) branch in 1889 from the Adirondack Railway, whose predecessor companies had built north from Saratoga Springs to tap the rich mineral resources of the Adirondack Mountains. D&H had been in control of the scenic Adirondack Railway, which hugged the Hudson River for much of its length, for several years prior to final takeover.

PASSENGER TRAFFIC

Being a carrier of moderate size, Delaware & Hudson's passenger services were likewise modest. Further, there was simply not enough population along D&H routes to support extensive passenger services. Ironically, though, D&H passenger service in a sense survived into the 2000s.

D&H competed with the Rutland Railroad, Central Vermont, and Boston & Maine for Montreal-bound passenger traffic—its mainstay passenger traffic market. Fortunately, D&H had a strong ally in the New York City–Montreal market, the New York Central System. D&H's Montreal trains

DELAWARE AND HUDSON

"the D&H"

NEW YORK
SARATOGA SPRINGS
ADIRONDACKS
LAKE CHAMPLAIN
FORT TICONDEROGA
PLATTSBURG
MONTREAL

EASTERN STANDARD TIME
TIME TABLE
EFFECTIVE OCTOBER 25, 1959

Route of the Famous
MONTREAL LIMITED

FACING PAGE: Alco PA passenger diesels built by Alco head up a Binghamton–Albany "deadhead" train (left in photo) shuttling equipment back home following a weekend of Binghamton–Albany excursions in the fall of 1973. The train is in the siding at Afton, New York, as a westbound freight behind Alco Century 628 locomotives smokes out for Binghamton. *Mike Schafer*

FACING PAGE, INSET: In honor of its 150th anniversary, D&H issued handsome commemorative plates that featured a canal scene and the road's then-newest General Electric diesels. *Mike Schafer*

LEFT: The look of D&H's public passenger timetables changed little over the years. The *Montreal Limited* was highlighted on the cover of this folder issued in October 1959 .

DELAWARE & HUDSON AT A GLANCE

Headquarters: Albany, NY

Route mileage:
1950: 765
2000: 1,381

Locomotive fleet as of 1963:
Diesels: 153

Rolling stock as of 1963:
Freight cars: 9,394
Passenger cars: 55

Principal lines circa 1950:
Albany–Troy–Mechanicville, NY–Montreal, Que. (trackage rights on Napierville Junction Railway, Rouses Point, NY–Montreal)
Albany–Schenectady–Binghamton, NY
Binghamton–Owego, NY (trackage rights on Erie)
Nineveh, NY–Wilkes-Barre, PA)
Hudson–Buttonwood Yard, PA
Delanson–Mechanicville, NY
Schenectady–Balston Spa, NY
Saratoga Springs–Tahawus, NY (trackage rights on U.S. Government track North Creek–Tahawus)
Troy–Castleton, VT (trackage rights on B&M Troy–Eagle Bridge, NY)
Whitehall, NY–Rutland, VT
Plattsburg–Lyon Mountain, NY
Plattsburg–Ausable Forks, NY
Fort Ticonderoga–Ticonderoga, NY
Oneonta–Cooperstown, NY
Cobleskill–Cherry Valley, NY

Routes added in 1976 via Conrail trackage rights
Owego–Buffalo/Niagara Falls, NY
Wilkes-Barre–Harrisburg, PA–Washington, DC
Scranton–Allentown, PA–Newark, NJ
Allentown–Philadelphia

Notable passenger trains:
Laurentian (New York–Albany–Montreal)
Montreal Limited (New York–Albany–Montreal)

NOTE: New York Central handled cars to and from New York City south of Albany.

This map from a 1934 public timetable shows most of the "classic"-era Delaware & Hudson in place, including the branch to Lake Placid, most of which was abandoned shortly after World War II. The map can also be used to trace the routes that D&H added at the time of Conrail's startup in 1976. At that time, D&H was extended to Buffalo over the former Erie; to Newark over the former Jersey Central and Lehigh Valley; to Philadelphia over the former Reading Railroad; and to Washington, D.C., over the former Pennsylvania Railroad. *C. W. Newton collection*

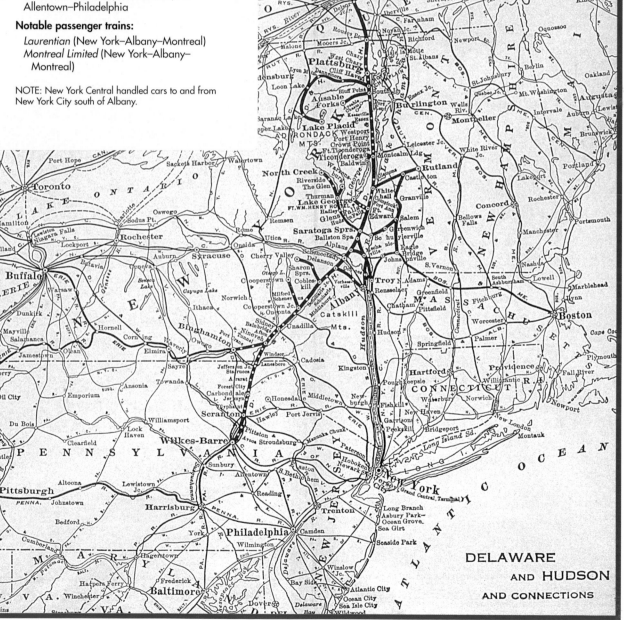

D&H's impressive headquarters in Albany, New York, in 1968 could have been mistaken for an esteemed ivy league university. *Mike Schafer*

originated and terminated at Albany where connection could be made with NYC trains to and from New York City, Chicago, St. Louis, and (via NYC subsidiary Boston & Albany) Boston. D&H and NYC coordinated through-car operation between New York and Montreal—an arrangement that would last until Amtrak took over most of the nation's intercity passenger trains in 1971.

The *Montreal Limited* and the *Laurentian* were the flagships of the railroad. The *Montreal Limited* provided overnight service between New York City and Montreal while the *Laurentian*, named for the Laurentide Uplands in the vicinity of the Great Lakes near the St. Lawrence River, provided scenic day service on the 375-plus-mile route. Into the 1950s, local-type trains provided supplemental service on the Montreal line to Fort Edward, Whitehall, Plattsburg, and Montreal. D&H also operated tourist-oriented services on the Lake George branch into the 1950s, as well as a suburban-type service between Carbondale and Scranton, 16 miles.

Until after World War II, the Albany–Binghamton main line featured double-daily passenger service, but by the 1950s this had been reduced to a single round trip that, until discontinued early in the 1960s, served as a connection to and from the *Laurentian*. Though the Albany–Binghamton line was critical to D&H's overall operations, low population along this beautiful route, which largely follows the Susquehanna River, rendered it incidental to the railroad's passenger earnings.

Post-World War II D&H management was not very pro-passenger, and the *Montreal Limited* and *Laurentian* thrived in relative obscurity (this could be said of the whole railroad) until 1967 when a new president, Frederic "Buck" Dumaine, came on board. Under his pro-passenger leadership, both trains, though mostly the *Laurentian*, were re-equipped with new (to D&H) secondhand locomotives and streamlined rolling stock. This happened at a time when most other U.S. railroads had tossed in the towel on passenger service and were discontinuing trains at a runaway rate.

The snow is gone and spring is imminent on this March day in 1949 at Cobleskill, New York, on the Binghamton–Albany line as the Cherry Valley local marches out of town under a roiling canopy of smoke and steam. A mile south, the 4-6-0 and its eight-car consist will turn north onto the short branch to Cherry Valley, New York. Milk seems to be a prominent commodity on this run, with nearly half of the train devoted to milk transport. Ten-Wheeler 536 was built by the D&H in 1905 and scrapped early in the 1950s when the steam era ended on the D&H. The Cherry Valley branch did not fare much better, becoming an early casualty of the boom in the trucking industry that swept the country in the 1950s. The branch was abandoned in 1956 and the Cherry Valley milk run—indeed, milk trains nationwide—became another page in railroad history books. *Jim Shaughnessy*

The New York Central was key to D&H passenger operations, forwarding through cars between Albany and New York City. At Albany in the spring of 1968, the *Laurentian* from Montreal has arrived and its through cars pulled off to be added to the Buffalo–New York City train on the next track over. *Jim Shaughnessy*

It's morning in Montreal as the *Montreal Limited,* behind a pair of Alco road-switchers, eases into Windsor Station at the conclusion of its overnight journey from New York in the 1950s. The *Montreal Limited* folder from 1961 reminded travelers that D&H was the shortest, fastest route between New York and Montreal. *Photo, Kevin J. Holland collection; brochure, C. W. Newton*

The *Montreal Limited* and *Laurentian* lasted until May 1, 1971, when they were discontinued concurrent with the startup of Amtrak. At the time, these two trains were the only ones linking New York with Montreal, and their loss was keenly felt. As a result, a grass-roots effort sanctioned by the D&H and championed (and partially funded) by the State of New York resulted in the resumption of New York–Montreal passenger service under Amtrak in 1974. Dubbed the *Adirondack*, after the mountain range skirted by D&H's Montreal main line, the new service pretty much picked up where D&H had left off in 1971; in fact, most of the equipment was provided by D&H.

As of 2000, D&H and Amtrak continued to provide daily *Adirondack* service to Montreal, along with new service to Rutland via D&H's former line out of Whitehall.

FREIGHT TRAFFIC

Having sold its historic canal in 1899 (it closed in 1904) and with much of its trackage established, the D&H was ready to face the twentieth century as an all-rail anthracite carrier. Because of its hard properties, anthracite coal burned much cleaner than bituminous coal and presumably would be in high demand for the foreseeable future. By the 1930s, anthracite accounted for more than half of the tonnage hauled by the D&H. The remainder included forest products (mainly newsprint), steel, and other mine-related products such as iron ore and cement. The railroad also hauled bituminous coal, much of it for export.

The bottom fell out of anthracite traffic during the Depression, however, and the railroad had to take a new direction to survive. It did so by becoming an "overhead" or "bridge" carrier—a railroad serving as a link between major carriers. In its new role, D&H became a conduit for traffic

Small railroad, big locomotives: D&H may have been overshadowed by surrounding giants like New York Central, Canadian Pacific, and Erie, but the railroad had nothing to apologize for in the motive-power department. To move heavy tonnage over Richmondville Hill on the Albany–Binghamton line, Ararat Summit on the Penn Division, and grades elsewhere, D&H relied on 40 Class J 4-6-6-4 Mallets and 14 big Class K Northerns such as the 308 at the top of the page; all were built by the American Locomotive during the World War II years, with the last 4-8-4 delivered in 1946. The big dual-purpose 4-8-4s also handled the *Laurentian* and *Montreal Limited*. The careers of these powerful steam locomotives were shortened by dieselization in 1952–53. In terms of heft, their diesel-era equivalents really didn't come along until 1964 when D&H began taking delivery of a fleet of nine Alco Century 628s, three of which are shown on train RW-6 near Richmondville in May 1965. Each of these hefty six-axle behemoths could drum up 2,750 hp. for mainline freight duties. *Steam photo, D&H; diesel photo, Jim Shaughnessy*

moving between Canada and New England and westward-bound railroads such as NYC and Erie. Connections in the Wilkes-Barre area with the Pennsylvania Railroad and Lehigh Valley also provided a gateway for traffic moving to and from the Southeast. D&H soon earned its new nickname, "The Bridge Line." Although the railroad continued to haul coal and even held onto some of its coal interests (notably the Hudson Coal Company) into the 1960s, its place in American railroading became—and remains—firmly established as a bridge line.

THE "NEW" D&H

The story of the D&H would probably have concluded in the 1970s with some sort of merger or acquisition had it not been for a series of events which drastically reshaped—rather than obliterated—the railroad. Until 1967 the D&H was pretty much an "also-ran" railroad—that is, a carrier overshadowed by other, more high-profile railroads in the region. After World War II, the D&H spent most of its efforts fulfilling its day-to-day duties and struggling to stay afloat while the railroad industry in general went into slow decline. All the while, D&H kept a relatively low profile.

This period of status quo began to change in 1967 when Buck Dumaine became D&H's new president and CEO. In short order, Dumaine upgraded the road's passenger service by buying five surplus Alco-built PA-type passenger diesels from Santa Fe and New Haven, along with several surplus passenger cars from the Rio Grande. Repainted in the D&H's handsome blue, silver, and yellow livery, the new equipment brought a whole new spirit—and a dynamic image—to the D&H.

Dumaine was very much an individualist and thus was a key figure in fighting to keep D&H an independent railroad. A condition of Norfolk & Western's 1964 merger/lease with the Nickel Plate and Wabash was that the D&H, B&M, and Erie Lackawanna be allowed to join the newly expanded N&W at a later date—mainly because the impending Pennsylvania-New York Central merger would probably result in several of D&H's connections becoming "unfriendly."

Insisting that D&H could survive while remaining independent, Dumaine staunchly opposed D&H's inclusion into anything—so much so that he resigned to lead a proxy fight. In an interesting twist, D&H and EL were acquired by Dereco, an N&W holding company. D&H and EL continued as affiliates until Hurricane Agnes

The *Laurentian* slinks along the precipitous walls of the Red Rocks area along Willsborough Bay on Lake Champlain on June 10, 1969. Leading the southbound train is Alco PA No. 18, one of five such locomotives purchased secondhand by the D&H in 1967, four from Santa Fe and one from New Haven for parts. D&H retained the "warbonnet" paint scheme pattern of the former Santa Fe units, substituting blue for red. Together with upgraded passenger train consists comprised of former Denver & Rio Grande Western rolling stock, the "new" *Laurentian* was a handsome-looking train. The locomotives became celebrities for students of diesel-era railroad history and were the last surviving Alco PAs in America. They occasionally performed in freight duties after D&H passenger service was discontinued in 1971 and eventually were sold to National Railways of Mexico. In 2000, two of the locomotives were returned to the U.S. where they were to be restored, with one destined for display at the Smithsonian Institution.
Jim Shaughnessy

Railroad Corporation—Conrail.

Under normal circumstances, this would have left the D&H high and dry, but these were not normal circumstances. The creation of Conrail had some caveats, and one was an expanded D&H. To maintain some semblance of competitiveness, D&H was granted trackage rights over Conrail west from Binghamton to Buffalo (where connection was made with Norfolk & Western to Chicago), and south to Atlantic ports at Newark, New Jersey, and Philadelphia, Pennsylvania, as well as to connections with the Southern Railway and Richmond, Fredericksburg & Potomac at Potomac Yard near Washington, D.C. When Conrail was formally born on that April day, the Delaware & Hudson more than doubled in size!

The new arrangement had its problems, such as finding enough locomotives to protect the train schedules of the newly expanded railroad; further, D&H trains moved over Conrail at the discretion of Conrail dispatchers, and the number of cars that could be interchanged to and from the D&H at terminals common with Conrail was limited.

But D&H soldiered on, and even embarked on yet another major transaction that again significantly altered its trackage map. In 1980 D&H purchased, from Conrail, the former Lackawanna main line between Binghamton and Scranton.

Representing a latter-day expanded D&H, train RPPY (Rouses Point–Potomac Yard) cruises along the Susquehanna River east of Binghamton on the former Lackawanna main line in late spring 1981. D&H purchased what became known as its "Lackawanna Side" route in 1980 to circumvent the heavy-grade route between Nineveh, New York, and Scranton, Pennsylvania, which was abandoned after the purchase.
Mike Schafer

wreaked havoc on the EL in 1972, forcing it to declare bankruptcy and leave Dereco. This led to a newly independent D&H under the leadership of Bruce Sterzing.

The 1970 collapse of Penn Central provided impetus to create a new governmental body, the United States Railway Administration, that would oversee the consolidation of all of the Northeast's bankrupt carriers, including PC, LV, Jersey Central, Reading, Lehigh & Hudson River, and, now, EL into a single new railroad. On April 1, 1976, these roads were combined to form the Consolidated

D&H was one of the few railroads to own rare "Sharknose" freight diesels, products of the long-defunct Baldwin Locomotive Works. Under the presidency of Bruce Sterzing, two Sharks were acquired from the Monongahela Railroad near Pittsburgh, Pennsylvania. The Monongahela had acquired them from New York Central in the late 1960s. The celebrity units are shown at Kenwood Yard, Albany, in February 1975 on an auto-rack train full of Volkswagens that had just entered the U.S. through the Port of Albany. *Jim Shaughnessy*

This well-engineered stretch of railroad, nearly 60 miles long, provided a shorter route for D&H traffic out of Buffalo destined for points south of Wilkes-Barre/Scranton. In addition, the purchase included major yard facilities at East Binghamton, which gave the D&H a more efficient, more centrally located hub for its recently expanded network. Until then, much classification had been handled by D&H's longtime major yard at Oneonta, New York, midway between Albany and Binghamton. The new line further improved operations by obviating D&H's trackage rights arrangement on Conrail (former Erie/EL) between Binghamton and Lanesboro, where trains had to traverse a steep, winding connecting track to reach the Scranton–Nineveh line.

In 1981, N&W's Dereco sold the D&H to financier Timothy Mellon's new railroad empire—Guilford Transportation—which included Boston & Maine and Maine Central. Labor unrest and other problems shortened the marriage, and Guilford sold the D&H. Canadian Pacific then acquired the D&H to gain access to U.S. markets and ports. Between Guilford and CP ownership, the Delaware & Hudson lost much of its identity, but technically it remains an entity, though owned by CP subsidiary St. Lawrence & Atlantic.

D&H has outlasted nearly all its contemporaries and often its competitors. For what had been a modest-size railroad for many decades, the Delaware & Hudson has led a remarkably convoluted, fascinating life.

The local from Whitehall en route to Albany stirs up the snow at West Waterford, New York, in January 1971. Ample snow comes with the territory in the land of Delaware & Hudson. *Jeremy Plant*

SERVING THE HEART OF
INDUSTRIAL AMERICA

Erie Railroad

The Erie Railroad was a powerhouse company when American railroading was in its infancy, but it was doomed to eventually take a back seat in the hotly contested New York–Chicago corridor. The Erie would also be among the first large "classic" American railroads to be merged out of existence, in 1960.

The Erie's birth was spurred by a canal, not another railroad. Amid much fanfare, the Erie Canal was completed across upstate New York in 1825, prompting the towns, merchants, and public living in southern tier of the state to want their own transportation artery. In response, New York Governor De Witt Clinton sanctioned the chartering of the New York & Erie Railroad in 1832 under the guidance of Eleazar Lord.

The sanction was not without caveats, among them that the railroad be entirely located within the State of New York and not be allowed to interchange with railroads in New Jersey and Pennsylvania without permission from the state legislature. To ensure this interchange condition, the NY&E's track gauge was set at 6 feet, considerably wider than the standard gauge of 4 feet 8½ inches. Although this would not prevent traffic from being interchanged at connecting points, it did prevent one railroad's cars from wandering on to another's lines. This wide gauge would prove both a bane and a blessing to the new railroad.

The eastern endpoint of the New York & Erie was established at Piermont, New York (not coincidentally the home of Eleazar Lord), on the Hudson River. The west end of the railroad would be at Dunkirk on Lake Erie some 40 miles west of Buffalo. Interestingly, the New York & Harlem Railroad offered to extend a line up the east side of the Hudson from New York City to a point opposite Piermont for purposes of interchange with the NY&E. Although this arrangement would have involved trans-Hudson packets to transfer cargo and passengers, it would have given the NY&E a friendly entrance into Manhattan.

Curiously, the NY&E refused the arrangement which—who knows—might have some day grown into a bridge or tunnel crossing of the Hudson and a direct line into Manhattan. Later, rail access to Manhattan would be severely thwarted by the growing empire of Cornelius Vanderbilt that would someday be known as the New York Central System. Erie's lack of a direct rail entrance into Manhattan would haunt the railroad to the end.

NY&E's first train ran in 1841 and bankruptcy soon followed due to unexpectedly high construction costs. The railroad reached Port Jervis, New York, 74 miles out of Piermont, in 1847 and Binghamton, New York, 201 miles, only a year later. In doing so, the NY&E had to break one of the conditions of its charter and detour through Pennsylvania, following the Delaware River between Port Jervis and Deposit, New York, to maintain an easy grade. At Deposit, the Delaware turned northeast while the Erie turned southwest, surmounting a mountain ridge to reach another waterway, the Susquehanna River, near Lanesboro, Pennsylvania. The resulting grade over Gulf Summit was the steepest on the Jersey City–Chicago main line. At Lanesboro an engineering landmark was built across the valley of Starrucca Creek: Starrucca Viaduct (sidebar). The New York & Erie was officially and entirely opened between Piermont and Dunkirk in 1851, an event attended by U.S. President Millard Fillmore.

A look a the Erie map reveals a gaggle of branches and alternate main lines at the eastern end of the railroad with Piermont now off the beaten path. Piermont was rendered impotent around 1852 when the NY&E leased what had been two thorns in its side: the Paterson & Hudson River Rail Road and the Paterson & Ramapo Railroad. Together these two upstarts had a shorter, more direct route between Jersey City—directly across the Hudson from Manhattan—and the NY&E at Suffern, New York, and an increasing amount of freight and passenger traffic off the NY&E had been using this route east of Suffern. With the lease, the NY&E's new mainline route to the Hudson east of Suffern became that via Paterson, New Jersey. Over the years, the railroad built or otherwise acquired numerous other lines in

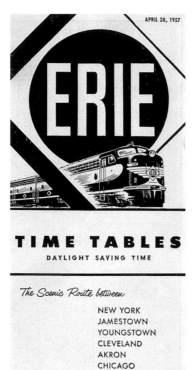

APRIL 28, 1957

ERIE

TIME TABLES

DAYLIGHT SAVING TIME

The Scenic Route between

NEW YORK
JAMESTOWN
YOUNGSTOWN
CLEVELAND
AKRON
CHICAGO

FORM 1

Erie Railroad

FACING PAGE: Back-to-back PA-series passenger diesels built by Alco (American Locomotive Company) head up an excursion train out of Hoboken on April 26, 1959. The train is shown posing for its riders on Erie's Newburgh (New York) branch. In the background is famous Moodna Viaduct on Erie's Graham Line, a bypass route around Middletown, New York. The Newburgh branch has since been abandoned, but a breathtaking view from Moodna Viaduct can today be enjoyed from the windows of New Jersey Transit commuter trains between Hoboken and Port Jervis, New York. *John Dziobko*

FACING PAGE, INSET: One of Erie's Alco road-switchers assigned to local switching duties in the Dayton, Ohio, area putts about town on a sunny early spring day in the 1950s. *Alvin Schultze*

LEFT: The public passenger timetable of April 28, 1957, touted Erie as "The Scenic Route between New York, Jamestown, Youngstown, Cleveland, Akron, Chicago."

Storming along on well-manicured right-of-way near Lanesboro, Pennsylvania, an Erie 2-10-2 "Santa Fe" type and a 4-6-2 Pacific doublehead train 22 on August 24, 1941. Two locomotives are necessary for the climb out of the Susquehanna River valley to Gulf Summit, New York. Nameless No. 22 was primarily a mail, express, and milk train (the second, third, and fourth cars are milk cars, and there some are behind the passenger-carrying cars as well) operating between Hornell and Susquehanna, New York. *C. George Krumm, Ed Crist collection*

northern New Jersey and southeastern New York State to serve the burgeoning population and industry of the region.

Things were changing at the west end of the railroad as well. Having been overshadowed by Buffalo, Dunkirk never became the important Great Lakes port that had been envisioned. Buffalo was the western anchor for the Erie Canal as well as the 11 newly affiliated companies that in 1853 opened as the New York Central Railroad between Albany and Buffalo. The NY&E built a branch to Buffalo (in part by acquiring NYC component road Attica & Buffalo between those two points) as well as to Rochester, New York. Dunkirk became a minor terminal on a branch of the Erie.

The railroad's growth was costly, and by the end of the 1850s the NY&E was in receivership despite having been lent money by railroad tycoons "Commodore" Vanderbilt and Daniel Drew, themselves adversaries. In 1859 the NY&E was reorganized as the Erie Railway.

The latter half of the 1800s became synonymous with railroading's "robber baron" era, and the

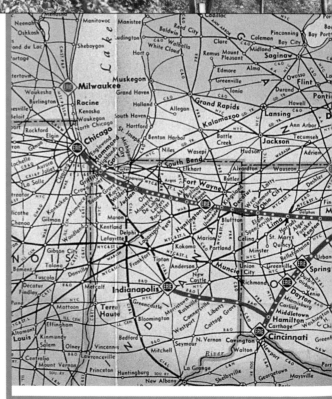

NY&E quickly became embroiled in a myriad of manipulations involving magnates whose names are well-known to railroad historians; aside from Vanderbilt and Drew, this included James Fisk and Jay Gould. The key player, of course, was Vanderbilt, of New York Central fame. Vanderbilt had a contempt for competition, in particular Drew and his cohorts, Fisk and Gould, who controlled the NY&E. After Vanderbilt had secured his NYC empire in 1864, he set out to conquer the Erie.

Vanderbilt underestimated his foes and lost his bid to seize the Erie. In a story of stock manipulation that deserves its own book, not only was Vanderbilt knocked out of the Erie picture, but so was Fisk and Drew. Jay Gould wound up as Erie president in 1868. Vanderbilt went back to concentrating on his New York Central System.

As with competitors NYC, Pennsylvania Railroad, and Baltimore & Ohio, Erie was eyeballing expansion into the Midwest, particularly the growing rail hub of Chicago. However, its first major push west from New York State took it to Cincinnati, Ohio, itself a growing gateway between East and West. The Erie reached Cincinnati in 1874 by leasing the Atlantic & Great Western, which ran

ERIE RAILROAD AT A GLANCE

Headquarters: Cleveland, OH

Route mileage circa 1950: 2,341

Locomotive fleet as of 1960:
Diesels: 695

Rolling stock as of 1960:
Freight cars: 20,372
Passenger cars: 519

Principal routes circa 1950:

Jersey City–Paterson, NJ –Middletown–Hornell, NY–Youngstown, OH–Chicago (Hammond– Chicago via trackage rights on the Chicago & Western Indiana)
Marion–Dayton–Cincinnati, OH (Dayton–Cincinnati via trackage rights on B&O)
Hamilton, OH–Indianapolis, IN (trackage rights on B&O)
Leavittsburg–Cleveland, OH
Pymatuning, A.–Leavittsburg, OH
Hornell–Buffalo–Niagara Falls, NY
Salamanca–Dunkirk, NY
Corning (Painted Post)–Attica, NY
Avon–Rochester, NY
River Junction–Cuba Junction, NY

Carrolton, NY–Eleanora Jct., NY (Brockway–Eleanora Jct. via B&O trackage rights)
Corning, NY–Newberry Jct., PA
Lanesboro–Wilkes-Barre/Scranton, PA
Lackawaxen–Avoca, PA
Newburgh Jct.–Campbell Hall–Graham, NY
Maybrook–Pine Island, NY
Croxton (Jersey City)–Nyack, NY
Piermont–Suffern, NY
NY&NJ Jct., NJ–Nanuet, NY
Rutherford Jct.–Ridgewood Jct.
Paterson (Newark Jct.)–Newark, NJ
Croxton–Midvale, NJ

Notable passenger trains (slash denotes dual destination or point of origin):

Erie Limited (Jersey City–Chicago/Buffalo)
Lake Cities (Jersey City–Cleveland/Buffalo; later extended to Chicago)
Pacific Express (Jersey City–Chicago)
Atlantic Express (Chicago–Jersey City)
Midlander (Jersey City–Chicago)
Southern Tier Express (Buffalo–Hornell–Jersey City)
Mountain Express (Jersey City–Hornell)
Tuxedo (Jersey City–Port Jervis)

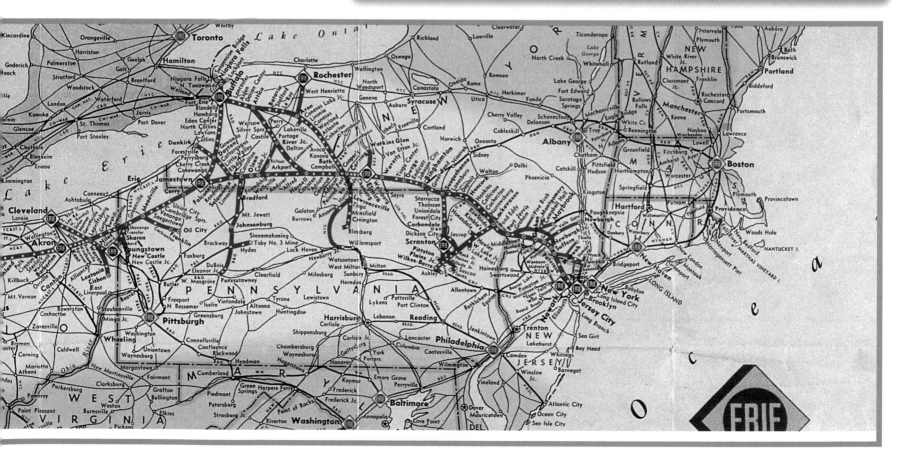

Erie freight NY-98 is near the end of its Chicago–Jersey City run as it eases across the Hackensack River on September 18, 1961; it will terminate at Croxton Yard only a short distance away. The Erie-Lackawanna merger has occurred, but with a nice matching set of Electro-Motive FT diesels at the helm still wearing Erie livery (though renumbered for the EL merger)this could easily pass for a scene from the late 1940s. Erie took delivery of its first FTs in 1944, and initially they were assigned to the most topographically challenged part of the New York–Jersey city route, that between Marion, Ohio, and Salamanca, New York. In later years the FTs tended to be concentrated on the eastern end of the system, as this photo reveals. *Robert R. Malinoski*

between Salamanca, New York (on the Erie), and Dayton, Ohio, via Meadeville, Pennsylvania, and Marion, Ohio; trackage rights took the A&GW on into Cincinnati. Later that year, the Erie gained a new president, Hugh Jewett, who soon reorganized the road as the New York, Lake Erie & Western and in 1880 converted it to standard gauge.

The A&GW lease ended when it entered receivership and it re-emerged as the New York, Pennsylvania & Ohio, which the Erie (NYLE&W) leased in 1883. By this time, the NYP&O had expanded into Youngstown and Cleveland, Ohio, among other places. During Jewett's reign, the Erie also finally reached Chicago by way of the Chicago & Atlantic Railroad which had opened between Hammond, Indiana, and Marion, Indiana, in 1880. Bankruptcy dogged the Erie and caught up with it (again) in 1893. In 1895, yet another reorganization happened, with the NYLE&W emerging as the Erie Railroad. The stage was now set for the Erie in its role as one of America's classic railroads of the twentieth century.

TWENTIETH CENTURY ERIE

Just before the turn of the century, Frederick Underwood became president of the Erie Railroad.

For the next quarter century or so, Underwood would develop the Erie into a respectable player in the ever-hostile New York–Chicago arena. Underwood double-tracked most of Erie's main routes, including some stretches of main line in Indiana where the eastbound and westbound main tracks were widely separated—by yards rather than feet—and sometimes entirely at different grades. Other physical plant improvements included the construction of low-grade freight bypass routes in mountainous areas and the electrification of some New York-area suburban passenger operations.

During the 1920s, the Erie had caught the attention of the Van Sweringen brothers, two highly successful real-estate moguls from Cleveland who had been buying and organizing rail properties since before World War I. One of these properties was the New York, Chicago & St. Louis—the Nickel Plate—and the brothers felt the Erie nicely complemented the Nickel Plate. By the end of the Roaring Twenties, the Van Sweringens had built an empire of cooperating railroads that included, aside from the NKP and its affiliate roads, the Chesapeake & Ohio, Missouri Pacific, Chicago & Eastern Illinois, and the Erie, and others.

These properties in general were well-managed and manicured under the Van Sweringen regime, which went so far as to apply a degree of standardization to some of their railroads' locomotives and rolling stock. However, the Depression was no kinder to the Van Sweringens than anyone else, and bankruptcy ran rife through the Van Sweringen lines in the late 1930s. Both brothers succumbed at a relatively young age to heart problems during that period, and the stress of the times may have been linked their deaths. Had they and their railroad empire survived the Depression, America's railroad history might have been significantly different, at least east of the Missouri River.

True to its nature, the Erie was one of those Van Sweringen roads that went bankrupt, in 1938. Yet another reorganization followed, in 1941 (the name stayed the same this time), and it included the outright purchase of a number of lines that until that time had been leased to the Erie or owned as subsidiaries.

The reorganization worked, and the Erie began to prosper—although World War II certainly helped to increase business. After the war, business flourished and Erie began an aggressive dieselization program that was completed in 1954—earlier than most of its competitors. The move bolstered earnings and improved operating performance, including the speedup of passenger schedules.

The prosperity was not all that long-lived, as Erie, like numerous other U.S. railroads, began to

Erie's flagship passenger run to the end of the railroad's existence was the *Erie Limited*, here featured on a colorized postcard from the 1940s. One of Erie's chunky K-5-class Pacifics is in charge of moving the *Limited* over the road. *Mike Schafer collection*

The throat of Jersey City Terminal was nearly always a busy place, with numerous Jersey Central and Erie commuter trains vying for track space with the intercity runs of Jersey Central, Erie, Baltimore & Ohio, and Reading. In this 1947 view that looks toward New York City (whose skyline on this day has been obliterated by haze), an Erie local behind Pacific 2750 eases out of the terminal as an early Alco switcher works a string of reefers. *Ed Crist collection*

Starrucca Viaduct

In this 1941 scene from the east end of Starrucca, Erie 2-8-4 No. 3370 serves as a pusher for the fourth section of train 98, slugging uphill toward Gulf Summit with 89 cars. *Robert F. Collins*

Starrucca Viaduct is one of America's most notable and elegant railroad engineering landmarks. When it was built by the New York & Erie in 1847–48, there was considerable doubt that the 110-foot-high stone structure would support the weight of a train. Not only did it support the first train across then, but more than 150 years later it was still carrying heavy-duty rail traffic! The viaduct's 17 masonry arches—which are hollow at the top—comprise a 1,200-foot long span over Starrucca Creek and at one time Delaware & Hudson Pennsylvania Division's main line. Located on Erie's 1.14 percent climb to the ridge of the Appalachian Mountains at Gulf Summit, Starrucca Viaduct looms over the village of Lanesboro in northeastern Pennsylvania. Though ownership of the breathtaking structure has changed three times since Erie days, it still is most closely associated with the dearly departed Erie Railroad.

feel the effects of increased competition from the newly emerging trucking industry and, on the passenger front, automobiles and airliners. Further, as the 1950s rock-and-rolled toward conclusion, the country was hit with a recession. Like fellow railroads, the Erie was forced to reconcile a venue of rising costs and sliding revenues. One of these fellow companies was the Delaware, Lackawanna & Western, a railroad whose route characteristics closely duplicated that of the Erie between the Hudson River and Binghamton. Though Erie and Lackawanna were obviously rivals in the railroading world that existed between the Jersey shore and Buffalo and many points between, the pair

early on recognized a much larger picture in which, united, they might stand a better chance against giants NYC and PRR.

This outlook led to a spirit of cooperation that began in the mid-1950s when the two roads began consolidating duplicate facilities, such as at Binghamton where they were literally only a few feet apart. The biggest such change came in 1956–57 when Erie moved its intercity and suburban passenger trains out of venerable Jersey City Terminal over to Lackawanna's stately terminal in Hoboken. Marriage was the next obvious step. On October 17, 1960, Erie and DL&W merged to form the Erie-Lackawanna Railroad.

An Erie Alco PA clad in its as-delivered black and yellow scheme takes a break from passenger duties to help with local freight duties at Lima, Ohio, in the late 1950s. The green-and-gray livery shown on the PAs on the first page of this chapter was introduced when Erie took delivery of its 14 E-series passenger diesels from Electro-Motive in 1951. The green/gray scheme was developed by Electro-Motive and later applied to some of the PAs. *Alvin Schultze*

An eastbound Erie freight threads its way through Akron, Ohio, late in the 1950s. The Erie passenger depot is at right in the distance, while the passenger platforms for the B&O depot are partially visible at left. Akron was one of the few intermediate on-line Erie cities where there was stiff competition for east-west freight and passenger traffic. *Alvin Schultze*

An A-B-B set of Alco FA freight locomotives drifts into the Hammond (Indiana) yard at the joint Erie-Monon depot with a short transfer freight from Chicago circa 1960. Although the Erie maintained a freight yard and engine facilities some 15 miles from here in Chicago at 51st Street, Hammond was really the west end of Erie's main line. West from Hammond, Erie trains utilized trackage rights on the Chicago & Western Indiana to reach downtown Chicago. Although a number of Erie's freights operated through to 51st Street, others terminated at Hammond and were reclassified into blocks that moved on transfers fielded out from Hammond to various other railroads' yards. *Dave Ingles*

TRAFFIC ON THE ERIE

Unlike competitors PRR, NYC, and B&O, Erie did not offer an extensive array of East Coast–Chicago passenger trains. Hampered by lack of a direct entrance into Manhattan, mountain grades, a long route between New York and Chicago (998 miles), and a Jersey City–Chicago timing of about 24 hours, at best (the fastest runs of NYC and PRR were about 16 hours), Erie was rarely the first choice for customers traveling through between America's largest and then-second-largest cities. Rather, the Erie best served as a link between intermediate on-line cities like Binghamton, Corning, Elmira, Jamestown, Meadeville, and Marion and New York or Chicago.

For many years, there was but two through trains in each direction between Jersey City and Chicago: the westbound *Pacific Express*; its eastbound counterpart, the *Atlantic Express*; and Erie's flagship train, the *Erie Limited*, in both directions. The *Pacific Express* and *Atlantic Express* had held

those titles since the 1800s but by the Depression had become primarily mail and express trains.

What the *Erie Limited* lacked in terms of speed, it made up for in offering good, solid equipment: sleeping cars, diners, Pullman parlor-buffet car, and deluxe "salon" coaches. Carrying the prestigious train numbers of 1 (westbound) and 2 (eastbound), the *Erie Limited* traversed the most scenic stretches of the railroad in daylight, that between Jersey City and Jamestown. During the night hours, the *Erie Limited* sped across the flatlands of Ohio and Indiana. The train also served Buffalo via split-off train out of Hornell, New York.

The *Lake Cities* provided overnight Jersey City–Cleveland and Jersey City–Buffalo service, likewise splitting at Hornell. In 1939, the Erie increased through east-west service with the addition of the Jersey City–Chicago *Midlander*, which ran combined with the *Lake Cities* between Jersey City and Salamanca, New York. Eventually, the *Midlander* name was dropped in favor of using the name *Lake Cities* for the Chicago leg as well as the Cleveland and Buffalo sections.

Additional service across New York's southern tier was provided by the *Southern Tier Express* and *Mountain Express*. Most Erie passenger service was concentrated east of Port Jervis, with numerous trains throughout the day, many of them scheduled for rush-hour duties aimed at metro New York. Passengers rode ferries between Jersey City and Manhattan.

A short but interesting passenger route on the Erie was its 67-mile Youngstown–Cleveland line. Aside from hosting the Cleveland leg of the *Lake Cities*, the line also served as a link in a Detroit–Pittsburgh–Washington passenger route

A rare scene on a branch long gone: Like several other Northeastern carriers, Erie relied on the economies of gas-electric cars to provide service on lightly patronized branch lines. One such car stands at New City, New York, at the end of the short branch out of Nanuet, New York, the latter on Erie's old New Jersey & New York line between Rutherford, New Jersey, and Spring Valley and Stony Point, New York. The date is February 5, 1938, and the conductor seems proud of his charge. Alas, this branch was abandoned a short time later. *Rod Dirkes, Ed Crist collection*

that provided through services coordinated by NYC, Erie, Pittsburgh & Lake Erie, and B&O. For many years the *Washingtonian* was the star train of the route, providing through-car service between Cleveland and the nation's capital. In the 1950s, the *Washingtonian* and the Cleveland leg of the *Lake Cities* became the *Morning Steel King* and *Evening Steel King*—new Cleveland–Pittsburgh runs jointly operated by Erie and P&LE. Erie also operated a modest commuter service between Youngstown and Cleveland.

After the 1960 EL merger, the *Erie Limited* became the *Erie Lackawanna Limited* and then finally took on an old DL&W name, the *Phoebe Snow*, lasting until 1967. Interestingly, the *Lake Cities* would outlast the Erie Railroad by ten years, making its final runs between Chicago and Hoboken in 1970 under the Erie Lackawanna banner. Even the lowly *Pacific* and *Atlantic Express* outlived the Erie, lasting into the late 1960s. Although the Cleveland commuter train was dropped in the mid-1970s, much of Erie's metro New York suburban services today survive under the direction of New Jersey Transit.

As with most other railroads, most of Erie's revenues by far were derived from freight traffic. Erie relied largely on the movement of automobiles and auto parts, steel, coal, and other products relating to heavy industry. Unfortunately, as with passenger service, in every major city served by the Erie, it had to share the freight pie with some big runners, notably NYC, PRR, and B&O. One of Erie's most notable virtues in freight transportation was that it was known for having wide clearances at tunnels, bridges, and other locations—perhaps the only good thing that came of having been built with broad-gauge trackage. Ample clearances made Erie a prime choice for "high/wide" freight whose movement was restricted on most other railroads.

Although the combined Erie-DL&W became very much a vaunted freight carrier against all odds, Hurricane Agnes in 1972 dealt a devastating blow to Erie Lackawanna, forcing it into bankruptcy and, four years later, inclusion into Conrail. Immediately upon Conrail's startup on April 1, 1976, almost the entire western half of the former Erie New York–Chicago main line was silenced as through traffic was rerouted to parallel Conrail lines. Shortly thereafter, most of the rails and ties were torn up, and the Erie today in Ohio and Indiana is largely a wide pathway of weeds through the farmlands and prairies.

Berkshire-type steam locomotives (2-8-4s) reigned on Erie freights after the Van Sweringen brothers embraced high-horsepower "Super Power" steam engines in the 1930s. This scene of Erie "Berk" 3319 on a coal train at an unknown location was probably staged, as the smiling engine crew seems to be hamming it up. *Don Furler, Railfan & Railroad collection*

A cab/booster/cab (A-B-A) set of Electro-Motive F3s has just ushered the pre-modernized *Erie Limited* into Binghamton, New York, circa 1950. Station personnel have wasted little time in swarming the head-end cars to load and unload mail and express while passengers assemble for boarding. *Johnny Krause, Railfan & Railroad collection*

Gulf, Mobile & Ohio

Of all the railroads featured in this volume, the Gulf, Mobile & Ohio was the newest—and shortest lived. The GM&O was, along with neighbor (and future merger partner) Illinois Central, a north-south railroad in an east-west industry.

The "Gee-Mo"—as it was sometimes called by its devotees—was chartered in 1938 to acquire the Gulf, Mobile & Northern and Mobile & Ohio railroads. Thus it could be said that the GM&O was among the first of the major players in the merger movement that would sweep across America in the later years of the twentieth century.

GULF, MOBILE & NORTHERN—A REBEL RAILROAD

The GM&N dated from 1917 when it was born through a reorganization of the New Orleans, Mobile & Chicago Railroad—itself having been created through a reorganization, in 1909, of the Mobile, Jackson & Kansas City Railroad. The MJ&KC and its predecessors had built north from Mobile, Alabama, to Middleton, Tennessee, not far south of Jackson, Tennessee, an important railroad center (and home to fabled IC engineer John Luther "Casey" Jones). Judging by the company's name, it had loftier goals than Middleton, but receivership halted further expansion.

A key figure in GM&O history was Isaac "Ike" B. Tigrett, a banker from Jackson, Tennessee, who joined GM&N's board of directors in 1919 and the following year became the road's president. A visionary railroader ahead of his time, Tigrett understood that, to survive, his railroad would have to expand through the acquisition of or merger with other key railroads. By 1927 he had extended the GM&N north to Jackson and then—via trackage rights on the Nashville, Chattanooga & St. Louis—to Paducah, Kentucky. At Paducah, the GM&N exchanged a large amount of traffic with the Chicago, Burlington & Quincy with which it shared a special traffic agreement.

By engineering mergers and leases with various other small railroads, the GM&N also extended itself northwest from Jackson to Dyersburg, Tennessee, in 1928. By the the time the Great Depression

had a full grip on America, Tigrett had expanded the GM&N southward to New Orleans via the South's "other" Jackson—that in southern Mississippi. This was accomplished through GM&N's merger with two shortlines and the lease of the New Orleans Great Northern.

THE MOBILE & OHIO

With its south end anchored at Mobile, Alabama, the Mobile & Ohio had goals similar to the GM&N and its predecessors: linking the Gulf to the North in general and the Ohio River in particular—hence the "Ohio" in the name. The M&O had been in service since the pre-Civil War era and by 1887 had been extended all the way to East St. Louis (formerly Illinoistown), Illinois, via Cairo, Illinois, at the junction of the Mississippi and Ohio rivers. St. Louis and East St. Louis together had become a major rail gateway between East and West, second only to Chicago.

In 1901, the M&O became a ward of the Southern Railway, but in 1938 SR sold the financially frail railroad to the Gulf, Mobile & Ohio. As a newly formed company, the GM&O—led by Ike Tigrett—in 1940 acquired the GM&N and M&O and consolidated all operations and trackage under the GM&O name.

Known somewhat as a maverick in a territory dominated by Illinois Central, the GM&O managed to weather World War II while eliminating redundancies that had resulted from taking on the M&O and GM&N. The result was a tightly run railroad eager to get to the nation's Number One railroad gateway: Chicago. And it did just that with the 1947 acquisition of the bankrupt Alton Railroad, which stretched from Chicago to St. Louis and to Kansas City.

THE ALTON ROUTE

The Alton's roots could be traced to 1847 with the charter of the Alton & Sangamon Railroad, which was built to link Alton, Illinois, some 25 miles north of St. Louis along the Mississippi, with agriculturally rich central Illinois. By the start of the Civil War in 1860, the railroad had been renamed as the St. Louis, Alton & Chicago, reflecting

FACING PAGE: Two generations of locomotives share the night lights at Gulf, Mobile & Ohio's yard at South Joliet, Illinois, in 1971. The railroad's new 700-series Electro-Motive GP38–2s wear the classy new red-and-white livery. In the background, Electro-Motive passenger F3 No. 880-B—a veteran of nearly a quarter century of service—defers to the new vanguard. *Mike Schafer/Joe Petric*

INSET: Passengers aboard the parlor-observation car of the *Abraham Lincoln* sip drinks and read their *Chicago Daily News'* prior to the train's departure from Chicago Union Station in 1965. *Ron Lundstrom*

LEFT: GM&O's colorful timetable from 1948 prominently featured "The Alton Route" slogan of merger partner Alton Railroad, perhaps as a way of lessening the confusion resulting from GM&O's 1947 takeover of the Alton.

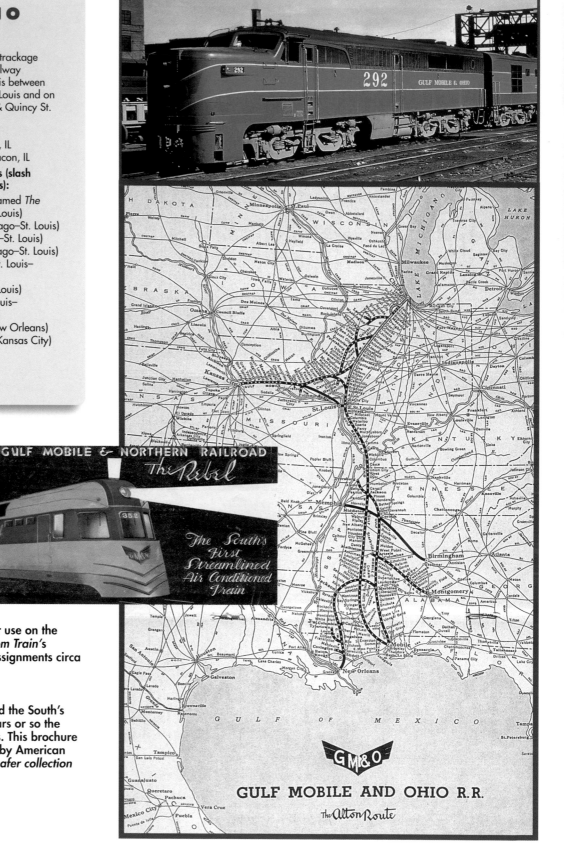

GULF, MOBILE & OHIO AT A GLANCE

Headquarters: Mobile, AL

Route mileage circa 1950: 2,900

Locomotive fleet as of 1963:
Diesels: 246

Rolling stock as of 1963:
Freight cars: 13,933
Passenger cars: 135

Principal lines circa 1950:
Chicago–Springfield–East St. Louis/St. Louis, IL–Corinth–Meridian, MS.–Mobile, AL
Springfield–Kansas City
Bloomington–Murrayville, Ill.
Dyersburg, Tenn.–Union, MS–Mobile, AL
Meridian–New Orleans
Artesia, Miss.–Montgomery, AL
Memphis, Tenn.–Birmingham, AL (trackage rights on Southern between Memphis and Corinth, MS, and on Illinois Central Corinth–Birmingham)
St. Louis–Mexico, MO (trackage rights on Terminal Railway Association of St. Louis between East St. Louis and St. Louis and on Chicago, Burlington & Quincy St. Louis–Mexico)
Godfrey–Roodhouse, IL
Springfield–East Peoria, IL
Dwight–Washington/Lacon, IL

Notable passenger trains (slash denotes dual destinations):
Alton Limited (later renamed *The Limited*; Chicago–St. Louis)
Abraham Lincoln (Chicago–St. Louis)
Ann Rutledge (Chicago–St. Louis)
Midnight Special (Chicago–St. Louis)
Prairie State Express (St. Louis–Chicago)
The Mail (Chicago–St. Louis)
Gulf Coast Rebel (St. Louis–Mobile/Montgomery)
The Rebel (St. Louis–New Orleans)
Night Hawk (St. Louis–Kansas City)

TOP RIGHT: GM&O Alco PA No. 292, built after World War II for use on the *Freedom Train*, was purchased by the GM&O after the *Freedom Train's* national tour. It stands at St. Louis between passenger-train assignments circa 1957. *Alvin Schultz*

ABOVE: GM&O predecessor Gulf, Mobile & Northern introduced the South's first streamliners, the *Rebels*, in 1935, and for the next 20 years or so the *Rebels* were fixtures on GM&N/GM&O lines south of St. Louis. This brochure introduced the striking red-and-silver trains, which were built by American Car & Foundry and powered by Alco prime movers. *Mike Schafer collection*

its new goals. In 1861, the StLA&C was purchased by the Chicago & Alton and by 1864 the C&A had reached Chicago proper. Through lease agreements with two smaller railroads, the C&A reached Kansas City in 1878, thereby opening what was billed as the shortest route between Chicago and Kansas City—at least until the Santa Fe opened its Chicago-K.C. line in 1888.

During the Civil War period, the C&A was the stage for two significant developments in American rail passenger service. In 1865, George M. Pullman built the first sleeping car—the *Pioneer*—for what would become a sleeping-car dynasty known as the Pullman Company. It operated on C&A trains between Chicago and St. Louis and also was drafted to carry the body of President Abraham Lincoln back to Illinois from Washington, D.C., following his assassination. In 1868, the C&A also played host to what is considered the first true railroad dining car, the *Delmonico*. Another Pullman-built car, the *Delmonico* was placed in regular service on the C&A. It was such a huge success that dining cars quickly became a feature service on passenger trains the world over.

The C&A was owned by various railroads early in the twentieth century, among them Rock Island, Nickel Plate, and Union Pacific. Finally in 1929 venerable Baltimore & Ohio purchased the C&A (at foreclosure) with hopes of creating an East Coast–Kansas City through route, and

In this aerial view of the Alton station at Bloomington, Illinois, circa 1940 looking south, the northbound *Prairie State Express* takes on water and passengers. Home to the railroad's main shop complex, Bloomington was the heart of the Alton; the stately depot building served as the railroad's headquarters and included the dispatcher's office. The line branching away to the right is the line to Kansas City, while the east-west intersecting lines belong to Nickel Plate and Peoria & Eastern. Note the streetcar that has just crossed the Alton main line. *Steve Smedley collection*

Clad in the original GM&O colors of crimson and silver (inherited from Gulf, Mobile & Northern), a new Alco S1 switcher poses for the company photographer at an unknown location in the 1940s. As the boxcar reveals, "Rebel Route" was an earlier slogan of the GM&O prior to its 1947 merger with the Alton Railroad, after which the GM&O became known as "The Alton Route." *GM&O*

An A-B-A set of weathered Alco FA freight cab locomotives have the nightly Memphis–Corinth, Mississippi, run in tow at Middleton, Tennessee, in June 1965. Operating on Southern Railway trackage rights, the train is at the intersection of SR's Memphis–Chattanooga line and GM&O's Jackson (Tennessee)–Mobile main, which crossed this side of Southern's depot. Pulpwood and other forest-related products were a prime traffic source on the railroad's lines below St. Louis. *Dave Ingles*

renamed the carrier Alton Railroad. B&O influence was strong, with B&O locomotives and rolling stock commonly seen on the Alton. The Depression and World War II took its toll on the Baltimore & Ohio, and shortly after the war the B&O decided to pursue other interests and sold the Alton to upstart GM&O. The formal date of the GM&O-Alton merger was May 31, 1947. Shortly after, GM&O became the first large Class 1 railroad to completely dieselize.

With its extremities anchored in Chicago, Mobile, New Orleans, and Kansas City, the new postwar Gulf, Mobile & Ohio was ready to compete with the big-league carriers, notably Illinois Central but also, to a lesser degree, Santa Fe, Louisville & Nashville, and Missouri Pacific. It would win some battles, and lose others, but the GM&O tenaciously hung on until 1972.

PASSENGER SERVICE

GM&O predecessor Gulf, Mobile & Northern was a pioneer in streamlining and internal-combustion motive-power. As early as 1924, GM&N began experimenting with motorized local passenger-train service. In 1935 the railroad launched the South's first streamliner, the *Rebel*, between New Orleans and Jackson, Tennessee. By the end of 1935, all GM&N passenger service had been motorized. *Rebel* service was eventually expanded to serve Mobile and St. Louis.

In the long run much more important in the realm of GM&O passenger service, though, was that which had been established by the C&A/Alton Railroad between Chicago and St. Louis. This was a hotly contested corridor where Illinois Central, Wabash, and Chicago & Eastern Illinois vied for customers. The Alton's Chicago–St. Louis route via Joliet, Bloomington/Normal, and Springfield was the shortest and fastest and served the largest population base. Longtime flag-bearer of the route was the *Alton Limited*—also known as the "Red Train" account of its eye-catching three-tone maroon scheme—but the flagship honor was arguably usurped with the 1935 introduction of the streamliner *Abraham Lincoln*, a train that would remain popular into the Amtrak era.

The *Abe* was joined in 1937 with a sister Chicago–St. Louis streamliner known as the *Ann Rutledge*, named for Abe Lincoln's childhood sweetheart who met an untimely death. Under Amtrak, "Annie" has been resuscitated and still plies the former GM&O main line between Chicago and St. Louis.

The long and short of GM&O passenger service: The *Limited* carefully treads over the UD High Line along the Mississippi River as it passes under Veterans Bridge and out of St. Louis for Chicago on a sunny summer afternoon in 1970. In the Chicago–St. louis market, GM&O passenger trains were always well-patronized, and even at this late date— Amtrak was less than a year away—the *Limited* fielded an impressive-size train that includes a diner-lounge and a parlor car. The *Limited* still survives, in a sense, under Amtrak, but today its run has been extended west from St. Louis to Kansas City, and it has been renamed with a former Alton Railroad moniker, *Ann Rutledge. Mike Schafer*

In contrast to the *Limited* and its brethren on the Chicago–St. Louis main line, GM&O's Bloomington–Kansas City route had but a single passenger train in each direction in later years, an all-day "doodlebug" run that operated until 1960. GM&O and its predecessor roads often employed gas-electric motorcars for lightly patronized routes. This motorcar and its coach trailer running as westbound train No. 9 are at Mexico, Missouri, not long before the run was discontinued. *George Speir*

Working their way west through central Illinois with train 233, the daily Bloomington–East Peoria freight, a pair of elderly Electro-Motive F3s curve into Delavan, Illinois, on a late summer's afternoon in 1972. At San Jose (pronounced San JOZ in these parts), the train will turn north on to the Springfield–North Pekin line to reach East Peoria, the railroad hub of central Illinois. The GM&O-IC merger is imminent, and its consummation eventually will render this run and the lines it traverses to the history books. *Doug Steurer*

The modern side of the GM&O is aptly portrayed in this 1966 scene of the new Commonwealth Edison unit coal train easing through Joliet (Illinois) Union Station. En route from ComEd's northern Indiana power-generating station, the empty train has traveled on the Elgin, Joliet & Eastern Railway to Joliet where it returned to home rails north of the station. From Joliet, the train will head back to southern Illinois coal mines at Percy to reload. *Mike Schafer*

The primary overnight train between Chicago and St. Louis for a time carried the legendary name *Midnight Special*, although the folk song of that name actually refers to a Texas & Pacific run.

GM&O's flagship passenger run south of St. Louis was the *Gulf Coast Rebel*, introduced in 1940 at the onset of the merger. Also nicknamed "Big Rebel" in deference to the "vestpocket" *Rebel* streamliners introduced a few years earlier under GM&N auspices, the *Gulf Coast Rebel* initially employed modernized heavyweight rolling stock and handled through sleeping cars between Chicago and Mobile.

GM&O also offered secondary passenger services throughout its system, much of it in the form of gas-electric motorcars and several of which had been inherited from GM&N's extensive collection of "doodlebugs." One motorcar run—that between Bloomington and Kansas City—lasted all the way until 1960 and was the longest motorcar operation in America. GM&O's secondary passenger services also included a modest commuter operation between Chicago and Joliet that not only is still in place, but, under the auspices of Chicago's Metra commuter rail agency, is growing.

Alas, passenger service south of St. Louis was an early casualty of the automobile era as well as

Northernmost point on the GM&O system was Chicago Union Station. On the morning of July 12, 1964, a southbound military special has just pulled away from the confines of Union Station's subterranean platforms under the U.S. Post Office building in the background as a set of Pennsylvania Railroad locomotives likewise head out from the station. The hefty GM&O train—at least 16 cars long—is bound for St. Louis where it will be handed over to the St. Louis–San Francisco Railway. Frisco will relay the train and its inductee passengers to Fort Leonard Wood, Missouri. GM&O also frequently operated student specials to Illinois State and Illinois Wesleyan universities at Bloomington/Normal and to the State Fair at Springfield, Illinois. *Jim Boyd*

Two Alco road-switchers bound past the tidy frame depot at Greenview, Illinois, with the "Jack Line local" out of Bloomington in the fall of 1970. GM&O's line between Bloomington and Murrayville, Illinois, where connection was made with the Springfield–Kansas City line, was known as the "Jack Line" account of its routing through Jacksonville. The train will do local switching at the towns along the 111-mile route to its home terminal, Roodhouse, including a stop at Jacksonville to switch the interchanges with Burlington Northern and Norfolk & Western. *Joe Petric*

the high-class service provided by Illinois Central between St. Louis and the Gulf. Service to New Orleans ended in 1954, and by the end of 1958, all *Rebels* had vanished. In a sense, GM&O did continue to offer passenger service south of St. Louis, but it was in the form of buses operated through GM&O subsidiary Gulf Transport.

North of St. Louis, the passenger story had a brighter ending—and in a sense it hasn't ended at all. Among all the players in the Chicago–St. Louis passenger market, GM&O came out the winner, largely because its high-speed direct route served the most population between Chicago and St. Louis. Indeed, as of the year 2000, GM&O's former Chicago–St. Louis route held status as a key "emerging high-speed corridor" in Amtrak's passenger-train network, although GM&O trains covered the route faster than today's Amtrak runs.

GM&O FREIGHT SERVICE

Naturally, GM&O's freight traffic was largely north-south in nature, but its east-west Kansas City arm fielded traffic to and from the St. Louis–Chicago and St. Louis–Gulf routes through the division-point hub of Roodhouse, Illinois. Here, traffic from the South could be transferred to Chicago–Kansas City trains and vice versa, making GM&O a direct competitor to Kansas City Southern and Missouri Pacific.

GM&O's former Alton lines generated much agricultural and chemical traffic, the latter largely from the Chicago–Joliet corridor and the St. Louis area. Chemical traffic, in fact, moved both ways between the north and south account of gulf port traffic and chemical companies which girdle the Gulf of Mexico. The southern lines also generated considerable lumber and pulpwood traffic, and forest-related products in general were once GM&O's most important single traffic source.

Four principal yards classified GM&O traffic: Glenn Yard, Chicago; Bloomington; Venice, Illinois, serving metro St. Louis; and Jackson, Tennessee. These were supplemented by smaller terminal and secondary yards at Kansas City; Mobile; New Orleans; Montgomery and Tuscaloosa, Alabama; and Meridian, Mississippi.

GM&O was an early proponent of dedicated unit-coal train service and in 1965—joint with Commonwealth Edison—inaugurated such trains between Percy Mine in southern Illinois and ComEd power-generating stations near Joliet, Illinois, and Hammond, Indiana. New ComEd coal cars and new GM&O Electro-Motive diesels clad in a striking new black-and-white paint scheme made for modern-looking trains that were in stark contrast to a railroad that, by the mid-1960s, was beginning to look a bit weary and weathered.

GM&O FAREWELL

It all came to an end on August 10, 1972, when GM&O and one-time rival Illinois Central merged to form the Illinois Central Gulf. Despite the disastrous Penn Central merger of 1968 in which the "parallel" (versus end-to-end) merger of the Pennsylvania Railroad and New York Central had resulted in the largest corporate bankruptcy to date, the Interstate Commerce Commission authorized the GM&O-IC union, itself another parallel merger. The success of the ICG merger remains controversial.

Following the merger, wholesale abandonments of duplicate trackage rendered much of the old GM&N and M&O to history, although nearly all principal former C&A trackage remains intact, having been divvied up by Union Pacific, the "new" Illinois Central, and Gateway Western. Amtrak operates the former GM&O Chicago–St. Louis service, including the *Ann Rutledge*.

Three Electro-Motive SD40s highballing over the Kankakee River near Lorenzo, Illinois, add a splash of color to an idyllic scene from the summer of 1972. The southbound train, No. 97 bound from Chicago to Bloomington and eventually Kansas City—was utilizing joint track with the Santa Fe; some GM&O traffic south of Joliet used this route to Coal City and then returned to the GM&O main line via a short cutoff line. This route bypassed grades and other rail traffic on the GM&O main line through Wilmington, Illinois. *Doug Steurer*

Kansas City Southern

The birth of the Kansas City Southern was contradictory to the industry pattern and occurred late in the game of railroad building. The seed railroad to what is today's KCS was born in 1890 when the nation was in its deepest depression yet encountered. It started as a terminal railroad in Kansas City—the Kansas City Suburban Belt Railroad—that one-time insurance salesman Arthur Stilwell had become involved with. It evolved into the Kansas City, Pittsburg & Gulf and began building south to the Gulf of Mexico. In short order the road was in trouble, and the rails had barely reached Pittsburg, Kansas, when the panic of 1893 sent investors running away.

Stilwell was not an easily daunted man. He sailed to Holland to sell securities and, with the help of his childhood friend, George M. Pullman (of sleeping-car fame), within six months had the $3 million necessary to keep his railroad project alive. He built the Gulf port facilities himself and named them after himself—Port Arthur, Texas. The final spike was driven 12 miles north of Beaumont, Texas, on September 11, 1897. Within two years of being completed, the railroad went into receivership, mainly as a result of being overcapitalized and underconstructed.

When the railroad was reorganized, Stilwell was squeezed out, and the railroad became the Kansas City Southern on April 1, 1900; it was still KCS when this book was first published a century later.

SAVED BY AN OIL WELL

The railroad was built to give Midwestern farmers a shorter route to an ocean, but it succeeded for an entirely different reason. To have been built to depend on grain shipments was a recipe for disaster, as grain shipments are unpredictable, seasonal, and often don't even cover their own costs. Further, the ship traffic in and out of Port Arthur never lived up to expectations as far as revenue was concerned. If the investors from Holland could have seen the territory the railroad ran through, Stilwell would likely never have gotten the capital to build the railroad. There was (and is) virtually nothing substantial as far as business and population from Joplin to Texarkana.

The key to KCS being a winner was simply referred to as "Lucas No. 9." Captain Anthony Lucas' drill, mounted on a salt dome near Beaumont, hit a gusher of oil on January 10, 1901. This birthed the Spindletop Oil Field and secured Kansas City Southern's future. Oil refineries grew around the new oil field, and later petrochemical plants sprung up all along the southern portion of today's KCS, thus providing some 37 percent of the railroad's revenue.

The KCS was led for 30 years (1906–1936) by Leonor Loree, who also led the Delaware & Hudson, and he was the first to look for mergers to improve the KCS's position in the industry. The first was an attempt to merge the KCS with the Missouri-Kansas-Texas (Katy) and the Cotton Belt in the mid-1920s. Though the KCS bought up the stock of these two roads, the Interstate Commerce Commission was never consulted, and KCS was forced to sell this stock. This stock sale proved a valuable asset to the KCS and helped the railroad weather the Depression.

Though the Katy and Cotton Belt merger failed, the KCS did add some other important railroads to its growing empire, the most important of which was the Louisiana & Arkansas, a road which had been formed with the merger of the original L&A and the Louisiana Railway & Navigation Company. These properties gave the KCS its trackage to southeast to New Orleans and west to Dallas from Shreveport, Louisiana. This merger gave the KCS access the ports of Baton Rouge and New Orleans, in turn providing the L&A an outlet to the North. The man responsible for the merger was Harvey Couch, who had assembled the L&A and had become chairman of the KCS in May 1939. Though he died in 1941, long before the real fruits of this merger could be seen, he left the pieces to his empire in the capable hands of William N. Deramus, who came up through the ranks of the KCS. Shortly after Couch died, Deramus took over the presidency of the KCS and

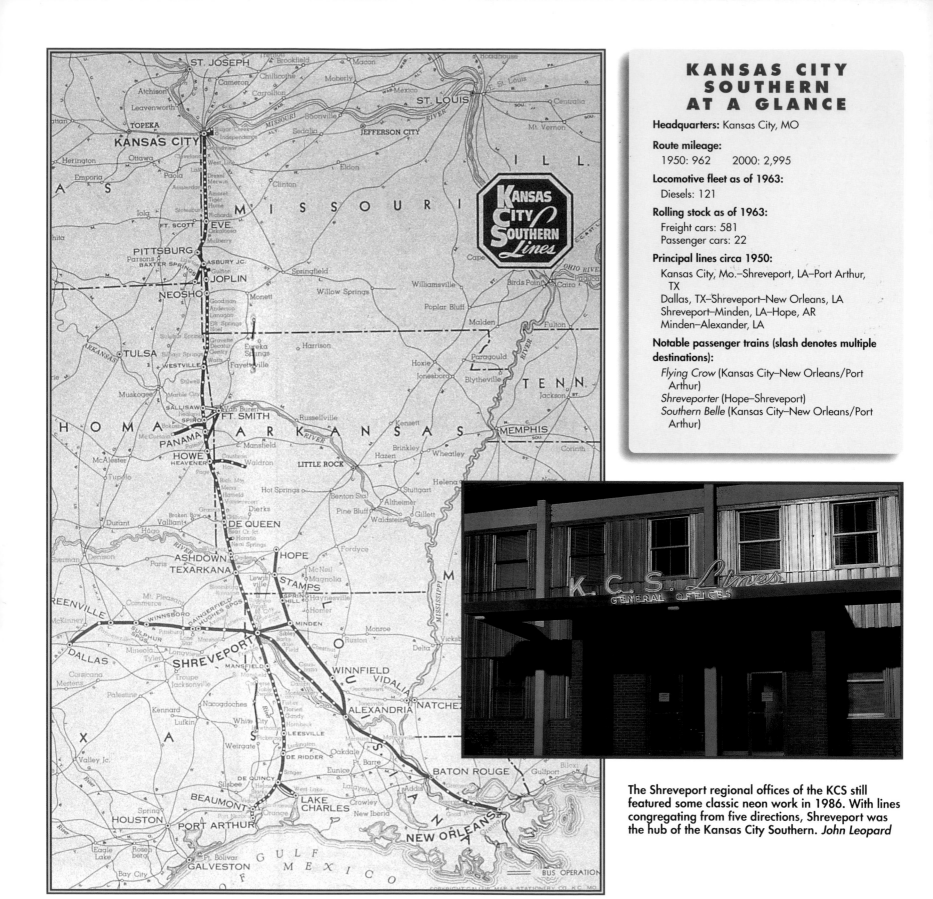

KANSAS CITY SOUTHERN AT A GLANCE

Headquarters: Kansas City, MO

Route mileage:
1950: 962   2000: 2,995

Locomotive fleet as of 1963:
Diesels: 121

Rolling stock as of 1963:
Freight cars: 581
Passenger cars: 22

Principal lines circa 1950:

Kansas City, Mo.–Shreveport, LA–Port Arthur, TX
Dallas, TX–Shreveport–New Orleans, LA
Shreveport–Minden, LA–Hope, AR
Minden–Alexander, LA

Notable passenger trains (slash denotes multiple destinations):

Flying Crow (Kansas City–New Orleans/Port Arthur)
Shreveporter (Hope–Shreveport)
Southern Belle (Kansas City–New Orleans/Port Arthur)

The Shreveport regional offices of the KCS still featured some classic neon work in 1986. With lines congregating from five directions, Shreveport was the hub of the Kansas City Southern. *John Leopard*

2-10-4 and 2-8-8-0 steamers off through freights on the more hilly portions of the railroad, and dieselization was completed in 1953.

Like many other railroads after the war, KCS revamped its passenger services, adding new cars to the *Southern Belle* as well as a Shreveport–Port Arthur connection, and adding a whole new streamliner (initially unnamed, but later taking on the *Flying Crow* name) between Kansas City and New Orleans, thereby providing double-daily streamliner service between those two points.

Centralized Traffic Control was implemented in 1943, the first installation being over the busy portion of joint track with the Missouri Pacific between De Quincy, Louisiana, and Beaumont. In 1956 Deramus Yard was opened in Shreveport, which put an end to the practice of running transfer drag freights between the separate, overcrowded yards in Shreveport that were part of the original two railroads. A 17-mile cutoff was built to connect the Texas trackage to the new yard, saving

Electro-Motive E6A No. 24 sprints along with what appears to be the Shreveport–Hope, Arkansas, *Shreveporter* in 1962 at an unidentified location. The paltry coach-only consist reveals that this train was living on borrowed time. The *Shreveporter* came off that same year. *Bill Ray, Kevin Eudaly collection*

KCS 808, a 4-6-2, and engine 905, a 2-10-4, are coming downgrade east of Page, Oklahoma, with a northbound drag freight of 62 cars. Black Fork Mountain is at left, while Rich Mountain is at right in this scene from August 31, 1946. *Preston George, courtesy Mrs. Preston George and Terry LaFrance*

persuaded a group of friends to help him buy enough KCS stock to gain control of the railroad.

Just before World War II, KCS made a big splash in the passenger market. Not that this was a big area of revenue for the KCS. Passenger operations between Kansas City and the Gulf had been modest prior to the stockmarket crash of 1929, the flagship train being the *Flying Crow*, introduced in 1928. During the Depression, this was the principal train on the railroad.

The fortunes turned a bit with the L&A merger, as there did seem to be a market for Kansas City–New Orleans service, and KCS addressed this with a new streamliner. On September 2, 1940, the new *Southern Belle* entered service between K.C. and New Orleans. The streamliner, pulled by Electro-Motive E-series passenger diesels, wore an understated but very attractive livery of Brunswick Green (a very deep green), yellow, and red.

THE DERAMUS ERA

After World War II, Deramus poured millions of dollars into the right-of-way, while reducing debt by $27 million between 1944 and 1950. During this era, the railroad replaced 75 percent of the railroad ties on the KCS and 95 percent of those on the L&A. Heavier rail was laid, and by the end of the war, Deramus was buying diesels, at first from the Electro-Motive Division of General Motors. These bumped

KCS dieselized its mainline freight operations after World War II with Electro-Motive F-units. The F7s shown here were dual-service locomotives, used in both freight and passenger service, and thus wore the road's classy yellow, black, and red passenger livery developed by Electro-Motive. The freight-only F7s wore a similar scheme, but with the red and yellow colors reversed. *EMD*

Though KCS has long been a devoted customer of Electro-Motive, the railroad did own Fairbanks-Morse products. Right after World War II, the railroad took delivery of F-M passenger cab units known as "Eries" or "Erie-Builts" (because they were assembled at General Electric's Erie, Pennsylvania, plant) as well as F-M road-switchers. Three Eries spliced by F-units roll a freight through Sheffield Junction in Kansas City in 1965. By this time, these big FMs had been re-engined with EMD power plants. *Jim Boyd*

12 miles on the Dallas run. By 1958, the Kansas City Southern was in super shape, and operations were nearly flawless.

The recession in 1957 and 1958 substantially changed how the KCS operated. Its penchant to run few and super-long freights became a dogma during this era, and existing trains were combined. Trains exceeding 200 cars became common, but the rugged north end of the railroad proved to be an operating challenge for these monstrous freights. In 1958 the standard freight was pulled by six EMD F-units. By 1959 it had grown to seven F-units, and by 1960, eight. The trains had become way too long, and the railroad began to experience operating problems. Trains started pulling apart, breaking couplers as more and more units were put on the trains. In 1961, these problems and the KCS presidency were passed on from William Deramus to his son, William Deramus III.

Interestingly, the passenger service hung on and had even garnered some high praise from the traveling public. The railroad bought more new passenger cars as late as 1965—one of the last purchases of new passenger rolling stock before Amtrak came along in 1971.

At the same time, KCS bought newer and larger freight locomotives designed to lug heavy tonnages on grades, and in 1966 began to use radio-controlled pushers on the steeper sections of the railroad. Deferred maintenance—the practice of putting off maintenance to the future to save money in the present—began in the late 1950s. By 1968 the railroad was really beginning to suffer. The theory was that, because of the massive influx of ties and rail put down between 1940 and 1953, maintenance would not be required at the same rate for "a while." Unfortunately for the KCS, this "a while" had lasted far too long, and the railroad slowly began a downward spiral. The discon-

tinuance of the nameless streamliner in 1968 was a signal that this was not the best of times, and in 1969 the *Southern Belle* made her last trips.

As the railroad got worse and worse, the operating people tried to convince top management that KCS was headed for disaster, but management was too involved in presiding over KCS's non-rail enterprises and trying to thwart takeover attempts. Indeed, between 1971 and 1973, the railroad completely fell apart. The ties and rail from the late 1950s had reached the point where they were just plain worn out. The change was sudden and dramatic.

On December 4, 1972, a southbound train went into emergency braking at Bridge A-206, near Sulphur Springs, Arkansas. The result was a

A quartet of Electro-Motive SD40 and SD40–2 locomotives grind upgrade out of Kansas City and over Gregory Boulevard on the Fourth of July 1982. This location was often used by KCS in the 1940s for publicity photos of the *Southern Belle* and *Flying Crow*. Despite the obvious drawbacks of having a white-based paint scheme in gritty railroad conditions, KCS's all-white look endured for more than a quarter century. *Kevin Eudaly*

The new image of KCS is that of gray locomotives with yellow striping and a bold, red "KCS" on their flanks. Three new Electro-Motive SD50s roll over the Red River south of Ashdown, Arkansas, in October 1993. *Tom Kline*

locomotive on the ground, three cars spilled into Butler Creek, and 17 more straddling the tracks, blocking the main line for 86 hours. Later that morning, while train No. 77 was detouring around the wreck, two cars and its caboose overturned while backing through an interchange track. A wrecker out of Pittsburg came to clean that up, and derailed in the attempt. Three days later another southbound derailed, just eight miles north of Sulphur Springs; and three days after that, train 77 dumped four cars within sight of that wreck. Within a few hours, No. 41 derailed at McElhany. All this occurred on the Second Subdivision between Pittsburg and Watts, Oklahoma, but within a few weeks, derailments began to spread across the system. The railroad had come apart, and during a time of record-shattering business.

A REVERSAL OF FORTUNES

There was nothing to do but to spend a hefty sum to rebuild the railroad, and a new president, Tom Carter, came in and recommended just that. The board of directors approved his plans, and the KCS set about to revamp essentially the entire railroad. The effort had an ersatz deadline: In November 1976, coal trains out of the Powder River Basin in Wyoming were to start moving down the KCS from Kansas City, where the Burlington Northern would deliver them to KCS. January 1974 proved to be a nightmare, as trains slowed to a crawl systemwide, resulting in motive-power shortages. During January, 41 mainline derailments cost the company just shy of $2 million.

The cure proved to include several elements. First, many of the derailments occurred to trains

that were running with mid-train slave locomotives, and it was determined the slaves were pushing too hard. By repositioning these locomotives more toward the front of the train so that they were pulling more than they were pushing, the derailments came to a stop. Secondly, the money for rebuilding slowly began to improve the track structure, and luckily for the KCS, revenues were coming in faster than expenses. By the end of 1975, the KCS had weathered the storm and was over the last of its financial woes.

Next, KCS completely restructured its approach to operating trains. The railroad improved the switching and blocking of its trains, and a host of other activities were monitored with efficiency in mind. Train statistics, engine-in-service hours, crew time, and locomotive utilization became the means to justify more—and shorter—trains. In May 1977, nearly 20 years after mammoth, infrequent trains had become the norm, additional manifests were added north of Shreveport. The management juggled schedules, connections, blocking, and train numbers in an attempt to find the right mix for the traffic base.

By late 1978, operations smoothed out, and by then the new coal trains were running. In 1979 these totaled 12 trains a week, which provided additional revenue to keep things running smoothly and to keep maintenance up. Through the 1980s the KCS continued to prosper. In the 1990s, the KCS expanded for the first time in years. First it bought regional railroad Mid-South, a railroad that had been created from ex-Illinois Central and Gulf, Mobile & Ohio trackage. This put the KCS solidly into Mississippi. Then KCS garnered control of the Gateway Western—a new railroad that had been parceled out of old GM&O trackage—which put KCS's reach into St. Louis and Springfield, Illinois.

The KCS had dieselized primarily with EMD locomotives, and they remained true to EMD throughout the diesel era. From the early 1960s on, KCS strictly bought EMDs, and by the 1970s every locomotive was EMD. Early diesel colors included the Brunswick Green, yellow, and red scheme for cab units, while early switchers and road-switchers wore a simple black scheme. Later, a solid red scheme with white lettering appeared,

and then, in the mid-1960s, the reverse—solid white with red lettering. In the early 1990s, a new gray-and-yellow scheme was introduced, and this remained the KCS image into the twenty-first century, although in 1995, the railroad put together a business-car train with three old F-units and painted them in a variation of the old *Southern Belle* colors using black, yellow, and red.

As of 2000, the Kansas City Southern remains an independent railroad while mergers have surrounded it with mega-systems like Burlington Northern Santa Fe and Union Pacific. In light of the North American Free Trade Agreement of the 1990s, the company has amalgamated itself with other regional carriers to form a conduit for the resulting increase in freight traffic to and from Mexico. Kansas City Southern stands poised to be one of the few railroads of the twentieth century to head into the new century essentially intact as they were in the steam era.

TOP: Now the sole passenger train on the railroad, the *Southern Belle* stands proud at New Orleans in 1969. E8 No. 23 wears the all-white image. *Jim Boyd*

ABOVE: A former New York Central lounge-observation car awaits passengers boarding train 9 about to depart Kansas City in 1967. *Mike Schafer*

ROUTE OF THE BLACK DIAMOND

Lehigh Valley

The photogenic Lehigh Valley Railroad was a classic Northeastern anthracite carrier that was hopelessly entangled in a long and challenging battle for self-preservation. LV's modest trunk line stretched from the eastern Great Lakes, through its namesake river valley, to metropolitan New York, and was supported by numerous branch lines. Although its original *raison d'etre* was King Coal, the "Valley" managed to build up a substantial bridge-freight and passenger network as well. But try as it might, the road was never able to fully overcome the losses stemming from a declining coal market. In its final years, the Valley's misfortunes were masked by a colorful, multi-hued diesel fleet.

The heritage of the Lehigh Valley Railroad is directly linked to the coal boom in northeastern Pennsylvania, which began about the time of the War of 1812. Anthracite, or hard coal, had been discovered near Mauch Chunk (now Jim Thorpe) prior to 1900 but didn't immediately gain popularity because it was so difficult to burn. Nonetheless, the Lehigh Coal Mine Company began an open-pit operation and shipped the "black diamond" product to Philadelphia by river barge.

Josiah White, who operated a foundry near that city, quickly realized that anthracite would burn exceptionally well under a forced-air draft, and he leased the mines to ensure a steady fuel supply. White was determined to eliminate the perils of river transport and constructed a primitive slackwater system along the Lehigh River, which would later become the Lehigh Canal. His mining and shipping affiliates were merged in 1820 as the Lehigh Coal & Navigation Co., a concern that would later have a substantial impact on Eastern railroading.

Increasing demand for anthracite created a greater need for improved transportation. A gravity railroad was constructed in 1827 to better move coal down the steep mountain slopes to the canal at Mauch Chunk. The concept of building a real railroad down the Lehigh River valley first appeared in the 1830s. The Beaver Meadow Railroad, already operating as a canal feeder line

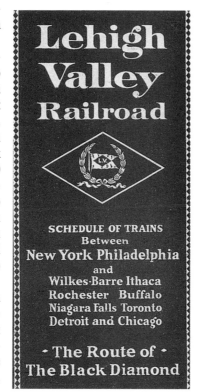

Lehigh Valley Railroad

LV

SCHEDULE OF TRAINS
Between
New York Philadelphia
and
Wilkes-Barre Ithaca
Rochester Buffalo
Niagara Falls Toronto
Detroit and Chicago

• The Route of •
The Black Diamond

north of town, began to grade a 45-mile line south to Easton, Pennsylvania, in 1835, to the complete chagrin of the LC&N. But political compromises, insufficient funds, and river floods scuttled that competitive threat.

The concept behind that ill-fated scheme would come back to haunt the canal interests. Despite opposition from the Pennsylvania Legislature, a charter was issued for the Delaware, Lehigh, Schuylkill & Susquehanna Railroad in 1846. Public response was poor, and the LC&N monopoly seemed secure. Finally, in 1851 some grading work was started, but the venture lacked sufficient funding and motivation. It was at this point that a Connecticut-born carpenter named Asa Packer stepped up to finance and guide the faltering company. Packer had a dream and was willing to risk his fortune on the lure of even greater profit. Ironically, he began to build his wealth through the construction and operation of LC&N barges, which generated capital for him to further invest. Packer gained control of the DLS&S venture and quickly hired Robert Sayre, also of LC&N background, as his chief engineer. The pair managed to overcome the canal stronghold, and in 1853 the charter was aptly reorganized as the Lehigh Valley Railroad.

An infusion of capital from some politically motivated backers of the Camden & Amboy Railroad in New Jersey stimulated construction, and the Lehigh Valley Railroad officially opened on September 12, 1855, with train service between Mauch Chunk and Easton, at the confluence of the Lehigh and Delaware rivers. Terminating at Easton would require coal shipments to be transferred into canal barges for continued shipment. Packer needed to bridge the Delaware River in order to interchange with the Central Railroad of New Jersey (CNJ) and Belvidere Delaware Railroad at Phillipsburg, New Jersey. The Jersey Central would provide access to tidewater at metropolitan New York, and the "Bel-Del" entry to Trenton and Philadelphia. The gap was promptly closed and the interchange became so successful that the LV paid a hefty 6 percent dividend by 1857. In fact, Packer's gamble paid off

FACING PAGE: **Following the railroad's namesake river and valley, a 117-car westbound Lehigh Valley freight behind a triple-unit set of Alco Century-series freight locomotives grinds through Oxbow, Pennsylvania, in August 1974. *Mike Nelson***

FACING PAGE, INSET: **Lehigh Valley business car No. 353 outlived the railroad for which it served for so many years. Built in 1915, this car was used by company officials as an office on wheels, traveling about the system until the Valley's demise into Conrail in 1976. The car was then purchased by Richard A. Horstmann and restored to its former grandeur, including a lighted *Black Diamond* drumhead. *Mike Schafer***

LEFT: **LV passenger timetable from 1934. *Kevin Holland collection***

so well that he quickly became a multi-millionaire and later founded Lehigh University.

The new railroad looked to expand operations beyond its namesake valley and began to build or consolidate numerous feeder and subsidiary lines. Extending the LV northward to White Haven in 1864 alarmed the LC&N, which quickly expanded its fledgling Lehigh & Susquehanna to foster competition on the opposite bank of the Lehigh River. Shortly thereafter, the LV absorbed the old Beaver Meadow line to tap several coal mines. Seeking to continue its northwesterly expansion, in 1867 the LV confronted Penobscot Mountain to gain access to the Wyoming Valley near Wilkes-Barre, Pennsylvania, where additional anthracite loadings could be derived. Packer then acquired control of the troubled North Branch Canal as an easy gradient for his New York & Pennsylvania Railroad to reach the New York & Erie Railroad, 105 miles distant at Waverly, New York, which happened in 1869. A brisk interchange of through traffic with the Erie was quickly established, despite that road's differing broad-gauge. Dual-gauging the Erie allowed the LV to operate direct service via trackage rights to Elmira, New York, and eventually Buffalo, New York, as an interim arrangement. Shortly afterward, a significant amount of trackage in the Finger Lakes region was obtained when the LV gained control of the Geneva, Ithaca & Sayre Railroad.

Meanwhile to the east, problems were developing with the Valley's friendly connections at Phillipsburg. Initially, the LV was quite content to rely on these connections to forward its anthracite shipments. The status quo was altered in 1868 when the Delaware, Lackawanna & Western leased the newly built Morris & Essex line. The CNJ lost traffic because of this and leased LC&N's Lehigh & Susquehanna to access Pennsylvania. Alarmed that the DL&W and CNJ now had competitive through

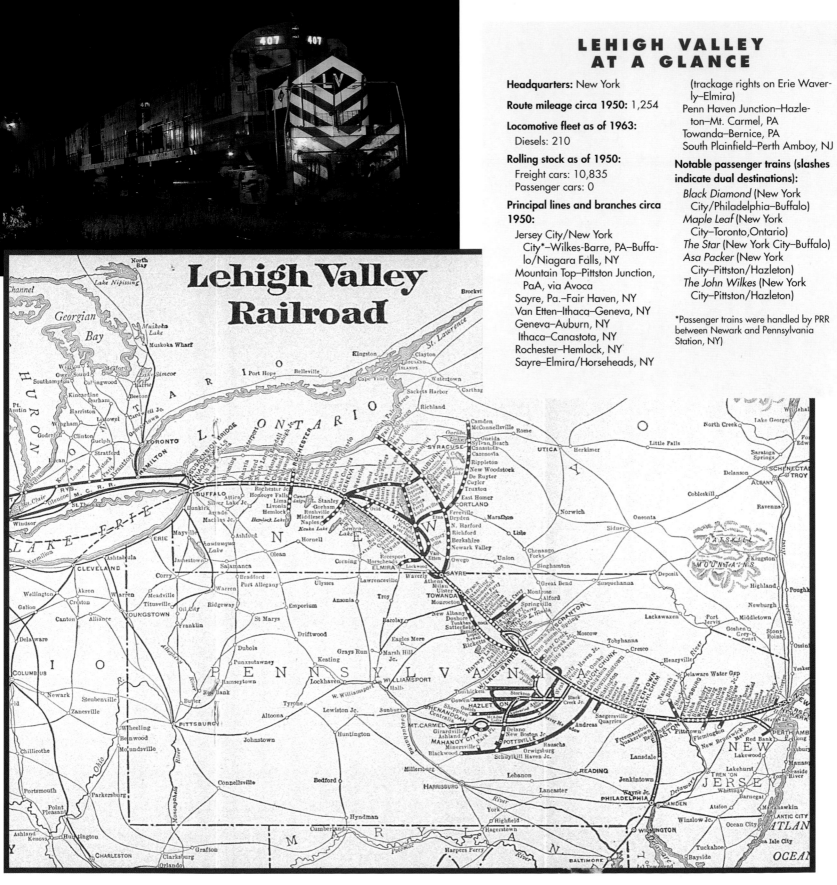

LEHIGH VALLEY AT A GLANCE

Headquarters: New York

Route mileage circa 1950: 1,254

Locomotive fleet as of 1963:
Diesels: 210

Rolling stock as of 1950:
Freight cars: 10,835
Passenger cars: 0

Principal lines and branches circa 1950:

Jersey City/New York City*–Wilkes-Barre, PA–Buffalo/Niagara Falls, NY
Mountain Top–Pittston Junction, PaA, via Avoca
Sayre, Pa.–Fair Haven, NY
Van Etten–Ithaca–Geneva, NY
Geneva–Auburn, NY
Ithaca–Canastota, NY
Rochester–Hemlock, NY
Sayre–Elmira/Horseheads, NY

(trackage rights on Erie Waverly–Elmira)
Penn Haven Junction–Hazleton–Mt. Carmel, PA
Towanda–Bernice, PA
South Plainfield–Perth Amboy, NJ

Notable passenger trains (slashes indicate dual destinations):

Black Diamond (New York City/Philadelphia–Buffalo)
Maple Leaf (New York City–Toronto, Ontario)
The Star (New York City–Buffalo)
Asa Packer (New York City–Pittston/Hazleton)
The John Wilkes (New York City–Pittston/Hazleton)

*Passenger trains were handled by PRR between Newark and Pennsylvania Station, NY)

Lehigh Valley Railroad

from South Plainfield, but the extension required CNJ trackage rights to reach the new port. In 1891, another extension brought the LV into Newark, where the Oak Island classification yard was established. The LV later crossed Newark Bay and by 1899 finally completed its own route to Jersey City, which became its new main line in eastern New Jersey, relegating the original Perth Amboy line to branch status.

The LV had long realized that its through-traffic would never be fully secure until it had its own route to Buffalo, which would offer better western traffic connections than its Southern Central line to Lake Ontario. The Valley pushed hard to complete its own route in order to replace the Erie trackage rights agreement, which was about to expire. When the LV completed its mainline extension to Buffalo in 1892, the railroad could finally offer competitive service entirely on its own rails.

Expansion costs and labor disputes weakened the Valley's financial situation and created an easy opportunity for financier J. P. Morgan to gain control. He began a resurrection program and acquired the Elmira, Cortland & Northern with the short-lived intention of reaching Watertown, New York. Following Morgan's improvements, the LV entered the new century in good form and continued to modernize its physical plant over the next 30 years.

STEAM POWER ON THE LV

Early LV steam power was a disorderly (and often unorthodox) assortment of locomotive types that were subject to the free will of each division superintendent. Common sense soon prevailed, and the railroad began a standardization program that resulted in the construction of the massive shop complex at Sayre, Pennsylvania.

Like most anthracite roads, the Lehigh Valley rostered numerous "Mother Hubbard" engines with over-sized Wooten fireboxes. The Valley pioneered the 2-8-0 Consolidation arrangement and clearly favored the 4-6-2 Pacific-type. In the modern steam era, the railroad relied on powerful Mikados and handsome 4-8-4s (called "Wyomings" by LV) to hustle merchandise and massive 2-10-2s to drag coal tonnage.

INSET: As with other anthracite carriers, Lehigh Valley's early steam roster was rife with "Mother Hubbard" locomotives whose cabs were positioned between the boiler and firebox, as in this view of a 4-6-0 hustling out of Communipaw Terminal with the *Black Diamond* in 1914. The cab is separated from the tender by the firebox, which on these locomotives had to be extra wide to facilitate the burning of anthracite coal. The width of the firebox would impair the crew's forward vision if the cab were behind the firebox. *K. E. Schlacter, Andover Junction Publications collection*

LV's Northern-type locomotives were known as "Wyomings," after the Wyoming Valley through which the railroad passed in the Scranton/Wilkes-Barre area of Pennsylvania. One of the big 4-8-4s bullies its way through Bethlehem, Pennsylvania, circa 1950. *Ed Crist collection*

routes to tidewater, the LV immediately sought out its own course across New Jersey. A combination of two smaller charters created the Easton & Amboy Railroad in 1872, which was intended to construct a 60-mile line to Perth Amboy, New Jersey, where the LV would develop port facilities. The key obstacle in the path of this new line was Musconetcong Mountain, where a nearly mile-long bore was required. The Pattenburg Tunnel took over two years to complete and delayed the opening of the New Jersey Division until May 28, 1875. Trackage rights on the PRR gave the LV access into Newark and Jersey City for the time being. The railroad bustled with coal tonnage, but the euphoria was diminished by the loss of guiding light Asa Packer, who passed away in 1879.

Perth Amboy provided a logical coal seaport, but a more direct link to metropolitan New York would greatly enhance the road's merchandise, freight, and passenger revenues. The LV had previously leased a section of the Morris Canal, which included an ideal waterfront terminal in Jersey City, New Jersey. A new line was built eastward

PASSENGER SERVICE

The Lehigh Valley boasted a modest fleet of mainline passenger trains, the best known of which was the *Black Diamond*, a luxury daytime parlor-car run between metropolitan New York and Buffalo introduced in 1896. Although fast, its running time still lagged behind competing trains run by the Lackawanna and New York Central. Nicknamed "the Handsomest Train in the World" and "the Honeymoon Express" (because it also served Niagara Falls), the *Black Diamond* embodied the spirit of the LV for many years.

In the 1930s, many American railroads were faced with the challenging problem of how to reverse declining passenger patronage. Many, including the LV, turned to streamlining as a means to create a modern image aimed at enticing new ridership. LV President Duncan Kerr hired famed industrial designer Otto Kuhler in 1938 to develop a new look for selected passenger trains. His work was performed in phases, the first being on a gas-electric motorcar set used in Mauch Chunk–Newark service. Kuhler created an orange-and-black scheme said to represent the orange glow of a blast furnace and black coal.

LV's *John Wilkes* represented an economical yet effective job of streamlining. Although most other railroads that joined the streamlining movement bought all-new trains, LV chose to restyle, upgrade, and otherwise modernize existing locomotives and rolling stock. Here, the newly streamlined *John Wilkes* is on display at Sayre, Pennsylvania, in 1939 just before it entered service between Pittston/Wilkes-Barre and New York. *Cal's Classics*

In this diesel era passenger scene from March 7, 1959, the westbound *Black Diamond* is taking on passengers and mail and express at the LV-Reading depot in Bethlehem (the Reading main line to Philadelphia can be seen branching to the right). Shortly, the *Diamond* will be discontinued. *John Dziobko*

The next phase replaced that motorcar set with a full steam-powered train. Two Class K-3 Pacifics were streamlined to match color-coordinated coaches in the orange-and-black scheme. The new streamliner was introduced as the *Asa Packer* on January 31, 1939. This new train's interior was the first in the U.S. to feature fluorescent lighting as a design element.

The final phases of the project streamlined five additional Pacific-types. However, at Kerr's suggestion, the original scheme was replaced with a handsome livery that would forever portray the Lehigh Valley image: Cornell red and black. The new look was unveiled in 1939 on a new day train, the *John Wilkes*, running between Pittston, Pennsylvania, and New York City. Pleased with the elegant image, the railroad applied the scheme to its best-known run, the *Black Diamond*, and added new lightweight coaches.

Hazleton, Pennsylvania, in the heart of the coal fields of central eastern Pennsylvania, was was at the end of a 23-mile branch, but the city was of sufficient importance that the railroad ran passenger trains there to the end of LV passenger service. In earlier days, through cars to New York and Philadelphia were handled out of Hazleton on conventional trains. In later years, Budd-built Rail Diesel Cars, such as this RDC at Hazleton on March 9, 1959, provided shuttle service to Lehighton where passengers changed to and from mainline trains. *John Dziobko*

The LV purchased many of its locomotives—steam and diesel—from Alco (American Locomotive Company). In August 1965, a three-unit set of Alco FA-type freight cab locomotives resume its eastbound journey following a stop at the yards at Sayre. This is the same depot at which the *John Wilkes* is pictured on the previous page some 25 years earlier. *Jim Shaughnessy*

DEPRESSION, WORLD WAR II, AND THE POSTWAR ERA

The Great Depression had been particularly hard on the Lehigh Valley. Tonnage decreased so drastically that the road was forced to slash labor costs and suspend dividend payments. World War II brought a dramatic upsurge in traffic, but the boom was too short-lived to greatly benefit a company already encumbered with over $8 million in Federal assistance loans. The railroad needed to further economize operations and launched a major dieselization program. Although the LV had previously experimented with early box-cab terminal switchers, serious dieselization began when the first set of Electro-Motive FT freight diesels was placed in pusher service in 1945. Various first-generation road-switchers and cab units quickly assumed mainline freight and passenger duties. Steam was totally vanquished by September 1951 when the last Mikado was retired.

Anthracite loadings continued to slide, but the loss was slightly offset with New England bridge traffic handled through connections with the Delaware & Hudson and Lehigh & Hudson River Railway. Despite a recent introduction of a new trailer-on-flatcar (TOFC) service, the LV's books were destined to show a profit for the last time in 1956. The end of the decade would bring an alarming 20 percent decline in revenues and a dramatic loss of cement traffic.

Passenger ridership declined as LV financial problems deepened. The Transportation Act of 1958 allowed LV to petition the Interstate Commerce Commission for the cancellation of all passenger service. A compromise was reached that maintained two mainline trains each way, the daytime *John Wilkes* and overnight *Maple Leaf*. The historic *Black Diamond* made its final run on May 11, 1959. The remaining trains were short-lived, though, being discontinued in 1961.

THE VALLEY IN TWILIGHT

The Valley's massive deficits of the 1950s forced the Pennsylvania Railroad—an LV stockholder since 1928—to purchase additional LV stock to help stabilize the road's sagging financial condition. Seeking to protect its investment, the Pennsy locked up nearly 90 percent of LV stock by 1963 but exercised little authority over the railroad, which continued to function as an independent operation.

The ailing LV quickly became known as an unwanted stepchild of the PRR, yet it was off limits

for merger consideration with other carriers. Norfolk & Western and Chesapeake & Ohio expressed some interest in the LV as a route to New York, but neither road tendered a purchase offer.

The Valley did manage to forge some new alliances. In 1964, a power-pool arrangement was reached with the Nickel Plate for runs between Sayre and Buffalo. When the N&W acquired the NKP shortly thereafter, the arrangement was extended to Bellevue (Ohio), Chicago, and Oak Island. This run-through service helped expedite the Valley's hot *Apollo* and *Mercury* TOFC runs.

The parallel CNJ was in even worse financial shape. Because of its light traffic density, the CNJ was seeking to reduce its mileage in Pennsylvania.

An Alco road-switcher works at Oswego, New York, on the North Fair Haven branch in June 1968. The Valley would be gone in eight years, but the old wooden depot in the background remained standing—and restored—in the year 2000. *Mike Schafer*

In a sense, the diesel-era equivalent of the Valley's 4-8-4 Wyomings were its fleet of Alco C628 ("C" for Century series) locomotives delivered early in the 1960s. Like the Wyomings, the Centurys were built by Alco and, at 2,750-hp. each, had ample pulling power. Some of the 628s wore the Valley's Cornell Red scheme (lead photo of this chapter) while others received a classy white-and-black scheme. Those that wore the latter were dubbed "Snowbirds." In this scene from the summer of 1970, Snowbirds lead an eastbound freight across the joint LV-Reading bridge over the Lehigh River at Bethlehem. *Mike Schafer*

In 1965, CNJ and LV entered into a joint trackage agreement in eastern Pennsylvania that would have both carriers utilize the CNJ from Bethlehem to Lehighton, the LV to White Haven, and CNJ again to Laurel Run.

Meanwhile, serious merger negotiations were in motion between long-time rivals New York Central and Pennsylvania. In 1966, the ICC approved the deal with the stipulation that the LV would again be offered to the N&W or C&O as a means to ensure "competition," but neither carrier expressed much interest in the faltering LV and its poor profit potential. The LV was forced to become an unwanted hostage in the catastrophic NYC-PRR merger of 1968. The new Penn Central monstrosity began to crumble almost immediately

and declared bankruptcy on June 21, 1970—an action that would literally bring down most Northeastern railroads. Unfortunately, the LV's financial security was so entangled in the PC debacle that the Valley followed the behemoth into Chapter 77 bankruptcy just three days later.

In 1971, the financially distressed CNJ made a drastic move to economize its operations with the complete discontinuance of service in Pennsylvania, thus creating a rare opportunity for the LV to enhance and economize its physical plant during lean times. By March 1972, LV assumed control of most CNJ property there, including the strategic Allentown Yard and the old Lehigh & New England subsidiary, which the CNJ had inherited in 1961.

The Lehigh Valley was virtually destitute by 1973. There simply wasn't enough traffic to overcome operating deficits, and deferred maintenance was beginning to take a serious toll on the road's trackage and motive power. LV trustees petitioned the Federal District Court for termination of all operations on October 1, 1973, unless additional Federal assistance could be secured. Although the ICC contested the proposed cessation of service, both the U.S. Department of Transportation and Federal Railroad Administration felt compelled to agree with the petition, citing that 90 percent of LV's traffic was handled on only 18 percent of the railroad.

In 1974, Congress approved the Regional Rail Reorganization Act, the Federal government's salvation plan for the failing Northeastern railroads. The newly formed U.S. Railroad Association was mandated to create a reorganization and consolidation plan for the LV, CNJ, RDG, L&HR, EL, and PC, all of which were threatening total shutdown. This Federal intervention created the Consolidated Rail Corporation, or Conrail for short, to stabilize Northeastern rail service.

The Lehigh Valley was formally incorporated into the new Conrail system on April 1, 1976. Almost immediately, nearly 160 miles of LV trackage in upstate New York was abandoned. Conrail was soon forced to reduce its freight traffic on the Northeast Corridor, and that tonnage was shifted onto the eastern end of the old Valley main line, making Allentown and Oak Island key hubs in the new system. Traffic density remained light north of Allentown, and portions of the LV line in the Lehigh Gorge were absorbed by the upstart Reading & Northern shortline in 1996. Norfolk Southern acquired most of the remaining LV trackage in 1999 when Conrail was divided between CSX and Norfolk Southern, which share the Oak Island terminal. The venerable Lehigh Valley Railroad may be gone, but happily, much of the famed "Route of the Black Diamond" continues to host a colorful parade of trains.

The Valley's main shops and yard were at Sayre, Pennsylvania, just below the New York State line. Locomotives abound at the Sayre engine facilities in the summer of 1975 as the joint Delaware & Hudson-LV train from Binghamton arrives with an endless string of interchange cars. D&H power is on the train today—the celebrity Baldwin "Sharks," no less—and they'll head back to Binghamton with interchange cars from the Valley. *Jim Boyd*

ROUTE OF THE EAGLES

Missouri Pacific

Until its merger with the growing Union Pacific System in 1982, there were two ways to describe the Missouri Pacific: it was standardized and it was a survivor. Like nearly all late twentieth century railroads, the Missouri Pacific, popularly known as the "MoPac," was a conglomerate of many predecessor railroads. The most important of these previous entities other than the MoPac itself were the St. Louis, Iron Mountain & Southern, the Texas & Pacific, the International-Great Northern, the Gulf Coast Lines, and finally the Chicago & Eastern Illinois after its merger with the MoPac in 1967.

The direct predecessor of the modern-day MoPac was the Pacific Railroad of Missouri which was chartered in 1849 to build west from St. Louis to the Missouri River. The plan was to connect there with any railroads being built from the West into what is now Kansas City—at that time known as Westport, a simple landing on the river. The original charter was later altered to allow the Pacific Railroad to build to the West Coast.

In January 1850, the railroad was organized with Thomas Allen as president and James Kirkwood as chief engineer. In July 1851, ground was broken and preliminary work began on the first railroad west of the Mississippi River. Kirkwood established a track gauge of 5 feet, 6 inches because he reasoned that the first railroad in the state could pick its own gauge and all the rest would follow. The State of Missouri did indeed legislate that gauge to be standard for the state, but in 1869 the Pacific Railroad went to 4 feet, 9 inches and later to the current standard of 4 feet, 8 1/2 inches.

In December 1852, construction officially began, and the railroad was slowly built westward. The construction was slowed by several factors, the most significant of which was the rugged terrain west of St. Louis along the Missouri River. Labor shortages and cholera epidemics also hampered early construction, and the railroad did not reach the state capital of Jefferson City until 1855. Construction continued, but Confederate raids and the general condition of war increased the

difficulty of expanding west, and Kansas City wasn't reached until September 1865 after the Civil War had finally ended.

In parallel, the St. Louis, Iron Mountain & Southern had been chartered the same year as the Pacific Railroad and began to build from St. Louis to Pilot Knob, Missouri, some 85 miles. The same leaders involved in the Pacific Railroad were also in charge of the Iron Mountain, with James Kirkwood's protege James Morely as the chief engineer. The railroad reached Texarkana, Texas, in 1878, absorbing the Cairo & Fulton into its empire along the way. Like the Pacific Railroad, the Iron Mountain built to the "Missouri standard" gauge, with car-hoist facilities in Texarkana transfering cars to wheel sets that matched the gauge of the International-Great Northern and the Texas & Pacific. The Iron Mountain was standard-gauged in 1879.

Even with its early success, the Pacific Railroad had faltered, and the State of Missouri foreclosed its lien on the property in 1868. The railroad was operated under state supervision until mid-1872 when it was leased to the Atlantic & Pacific Railroad Company, a predecessor of the St. Louis–San Francisco Railway (Frisco). In 1876 the A&P defaulted, and in 1879 controlling interest in the A&P was purchased by Jay Gould, a financier with an ever-growing railroad empire, and the Missouri Pacific was born. By chance, Gould got control of the Texas & Pacific that same year.

Over the next few years the MoPac consolidated a number of subsidiaries, including lines in Missouri, Nebraska, and Kansas, and the Missouri Pacific name was retained with each transaction. Jay Gould then went after the Iron Mountain and in 1881 purchased a controlling interest in it. Though he owned both the MoPac and the Iron Mountain, he would never live to see their integration, which did not come about until 1917, 25 years after his death. By the time he acquired his interest in the Iron Mountain, it had expanded into Illinois, Arkansas, Tennessee, and Louisiana.

In the meantime, the stage was being set for a shoot-out in Texas, as the Gould-controlled T&P crews ran head-on into crews of the Collis

FACING PAGE: The Missouri Pacific was an institution in St. Louis, Kansas City, and nearly all points south from those rail centers to Texas and the Gulf of Mexico. Fondly remembered for its *Eagle* streamliners, impressive steam locomotive fleet, and blue-and-gray diesels, the "MoPac" vanished in a merger with the Union Pacific early in the 1980s. This scene in Ozark country just west of St. Louis turns the clock back to September 1951 as a four-unit set of Electro-Motive and Alco diesels highball manifest train No. 75 through Eureka. *Kevin EuDaly collection*

FACING PAGE, INSET: Missouri Pacific ticket coupon books were among the most attractive of any railroad, sporting flashy artwork of an *Eagle* streamliner.

LEFT: For years, MP passenger timetables featured an artist's rendering of an *Eagle* streamliner and the road's "buzzsaw" herald.

Huntington-controlled Southern Pacific. The resultant court settlement cut off the T&P to the west, so the T&P turned its attention eastward and built toward New Orleans, completing the line in 1882.

As with so many railroads during the rapidly expanding railroad scene in the formative years, MoPac's history is punctuated with countless defaults, reorganizations, bankruptcies, and the like. The MoPac itself was reorganized in 1868 and again in 1876. The I-GN saw reorganizations in 1878, 1889, and 1908, and the Missouri Pacific and the Iron Mountain both in 1915. The MoPac's final bankruptcy lasted from 1933 until 1956. After this trusteeship ended, the I-GN and the Gulf Coast Lines were officially merged into the Missouri Pacific, their parent company. The GCL had been formed from the St. Louis, Brownsville & Mexico Railway and the New Orleans, Texas & Mexico Railway in the very early 1900s. They were merged into the MoPac in 1925, the same year that MoPac also got control of the I-GN. Several other small roads were absorbed in the same era, and the

The Texas & Pacific roundhouse at Texarkana hosts that road's Electro-Motive GP7s and F-units in 1955. The F-units wore the Eagle Blue and Mist Gray scheme of parent MoPac, but the road-switchers got T&P's own Swamp Holly Orange and black scheme. After being folded into the MoPac, all diesels on the T&P became blue. *R. S. Plummer photo*

MoPac 2-8-0 switcher No. 129 gets "spun" on a manual turntable in the early 1940s. These little locomotives held down numerous branch and secondary line runs until the end of steam. Two of this class, Nos. 40 and 124, have the dubious honor of handling the last steam run on the MoPac on April 7, 1955, a train that consisted of nine other dead 2-8-0s and a lone 2-8-2 being hauled to scrap at Dupo, Illinois. To add insult to injury, the two little Consolidations ran out of water two miles from Dupo and had to be hauled in by diesel switchers. *Kevin EuDaly collection*

MISSOURI PACIFIC AT A GLANCE

Headquarters: St. Louis, MO

Route mileage circa 1950: 9,700

Locomotive fleet as of 1963:
Diesel: 724

Rolling stock as of 1950:
Freight cars: 44,923
Passenger cars: 533

Principal lines circa 1950:
St. Louis–Sedalia–Kansas City, MO–Omaha, NE
Jefferson City–Boonville–Kansas City
St. Joseph, MO–Stockton, KS
Kansas City–Pueblo, CO
Osawatomie, Kan.–Wagoner, OK–North Little Rock, AR
Pleasant Hill, MO–Wichita–Geneseo, KS
Fort Scott–Larned, KS
Rich Hill–Joplin, MO
Carthage, Mo.–Diaz, AR
St. Louis–Little Rock, AR–Texarkana, TX
East St. Louis, IL–Poplar Bluff, MO
Bismarck, MO–Salem, IL
Bald Knob, AR–Memphis, TN
Little Rock–McGehee, AR–Lake Charles, LA
Memphis–McGehee
McGehee–Vidalia, LA
Pine Bluff–Hot Springs, AR
Gurdon, Arkansas–Clayton, LA
Longview–Laredo, TX
Palestine–Galveston, TX
Brownsville, Texas–Baton Rouge, LA–New Orleans
New Orleans–Donaldson–Alexandria, LA
Fort Worth–Spring (Houston), TX
San Antonio–Corpus Christi, TX
El Paso–Longview, Texas–Livonia, LA–New Orleans (T&P)

Fort Worth, TX–Cypress, LA, via Texarkana and Marthaville, LA (T&P)
Texarkana–Longview (T&P)

Notable passenger trains (slash indicates dual destination):

Aztec Eagle (San Antonio–Mexico City)
Colorado Eagle (St. Louis–Denver)
Houstonian (New Orleans–Houston)
Louisiana Sunshine Special (Little Rock–Lake Charles)
Missouri River Eagle (St. Louis–Omaha)
Missourian (St. Louis–Kansas City/Wichita)
Orleanean (Houston–New Orleans)
Ozarker (St. Louis–Little Rock)
Pioneer (Houston–Brownsville)
Rainbow Special (Kansas City–Little Rock)
Royal Gorge (Kansas City–Pueblo)
Southerner (St. Louis–El Paso/San Antonio/New Orleans)
Southern Scenic (Kansas City–Memphis)
Sunflower (St. Louis–Kansas City/Wichita)
Sunshine Special (St. Louis–Hot Springs/San Antonio)
Texan (St. Louis–Fort Worth)
Texas Eagle (Nos. 1 and 2: St. Louis–El Paso, TX)
Texas Eagle (Nos. 21 and 22: St. Louis–Houston/San Antonio)
Valley Eagle (Houston–Brownsville)

(NOTE: *Aztec Eagle* operated by National Railways of Mexico, Nuevo Laredo–Mexico City; El Paso trains were operated by T&P out of Texarkana; T&P handled all trains moving between Texarkana and Longview; Denver & Rio Grande Western handled Denver trains out of Pueblo)

resulting system sprawled across the southern Midwest from St. Louis to Pueblo, Colorado, to Brownsville, Texas, and to El Paso and New Orleans through MP's T&P subsidiary.

In 1967, the Chicago & Eastern Illinois was acquired by the MoPac, thus providing a main line from St. Louis to Chicago, and in 1969, MP sold the Woodland Junction, Illinois–Evansville, Indiana, line to the Louisville & Nashville as a condition of the merger. The two new owners shared trackage between Danville and Chicago. The final

visible reorganization took place in 1976, when the C&EI and T&P subsidiaries were formally merged into the MoPac, and a final paper shuffle eliminated the Missouri-Illinois Railroad Company ("Mike & Ike") and six other subsidiaries.

On April 18, 1980, MoPac's stockholders approved a merger with the Union Pacific, and in 1982 the MoPac as an entity finally came to an end when it became a subsidiary of the Union Pacific. Though the MoPac name still legally exists, its presence has been obliterated at trackside.

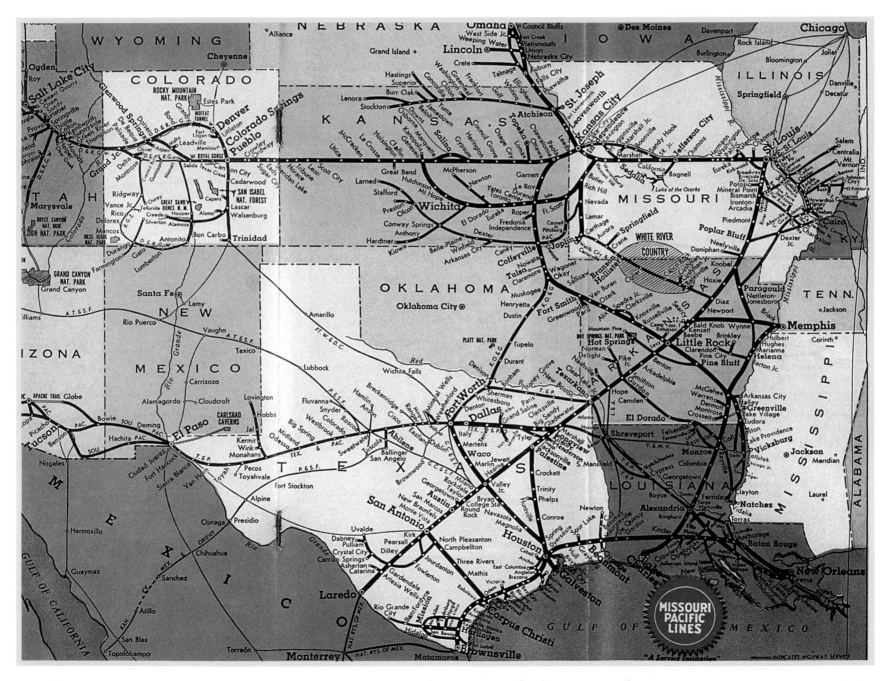

MOPAC AND ITS PASSENGER TRAINS

The MoPac fielded an impressive array of passenger trains in its heyday, the best known in the pre-streamliner era being the *Sunshine Special* between St. Louis and Texas. Other MoPac runs included the *Sunflower* between St. Louis and Kansas City and Wichita, the *Southern Scenic* between Kansas City and Memphis, the *Southerner* and *Rainbow Special* linking Kansas City and Little Rock, Arkansas, the *Houstonian* and *Orleanean* pair on the Houston–New Orleans route, and—in conjunction with the Denver & Rio Grande Western and Western Pacific—the *Scenic Limited* (later renamed *Royal Gorge*) between St. Louis and San Francisco. In terms of passenger service, though, MoPac is perhaps best remembered by its fleet of *Eagle* streamliners.

Streamliners debuted on the MoPac with the delivery of the first *Eagle* trainset in 1940. Following ceremonies in St. Louis, the new trainset from American Car & Foundry set off on a whirlwind tour on MoPac's Eastern Division. On March 10, 1940, the new *Eagle* began service between St. Louis, Kansas City, and Omaha, and from this grew an extensive fleet of Eagle Blue and Mist Gray trains that would grace the rails for the next quarter century. The *Eagle* was chosen from hundreds of entries in an employee naming contest, and the train's styling was developed by famous industrial designer Raymond Loewy.

Next came the little two-car *Delta Eagle* streamliner in 1941, linking Memphis and Tallulah, Louisiana. Now with the fleet expanding, the original *Eagle* was renamed *Missouri River Eagle* to differentiate it from newer *Eagle* services.

Arguably the most famous of all MoPac streamliners was the *Colorado Eagle*—a train which almost never saw the light of day, as World War II restrictions began to impact the nation's

It has been said that every significant steam-era passenger train on the MoPac was inaugurated behind a 6401-class Pacific. Here the *Sunshine Special* poses for the company photographer a few miles out of St. Louis shortly after its inauguration behind 4-6-2 No. 6423. The "Pacific" nomenclature for 4-6-2s originated on the MoPac. *MP*

Two Sedalia-rebuilt Northerns are at speed with a coal train at an unidentified location shortly after their outshopping. Built to Denver & Rio Grande Western specifications, these locomotives were acquired during World War II and operated less than 15 years before they were scrapped, having been bumped from service by the ever-increasing tide of diesel power. *C. T. Wood*

economy. In the end, the government sanctioned the completion of the new trains if for no other reason than to free up older MP equipment for troop train use. The first run of the newest streamliner in MoPac's fold occurred on June 21, 1942, with little publicity—an agreement the railroads had made with the government so as to keep additional demand for rail travel at a minimum. The *Colorado Eagle* ran from St. Louis to Pueblo, Colorado, on the MoPac and then on the Rio Grande beyond to Denver—and vice versa.

After World War II, a number of railroads introduced new or re-equipped streamliners, including Frisco-Katy's *Texas Special*, Southern Pacific-Rock Island's *Golden State*, and Santa Fe's *Super Chief*. MoPac was among the many carriers to launch new services during these heady postwar years, introducing the *Texas Eagle* on August

15, 1948. Two pairs of *Texas Eagle*s began service, unofficially known as the *West Texas Eagle* (St. Louis–El Paso) and the *South Texas Eagle* (St. Louis–San Antonio/Houston). Also in 1948, MoPac introduced the *Louisiana Eagle* between New Orleans and Fort Worth on subsidiary T&P, and the *Valley Eagle* between Houston and Brownsville, Texas. The operation of both these trains dovetailed with those of the *Texas Eagle*s.

During the 1960s the *Eagle*s were victims of retrenchment. The *Colorado Eagle* operated as a full-service through train into the 1960s when MoPac began to trim its feathers. In March 1964 the *Colorado Eagle* name disappeared along with many of the train's amenities. The nameless pair of remnant liners ran until April 2, 1966, when the MoPac finally dropped the train, ending all MP passenger service west of Kansas City. The west

The southbound *Texas Eagle* has arrived at Texarkana in the wee hours of a spring morning in 1968. At this crew division point, MoPac subsidiary Texas & Pacific takes over for the run to Longview, Texas, where the *Eagle* will be switched into two trains, a Fort Worth section and a San Antonio section. MoPac will handle the San Antonio train from Longview to San Antonio while T&P takes the Fort Worth section all the way home. *Jim Boyd*

This rare view from 1959 shows five Alco RS11s loading iron ore within plant property belonging to Pea Ridge Iron Ore Company near Sullivan, Missouri, southwest of St. Louis. The branch was built in 1959 to haul iron ore from the recently completed plant, which was built to tap ore discovered by magnetic surveys conducted during World War II as part of the war effort. The ore body contains ore that is 56 percent iron—a staggering percentage when one considers that Minnesota's famous Iron Range contains ore of only 38 percent. *Kevin EuDaly collection*

MOPAC MOTIVE POWER

The history of the MoPac's motive power is a study in contrasts. The road's steam power rose in interest and volume until there were over 1,150 locomotives in service on over 7,000 miles of track in the late steam era. MoPac motive power from the beginning seemed to be somewhat business-like, an early trait of the railroad in general. In 1923, right after MP President Lewis Baldwin took office, he decreed that the only proper color for a steam locomotive was black, and from then on black it was. The early bold yellow lettering was replaced by a more conservative dull silver enamel which lasted until the demise of steam. MP steam power revealed, however, an incredible array of details to the point that no two engines seemed exactly alike.

section of the *Texas Eagle* was discontinued altogether on May 31, 1969. As of autumn 1970, the *Texas Eagle* was but a single train between St. Louis and San Antonio. By the time Amtrak took over most of the nation's intercity passenger trains on May 1, 1971, the mighty *Texas Eagle* had been reduced to a "sparrow"—a coach-only run between St. Louis and Texarkana. Though earlier having been retrenched from Omaha to Kansas City, the *Missouri River Eagle* fared somewhat better, becoming a part of a new New York–Kansas City run under Amtrak. Today, Amtrak runs a revived *Texas Eagle* while the *Kansas City Mule* follows the route and nearly the schedule of the old *Missouri River Eagle*.

MoPac employed a large array of steam engine types, including smaller locomotives such as 2-8-0 Consolidations, 0-6-0 and 0-8-0 switchers, prim and high-stepping 4-6-0 Ten-Wheelers, 4-4-2 Atlantics, and 4-6-2 Pacifics. The Pacific design is credited to the MoPac, and hence its name. MoPac's most common locomotive, the 2-8-2 Mikado, was also by far the most common locomotive wheel arrangement in the U.S. and a staple of freight runs. MoPac's most impressive machines were undoubtedly the 2201-series 4-8-4 Northerns, though earlier Northerns and beautiful 4-8-2 Mountains could also be seen on the road's most important trains. MoPac's only Mallet—a 2-8-8-2 on small, 55-inch drivers—was purchased by the St. Louis, Iron Mountain & Southern to shove cars

It's the very first day of 1957 as local train 425 pauses at Eldorado, Kansas, behind an Electro-Motive GP7. At one time a Fort Scott–Wichita run that connected with a Kansas City–Little Rock train at Durand, Kansas, No. 425 and its eastbound counterpart, train 426, eventually were reduced to a Durand–Wichita run. *Kevin EuDaly collection*

in the hump yard at Dupo, Illinois, and rarely ventured out of the St. Louis area.

The 4-8-2 Mountain-type locomotives were quite varied on the MoPac roster. They ranged from 80 feet long to 102 feet long, and from 296,000 pounds to 396,000 pounds. The first Mountains were built for passenger service on the Chesapeake & Ohio in 1911, and presumably the "Mountain" terminology came from the fact that the C&O bought them for the mountainous climb west of Clifton Forge, Virginia. MoPac old-timers have long argued that the wheel arrangement went unnamed until it arrived on the Iron Mountain in 1913. Either way, the locomotives were purchased to conquer the grades on the Iron Mountain main line, specifically at Gads Hill and Tip Top, where the ruling grades exceeded 2 percent—quite steep for a mainline route.

As competition increased from Union Pacific and Burlington streamliners between the Midwest

After World War II, MoPac dieselized largely with locomotives from Alco and Electro-Motive, although EMD would emerge as the victor when MP later standardized on one builder. Among the numerous freight-cab diesels purchased by MP were a fleet of Alco FA-series, four-axle cab units. FA No. 388 is seeing passenger duties, however, on a July day in 1958 as it leaves St. Louis Union Station with MoPac's sole commuter train, operating between St. Louis and Pacific, Missouri. *Richard J. Solomon*

Big brother to the Alco FA freight units were the Alco PA passenger diesels one of which—paired with an Electro-Motive E-series passenger diesel— heads train No. 238 arriving Texarkana in July 1956. This was primarily a mail-and-express train operating between Longview, Texas, and Texarkana where connection was made with MP's *Southerner* for St. Louis. *R. S. Plummer Sr., Kevin EuDaly collection*

Downtown Fort Worth (at right in photo) and Texas & Pacific's impressive headquarters building (at left) serve as a backdrop for train 62 starting its journey to East St. Louis, Illinois, in the mid-1960s. Three Electro-Motive units are in charge, led by a GP18.
Thomas Hoffmann

of only two overall conversions of older power into modern-day 4-8-4s, the other being a Reading conversion of aged 2-8-0s. Sedalia turned these locomotives into 25 of the raciest, trimmest, and absolutely beautiful 4-8-4s yet to be built. With the wartime effort well under way, these locomotives immediately went into fast freight service between St. Louis and Pueblo. They were allowed 60 MPH on freights but often drew duty on passenger runs, troop trains, and mail/express "Extras" where they would hit 90 MPH. Only eight years after the rebuilding, the scrapping began, and the last five were gone by late 1953.

Missouri Pacific's last steam power came in the form of 15 new 4-8-4 Northerns built by Baldwin in mid-1943 to alleviate traffic pressure resulting from the war effort. They first saw service on redball freights and heavyweight passenger runs. After 1950, they were sent to Arkansas as the Eastern Division was dieselized, and finally they were scrapped in 1956.

and Colorado, MoPac had to shorten running times on its St. Louis–Denver *Scenic Limited/Royal Gorge*. MoPac shops at Sedalia, Missouri, went to work and built an entirely new series of 4-8-2s in 1939, the most modern locomotives on the system at the time. They were assigned to the *Scenic Limited*—where they regularly ran 90 MPH—and other notables such as the *Sunflower* and the *Texan*. MP's final group of 4-8-2s were not the most modern, but they were the heaviest and most powerful and routinely saw service on the *Sunshine Special*. They were the big guns of MoPac's passenger steam fleet, but, after being bumped by new diesels, worked their remaining days in high-speed manifest freight service.

MoPac's first group of 4-8-4s came out of Lima Locomotive Works as 2-8-4s. They were good enough on their own ground, but motive-power officials saw 4-8-4s as the wave of the future. In 1940 Sedalia shops began what proved to be one

The variety seen in the steam era changed quickly with the advent of the diesel locomotive. Though the early diesel era saw another vast array of model types, chief mechanical officer Downing Jenks reduced the variety that had developed on the MoPac from its first diesel locomotive in 1937 to the late 1950s. Under his direction, the railroad standardized on Electro-Motive diesels. After 1964, railroad remained true to Electro-Motive for new orders until the first General Electric locomotives were ordered in 1967. Jenks also put an end to the handsome blue-and-gray passenger scheme by the mid-1960s. His much simpler dark blue with white chevron scheme was certainly less expensive in the paint shop, but was also less dramatic at trackside.

Despite the eventual standardization, MoPac initially rostered a wide array of diesel power, beginning with an ever-growing fleet of switchers from numerous builders in the early diesel era.

The passenger locomotive roster began with slant-nosed E-units from Electro Motive, modernistic PAs from Alco, and a host of other smaller locomotives. Freight diesels began with EMD FTs delivered during World War II, and would see the typical early variety with road freight locomotives from EMD, Baldwin, Alco, and finally GE. When it was all over, the MoPac had rostered 3,062 diesel units between 1937 and 1985.

It is interesting to note that even in defeat the MoPac proved a fighter. When the Union Pacific merged the Missouri Pacific into its system in 1982, the MoPac had more locomotives and route-miles than did the UP. Further, most of the top management of the newly expanded Union Pacific came from the MoPac. In a brief respite, the Missouri Pacific name still graced the sides of locomotives that were repainted in UP's Armour Yellow and Harbor Mist Gray during the early years of the merger. All too soon though, "Missouri" fell to "Union," and the MoPac became yet another fallen flag in America's heartland.

North of Norfork, Arkansas, on the line between Rich Hill, Missouri, and Diaz, Arkansas, the MoPac skirts the White River under a towering hillside, and one set of rock ledges nearly overhangs the tracks. From these ledges a Kansas City–Memphis freight can be seen rolling along White River on October 24, 1982. *Kevin EuDaly*

NICKEL PLATE HIGH SPEED SERVICE

New York, Chicago & St. Louis

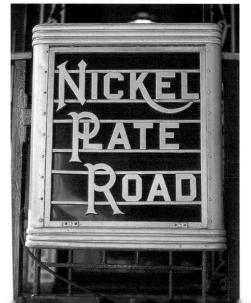

If ever there was a "David" to the "Goliath" that was the New York Central System, it was the New York, Chicago & St. Louis Railroad (NYC&StL). Known for most of its 83-year existence (1881–1964) as the Nickel Plate Road, the NYC&StL emerged from New York Central control during the World War I and went on to earn a nationwide reputation as an efficient, high-speed "bridge route" between the Midwestern gateways of Chicago, St. Louis, and Peoria, and Northeastern connections at Buffalo, New York.

The Nickel Plate's original Buffalo–Chicago route was surveyed and built for little other reason than to be a thorn in the side of the parallel Lake Shore & Michigan Southern (a New York Central predecessor), one of several holdings of the great Vanderbilt empire of Cornelius "The Commodore" Vanderbilt. The threat to their monopoly was not lost on Vanderbilt interests, and they gained control of the NYC&StL days after its October 23, 1882, opening. Having thus become a ward of the LS&MS and, later, the New York Central, the Nickel Plate languished in the shadow of its owner for over 33 years. While the multiple-track NYC offered the last word in freight and passenger services, the single-track Nickel Plate initially was very much the neglected stepchild.

The NYC&StL's nickname was bestowed in 1881 by an Ohio newspaper editor commenting on the new line's high construction standards—to label something as "Nickel Plated" in the late nineteenth century was high praise—but by the time the NYC&StL emerged from NYC control in 1916 it was an antiquated property ill-equipped to compete for the lucrative Midwest-Northeast bridge traffic it would need to survive. Had NYC been left to its own devices, the Nickel Plate (NKP) would have remained "in the family." In the wake of federal government anti-trust efforts, the NYC was forced to divest itself of the LS&MS, the Michigan Central Railroad, or the Nickel Plate. In 1916 NYC chose its Nickel Plate and sold it to the Van Sweringen brothers of Cleveland, setting the stage for one of the classic comebacks of American railroading.

NICKEL PLATE'S VAN SWERINGEN ERA

When they bought the Nickel Plate, Oris and Mantis Van Sweringen were not railroaders, but real-estate developers and financiers who saw a small piece of the Nickel Plate's right-of-way as a solution to the problem of connecting their suburban Shaker Heights development to downtown Cleveland. They entrusted the management of the Nickel Plate to John J. Bernet, an experienced railroader whom they had lured away from NYC. Under Bernet's guidance, the Nickel Plate's single track and sparse passenger schedules—legacies of NYC's benevolent neglect—became hallmarks of a lean, freight-oriented carrier out to give its former owner a run for its money. In the two decades following their purchase of the Nickel Plate, the Van Sweringens became rail barons in their own right, amassing through their Alleghany Corporation a 23,000-mile empire which, at its peak, included the NKP, Chesapeake & Ohio, Erie, Pere Marquette, Wheeling & Lake Erie, Rio Grande, Chicago & Eastern Illinois, and Missouri Pacific railroads.

The 523-mile Nickel Plate itself also grew under Van Sweringen ownership when the Lake Erie & Western and the Toledo, St. Louis & Western (nicknamed the "Clover Leaf") railroads were merged in 1922. The LE&W contributed its 713-mile network, comprising an east–west trunk between Sandusky, Ohio, and East Peoria, Illinois, and north–south Michigan City–Indianapolis and Fort Wayne–Connersville feeders in Indiana. The Clover Leaf's 449 miles gave the NKP access to important connections at Toledo and St. Louis, as well as a half-interest (with Grand Trunk Western) in the 48-mile Detroit & Toledo Shore Line. The former LE&W and Clover Leaf main lines crossed at Frankfort, Indiana, which became a major classification and shop location for the Nickel Plate. The road's primary locomotive and cars shops were in Conneaut, Ohio, while Bellevue, Ohio, with its major classification yard, was generally regarded as the heart of the Nickel Plate. The complex today remains a strategic point on the vast Norfolk Southern system.

FACING PAGE: **The location is Conneaut, Ohio, a division point on the Nickel Plate and the location of a major backshop where repairs kept the railroad's fleet of steam locomotives in top running condition. The presence of one of NKP's mighty Berkshire locomotives steaming in the early morning sun suggest that we're perhaps witnessing NKP steam in its final months of glory. But the date is 1968—not 1958 when Nickel Plate was in the process of ending all steam operations. However, the Berk—No. 759—is quite real and the folks milling about the imposing 2-8-4 are preparing to board a special excursion to Buffalo, which the 759—lovingly restored to operating condition by volunteers—will power, bringing the Nickel Plate back for an encore.** *Mike Schafer*

FACING PAGE INSET: **This handsome drumhead graced the trailing car of many a Nickel Plate passenger train through the years and now stands proudly on display on a NKP office car at Lima, Ohio.** *Mike Schafer*

LEFT: **The Nickel Plate passenger timetable from February 1945 shows that steam still ruled.** *Kevin Holland collection*

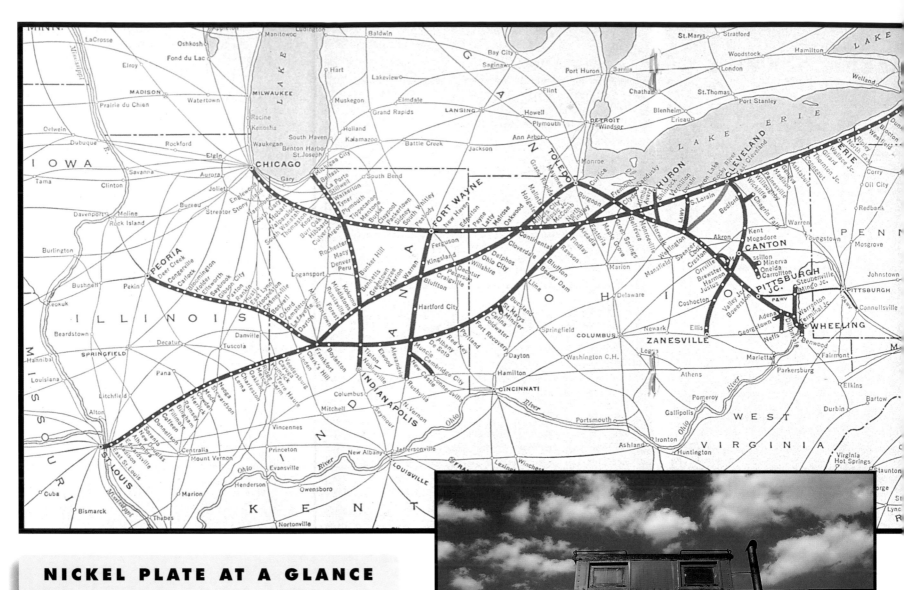

NICKEL PLATE AT A GLANCE

Headquarters: Cleveland, Ohio

Route mileage circa 1950: 2,192

Locomotive fleet circa 1950:
Steam: 392
Diesel: 117

Rolling stock as of 1950:
Freight cars: 29,229
Passenger cars: 117

Principal lines circa 1953 (following W&LE merger):
Chicago–Buffalo, NY, via Fostoria and Lorain, OH
Toledo, OH–East St. Louis, IL
Toledo–Wheeling, WV, and Steubenville, OH
Cleveland–Zanesville, OH
Sandusky, OH–East Peoria, IL,

via Lima, Ohio
Indianapolis–Michigan City, IN
Fort Wayne–Connersville and Rushville, IN
Norwalk–Huron, OH
Cleveland–Wellington, OH

Notable passenger trains:
Blue Arrow (Cleveland–St. Louis)
Blue Dart (St. Louis–Cleveland)
City of Chicago (Buffalo–Chicago)
City of Cleveland (Chicago–Buffalo)
Commercial Traveler (Toledo–St. Louis)
New Yorker (Chicago–Buffalo)
Nickel Plate Limited (Chicago–Buffalo)
Westerner (Buffalo–Chicago)

The map from a 1954 Nickel Plate public passenger timetable shows the railroad shortly after its Wheeling & Lake Erie expansion, which greatly opened up traffic sources account of the W&LE's proximity to the Pittsburgh gateway and its strong base in mineral traffic—coal north to the Great Lakes and iron south from the Great Lakes to Pittsburgh-area steel mills. A hallmark of Nickel Plate freight service in general was its short, high-speed trains, nearly all of which were punctuated by one of the road's famous "High Speed Service" cabooses, so lettered on a highly visible white band across their top sides. NKP caboose 700 is at the Mad River & Nickel Plate Railroad Museum in Bellevue, Ohio. *Mike Schafer*

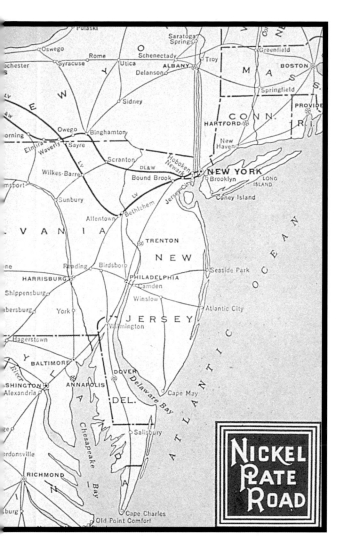

and stations to signs and tools. In 1934 the AMC designed the locomotive that would shape the fortunes of the Nickel Plate for the following quarter century. Modifying their own 2-10-4 design produced in 1930 for C&O, the AMC created the S-class 2-8-4 Berkshire, of which the Nickel Plate eventually would buy 80 copies from two builders. The AMC's 2-8-4 design, with minor modifications, also saw service on the C&O, Pere Marquette, and Virginian. These locomotives, the first 15 of which were built by Alco in the depths of the Depression, brought the "Super Power" era to the Nickel Plate and provided the speed and sustained horsepower necessary to propel the NKP to the front ranks of American railroading.

POST-DEPRESSION—ANOTHER NEW ERA FOR NICKEL PLATE

By 1937, with both Van Sweringen brothers dead and control of their Alleghany Corporation in the reluctant hands of Muncie, Indiana, glass manufacturer George Ball, flamboyant financier Robert R. Young saw the opportunity to achieve his longstanding goal of controlling Alleghany Corporation and acquired Ball's holdings. The C&O, then under Young's management, acquired stock control of the Nickel Plate in December 1937. Young's ambition at the time was to merge the NKP, C&O, W&LE, and PM, but a September 1945 attempt met with such resistance that Young's C&O relinquished its stock control of the

Flagship passenger train of the Nickel Plate in the late steam era was the *Nickel Plate Limited* between Chicago and Buffalo with through cars to Hoboken, New Jersey, handled by the Delaware, Lackawanna & Western east of Buffalo. Here, the westbound *Nickel Plate Limited* is at the Englewood station stop less than seven miles out of Chicago's La Salle Street Station on August 30, 1936. Leading the train is Hudson No. 170, an L-1a-class 4-6-4 built by Brooks Locomotive Works. This was the NKP's first Hudson. *The Sirman collection*

Locomotives were the weak link in the Nickel Plate's ability to compete with NYC and the other half-dozen railroads heading east from Chicago in the 1920s. Several classes of 2-8-2 Mikados had been delivered to the NKP in the early years of Van Sweringen control, and the road's 4-6-4 Hudsons missed the distinction of being the first in-service locomotives of that wheel arrangement by a matter of weeks. Each type was a vast improvement in power and reliability over the obsolete engines which they replaced, but the Mikados could still not provide the combination of speed and sustained power necessary for the Nickel Plate to break out of the "drag era" and compete with its larger neighbors.

The Van Sweringen roads benefitted from the engineering efforts of their Advisory Mechanical Committee (AMC), a clearing-house for development and design of everything from locomotives

One of Nickel Plate's famous high-speed freights lives up to its name as it pounds over the crossing of Baltimore & Ohio's Lake Erie branch at Paynesville, Ohio, east of Cleveland on the morning of August 15, 1956. In charge of keeping the merchandise on time is NKP Berkshire No. 778. *John Dziobko*

Morning sun bathes the "Bluebirds"— Nickel Plate's blue-and-silver Alco PAs— on the approach to Cleveland Union Terminal with the *City of Cleveland* on August 15, 1956. The gray-and-maroon car toward the rear belongs to Delaware, Lackawanna & Western and is one of the through cars to Hoboken. *John Dziobko*

Nickel Plate in November 1947. Related to this divestiture, the Interstate Commerce Commission authorized the Nickel Plate to acquire C&O's holdings in coal-hauling Wheeling & Lake Erie. The C&O, in turn, was authorized to merge its other long-time affiliate, Pere Marquette.

When the Nickel Plate formally leased the W&LE in December 1949, it acquired a property with healthy originating traffic, something which the bridge-route NKP had never enjoyed in any appreciable amount. Wheeling's strength lay in mineral traffic, with southern Ohio coal destined for the Lake Erie docks at Huron, Ohio, and southbound iron ore heading from lake boats to the steel mills of Cleveland, Wheeling, and Pittsburgh.

PASSENGER SERVICE

The Nickel Plate is not generally remembered as a major passenger train operator. During the years of NYC control, the Nickel Plate's modest mainline schedules—three Buffalo–Chicago trains known on the railroad as the "Peerless Trio"—paled against the extra-fare limiteds of its parent. Beginning in 1893, Nickel Plate passengers had the option of through sleeping cars to New York City, via the West Shore Railroad from Buffalo. The Nickel Plate's longest-running through sleeper operation commenced in 1897 when cars were forwarded between Buffalo and Hoboken, New Jersey (across the Hudson River from Manhattan), via the Delaware, Lackawanna & Western.

Nickel Plate's premier train, the *Nickel Plate Limited*, provided overnight service in both directions between Chicago, Cleveland, and Buffalo, and through-car service between Buffalo and Hoboken. The Buffalo–Chicago day train, with overnight through cars from Hoboken via the Lackawanna, was known as the *Westerner*. The eastbound counterpart run remained nameless until the 1950s when it was christened *New Yorker*.

There may have been faster ways to travel by train between New York and Chicago and Cleveland and St. Louis, but the Nickel Plate's offerings were noted for a homespun warmth sometimes lacking aboard the competition's more famous limiteds. Supporting the Nickel Plate's mainline trains were a host of accommodation runs and mixed trains, but these gradually withered after World War II as Midwesterners embraced the automobile. One of the first to go was the *Commercial Traveler*, a Toledo–St. Louis train inherited from the Clover Leaf, which made its final run in 1941.

A westbound freight out of Buffalo behind Berkshire 772 has just crossed from the state of New York into North East, Pennsylvania, where it approaches a typical NKP crossing watchman's shanty—and a watchman—guarding a street crossing. The skies are absolutely clear on this March day in 1957, but clouds are on the horizon for the future of steam on the Nickel Plate Road. *Jim Shaughnessy*

Nickel Plate was one of the few Class 1 railroads to purchase General Electric's 44-ton switcher model; most of these little center-cab diesels went to shortline and industrial railroads. NKP 90, shown prowling about the outskirts of Bloomington, Illinois, in April 1959, was the only 44-tonner purchased by NKP. *Monty Powell*

With high-performance Berkshires successfully serving as its mainstay freight (and sometimes passenger) power after the Depression, Nickel Plate was hesitant to completely dieselize as early as most of its contemporaries. In 1942, the Plate took delivery of its first diesels—Electro-Motive NW2 and Alco S2 switchers intended for yard assignments. The railroad was still not convinced that diesels were the way to go for over-the-road service, however. The 29 in this scene at Cleveland in 1959 is an S2 switcher that was delivered in 1947. At right is GP9 No. 477, an Electro-Motive "General Purpose" road-switcher intended for road and switching service. These "Geeps" (pronounced "jeeps") and their Alco equivalents—RS3s, DL701s, and DL702 models—would render steam a vanished breed on the NKP by the end of the 1950s. *John S. Ingles*

The Berkshire locomotives had enabled the Nickel Plate to perform yeoman's service during World War II, but at war's end the road found itself rostering freight and passenger equipment literally worn out by the war effort. Still under the influence of C&O's Robert Young, the Nickel Plate was caught on the fringes of the postwar boom in passenger train re-equipping. When Young placed his overly optimistic November 1946 order for 287 stainless steel-sheathed Pullman-Standard passenger cars for C&O, the Nickel Plate added 25 of its own cars to the order. When they were delivered in 1950, they went to work behind the 11 Alco PA1 passenger diesels that had been on the property since 1947–48. Nickel Plate's passenger trains, which had presented a conservative Pullman green exterior prior to the war, now wore a sparkling cloak of stainless steel and dark blue, although the continuity was often interrupted by cars still painted in Pullman Green or through cars bearing Lackawanna livery.

Following the upgrading of passenger services, the St. Louis trains even received names. The westbound Cleveland–St. Louis run became known as the *Blue Arrow* while its eastbound counterpart became the *Blue Dart*.

A NEW POSTWAR NICKEL PLATE

New equipment—to the tune of over $35 million—was far from the only postwar rehabilitation. Between 1943 and 1949, the Nickel Plate invested more than $25 million in such physical plant improvements as Centralized Traffic Control (CTC), radio installations, and shop and yard modernization.

Nickel Plate was late to embrace the diesel locomotive. The road's first yard units arrived in 1942 mainly to comply with smoke abatement ordinances in Buffalo and Chicago. Switchers remained the only diesels on the roster until the first PAs arrived in December 1947. Freight service was still completely steam-powered, with NKP management so convinced of the Berkshires' abilities that they ordered ten more in 1948—even before comparative tests of Electro-Motive F3 demonstrators had been concluded. NKP S-3 Berkshires Nos. 770–779 were delivered in 1949 and would soon prove to be the Nickel Plate's final new steam purchase, with the 779 earning the dubious honor of being the last steam locomotive produced by the Lima Locomotive Works.

Embarrassed by the defeat of its 1948 Nickel Plate F3 demonstration—in which the final ten

Berkshires had been ordered while the diesel assessment was still under way—General Motors' Electro-Motive Division persevered with tests by a pair of F7 demonstrators on NKP's Peoria Division in the spring of 1949. These tests, while unsuccessful in the short term, paved the way for NKP's first diesel road-switcher order in 1950. When EMD delivered GP7s Nos. 400–412 to the Nickel Plate in early 1951, the new units went to work on the Indianapolis-Michigan City Division.

Dieselization progressed steadily, but slowly enough for the Nickel Plate to achieve notoriety—along with coal roads Norfolk & Western and C&O—as one of the last railroads operating mainline steam power in the U.S. Remarkably, steam still accounted for over 52 percent of Nickel Plate freight gross ton-miles in the spring of 1957. Nickel Plate management was on record as expecting steam to survive into the early 1960s, but an economic recession in 1957–58 brought mainline steam to an end, with enough diesels on the property to handle existing and anticipated traffic. The final operation of a Berkshire on a Nickel Plate freight occurred on July 2, 1958, when S-2 No. 746 ran from Bellevue to Conneaut, Ohio. Steam switchers made a brief curtain call in Conneaut yard in 1959, but with the banking of their fires, the steam era on the Nickel Plate Road had finally come to an end.

The Nickel Plate, which had diversified its own traffic mix with the 1949 W&LE acquisition,

Nickel Plate's passenger service on the Chicago–Buffalo main line was greatly overshadowed by the multitude of trains operated by the parallel New York Central. Further victimized by the increase in popularity of the automobile and the proliferation of government-subsidized highways, NKP passenger runs had withered as the 1960s got under way. In this scene at Erie Lackawanna's Babcock Street Station in Buffalo in April 1964, a three-car *City of Cleveland* has just arrived from Chicago. A single baggage car and two coaches are more than ample for the paltry number of passengers aboard. Although through-car operations to and from Hoboken had ended by this time, it was still possible to connect with Erie Lackawanna trains, the equipment for which is being held by a switcher in the distance. *Brian J. Bentley*

Though Nickel Plate's home states of Illinois, Indiana, and Ohio are assumed by many to be entirely frying-pan flat, all three do have their scenic moments. West of Cleveland in April 1958, two Bluebirds cruise high above the Rocky River at Rocky River, Ohio, with the eastbound *Blue Dart. Bruce McCaleb, Jay Williams collection*

continued to tap new markets through the 1950s. It was an early proponent of trailer-on-flatcar (TOFC, or "piggyback") service, affording the relatively rare sight of piggyback cars speeding along behind steam locomotives. Speed was paramount to the road's postwar success, and, lest anyone forget, the road's piggyback trailers and cabooses were emblazoned with a "Nickel Plate High Speed Service" banner. Solid eastbound "reefer blocks" of meat- and produce-laden refrigerator cars were a staple of the Nickel Plate's bridge traffic. These were augmented in the road's diesel era by such then-novel concepts as unit coal trains from on-line southern Ohio mines.

Changing traffic patterns and the emerging Eastern merger movement were clouds on the horizon for many Eastern railroads as the 1950s drew to a close, the Nickel Plate among them. The same 1957–58 recession that led to the demise of Nickel Plate steam power also affected

the road's passenger operations. After April 28, 1952, the Nickel Plate's passenger schedules comprised just six daily trains—a day train and night train in each direction between Chicago and Buffalo (still with through service to Hoboken), and an overnight Cleveland–St. Louis service. The economic downturn precipitated the end of trains 9 and 10 between Cleveland and St. Louis, which were actually cut back in awkward segments as the states involved (Illinois, Indiana, and Ohio) allowed the Nickel Plate's request to discontinue the service. The last vestiges of Nickel Plate passenger service over the former LE&W and Clover Leaf routes disappeared on October 17, 1959.

The Chicago–Buffalo mainline passenger trains fared somewhat better, but were still fighting a losing battle with growing airline and highway travel. The colorful PA1 locomotives, dubbed "Bluebirds" on the Nickel Plate for their unique blue-and-gray paint scheme, were replaced with steam-generator-equipped GP9 and RS36 hood units after 1962. In June 1963 the *Westerner* and the *New Yorker*, trains 7 and 8, were discontinued. Their discontinuance left only the former *Nickel Plate Limited*, now known westbound as the *City of Chicago* and eastbound as the *City of Cleveland*, in the Nickel Plate's timetable. These last remnants of Nickel Plate passenger service operated on an overnight schedule between Chicago and Cleveland, and as a truncated coach-only train between Cleveland and Buffalo.

NICKEL PLATE MERGES INTO HISTORY

As pathetic as the last Nickel Plate Road passenger trains may have been—rarely more than a GP9, a grubby baggage car, and a solitary lightweight coach east of Cleveland—they managed to outlive the Nickel Plate itself. On October 16, 1964, the 83-year-old Nickel Plate was merged into the Norfolk & Western Railway, which also leased the Wabash Railroad and several smaller companies to diversify its traffic base and extend its reach from Appalachian coal fields to the growing markets of the Northeast and Midwest.

The Nickel Plate Road owned a total of 440 diesel locomotives, and contributed 407 of them to the N&W roster. While most were first-generation road-switcher models like GP7s, GP9s, RS3s, and RS11's, the Nickel Plate survived long enough to sample a few second-generation locomotives. Among the last models purchased were 11 Alco RS36s (which incorporated components from the traded-in Bluebirds), and ten of EMD's distinctive GP30s. Wreck replacements just before the merger added a single EMD GP35 and an Alco Century 420 to the Nickel Plate roster.

Everyone loves an underdog, and that may explain the perennial interest in the Nickel Plate Road even decades after it disappeared. "Doing more with less" is a fair characterization of how the Nickel Plate held its much larger competitors at bay, and was just as true when the company emerged from NYC control in 1916 as it was through the economically turbulent 1950s and early 1960s. Tangible reminders of the Nickel Plate are plentiful, with a number of steam locomotives, diesels, freight, and passenger cars having been preserved and restored by museums and individuals. A few Nickel Plate structures survive, but the road's greatest legacy is the key role its original Chicago-Buffalo route still plays as a high-speed artery for N&W successor Norfolk Southern.

En route back to Calumet Yard on Chicago's south side, an NW2 switcher comes face to face with symbol freight CB-12, the erstwhile Nickel Plate's hot Chicago–Buffalo train, at State Line interlocking, Hammond, Indiana. It's the autumn of 1965 and the N&W-NKP happened a year earlier—yet, it still looks like the Nickel Plate. *Mike McBride*

Nickel Plate began acquiring second-generation diesels from Electro-Motive in 1962 when it took delivery of ten turbocharged GP30s. One of the burly units hammers across the Illinois Central crossing at Dean tower, Bloomington, Illinois, with the westbound Frankfort–East Peoria train on May 3, 1964. *Jim Boyd*

SERVING NEW YORK AND NEW ENGLAND

New York, New Haven & Hartford

The fabled New Haven Railroad was an institution, not only in New England but also in metropolitan New York. It was a compact railroad—about 1,800 route-miles as of 1950—dense with lines that webbed Connecticut, Rhode Island, and Massachusetts. And, unlike all the other railroads featured in this volume, it derived a large amount of its revenues from passenger trains.

The Hartford & New Haven Railroad, one of the earliest predecessor lines of the modern-day New Haven, was chartered in 1833. The H&NH extended north from New Haven, Connecticut, to Springfield, Massachusetts, via Hartford, Connecticut. Another key road was the New York & New Haven, chartered in 1844 to operate between its namesake cities, using trackage rights on the New York & Harlem (New York Central System) to enter Manhattan.

The NY&NH, which considered the H&NH a competitor, grew by taking over various other area railroads, among them the New Haven & Northampton between New Haven and Plainville, Connecticut. In 1870 the NY&NH also acquired control of the Shore Line Railway which ran east from New Haven to Stonington, Connecticut, near the Rhode Island border.

A turning point came in 1872 when the NY&NH and rival H&NH merged to form the New York, New Haven & Hartford Railroad—a name and railroad that would survive nearly a century. Although the "New Haven" had now officially been formed, it was far from complete, and the new company entered a period of rapid expansion.

Among the key companies acquired by the fledgling company were: the Boston & New York Air Line (New Haven–Willimantic, Connecticut); Hartford & Connecticut Valley (Hartford–Saybrook via Middletown); the New York, Providence & Boston (Stonington–Boston via Providence, Rhode Island); the Housatonic (Norwalk, Connecticut–Pittsfield, Massachusetts); the Naugatuck Railroad (Devon–Winsted, Connecticut); and the Old Colony lines around Boston. Nearly the same size as the NYNH&H, the Old Colony

had opened between Boston and Plymouth, Massachusetts, in 1845 and quickly grew by swallowing up a number of other Massachusetts-based railroads fanning out toward Cape Cod, Fall River, and New Bedford.

Another important NYNH&H component, the New York & New England, was also a major competitor before its acquisition. Separate lines from Boston and Providence joined at Willimantic to form a through route through Hartford, Waterbury, and Danbury to the east bank of the Hudson River at what is now Beacon, New York. From there, car floats made a connection with the Erie across the river at Newburgh, New York. NY&NE also bought the Norwich & Worcester (Groton, Connecticut–Worcester, Massachusetts).

The Central New England was yet another railroad of note in the New Haven network, not so much for size, but for its strategic location. The CNE was formerly the Philadelphia, Reading & New England, which entered New England by circumventing New York City to the north, crossing the Hudson River on a huge bridge (still standing) at Poughkeepsie, New York. Normally, most rail freight moving into New England had to pass through the tangle of New York City, with much of it being moved on car floats across the Hudson and East rivers. The PR&NE was reorganized as the Central New England in 1899 and NH purchased it in 1904.

The carriers mentioned here are just a few of the more than 200 that fell into a great swirl of business transactions that eventually grew the NYNH&H to blanket southern New England.

At the threshold of the twentieth century, the New Haven had become a powerful force in New England transportation. Part of this could be attributed to the famous financier J. P. Morgan, who with his associates—including New Haven president Charles Mellen—had gained control of the New Haven at the end of the 1800s. Soon the New Haven controlled the Boston & Maine, Maine Central, New York, Ontario & Western, Rutland Railroad (with NYC), various steamboat companies, and local utilities and streetcar companies.

TIMETABLE
Effective September 26, 1948
EASTERN STANDARD TIME

The New York New Haven and Hartford RAILROAD CO.

THE SCENIC SHORELINE ROUTE SERVING NEW YORK AND NEW ENGLAND

FACING PAGE: Diesel-electric/electric and straight electric locomotives lay over at the engine terminal in New Haven, Connecticut, between assignments on a June night in 1968. Until the year 2000, when Amtrak extended electrification to Boston, New Haven was the point at which steam or diesel locomotives were exchanged for electric locomotives for the trip into New York City. The locomotive at left is an Electro-Motive FL9, a dual-mode unit. It can operate as a regular diesel-electric or, in third-rail territory, as a straight electric locomotive, hence its designation as a "diesel-electric/electric." *Mike Schafer*

FACING PAGE, INSET: A New Haven rectifier electric freight locomotive noses through Fresh Pond Junction, New York, in 1964. *Richard J. Solomon*

LEFT: New Haven's public timetable issued in September 1948 featured an artist's rendering of the dual-service Alco diesels purchased prior and during World War II for freight and passenger service.

NEW YORK, NEW HAVEN & HARTFORD AT A GLANCE

Headquarters: New Haven, CT

Route mileage circa 1950: 1,800

Locomotive fleet as of 1963:
Diesel: 381
Electric: 22

Rolling stock as of 1963:
Freight cars: 6,925
Passenger cars (includes self-propelled cars): 1,055

Principal routes circa 1950 (slash denotes branched end points):

New York City (Grand Central)–New Haven–New London, CT–Providence, RI–Boston, MA

New York City (Pennsylvania Station)–New Rochelle, NY

New Haven–Hartford, CT–Springfield, MA

New Haven–Middletown–Putnam, CT–Boston (Readville)

New Haven–Northhampton/Holyoke, MA

Devon–Winsted, CT

Waterbury–Hartford–Plainfield, CT–Providence

Providence (Valley Falls)–Worcester, MA

Norwalk, CT–Pittsfield/State Line, MA

Derby, CT–Campbell Hall/Beacon, NY

New London–Worcester

New Bedford/Fall River–Framingham–Lowell/Fitchburg, MA

Boston–Brocton–Provincetown/Hyannis/Woods Hole, MA

Attleboro–Taunton–Middleboro, MA

South Braintree–Plymouth, MA

Notable passenger trains :

NEW YORK–BOSTON
Bay State | Bostonian

Commander | Forty-Second Street
Gilt Edge | Hell Gate Express
Merchants Limited | Murray Hill
Narragansett | New Yorker
Owl | Puritan
Roger Williams | Shoreliner
Yankee Clipper

BOSTON–PHILADELPHIA–WASHINGTON
(Operated by Pennsylvania Railroad west of New York/Pennsylvania Station)
Colonial | Federal
Patriot | Pilgrim
Quaker | Senator
William Penn

OTHER RUNS
Bankers (New York–Springfield)
Berkshires (New York–Pittsfield)
Connecticut Yankee (New York–Springfield)
Day Cape Codder (New York–Hyannis/Woods Hole)
Day White Mountains (New York–Berlin, New Hampshire; operated by Boston & Maine north of Springfield)
Montrealer (New York-to-Montreal, operated by B&M, Central Vermont, and Canadian National north of Springfield)
Nathan Hale (New York–Springfield)
Naugatuck (New York–Winsted)
Night Cap (New York–Stamford, Connecticut)
State of Maine (New York–Portland, Maine, via Providence and Worcester; B&M beyond)
Washingtonian (Montreal-to-Washington counterpart to *Montrealer*)

Eventually all this activity garnered the attention of the federal government, and anti-trust suits brought indictments against Mellen, Morgan, and their cohorts, although Morgan "escaped" much of the commotion by dying in 1913. Regardless, Mellen's leadership had considerable positive impact on the New Haven. The Mellen administration electrified the all-important main line from New Haven west to New York City as well as the New Canaan branch between 1907 and 1915. Under Mellen, the New York Connecting Railroad and its Hell Gate Bridge opened in 1917, providing the New Haven with a high-speed path into Pennsylvania Station and allowing for service through Manhattan in conjunction with the Pennsylvania Railroad. Without Hell Gate Bridge, high-speed Amtrak *Acela* service between Washington, New York, and Boston would not be possible today.

The Mellen administration also oversaw the strengthening of the Maybrook gateway—the "Poughkeepsie Bridge Route"—for freight traffic moving in and out of New England. Utilizing the trackage of CNE and other New Haven predecessors, a high-speed freight route was established between New Haven and Maybrook, New York, some 50 miles above New York. At Maybrook Yard, NH connected with the NYO&W, Erie, NYC, Lehigh & New England, and Lehigh & Hudson River.

Unfortunately, all these improvements overextended the New Haven and nearly put the road into bankruptcy. However, the boom in traffic resulting from World War I helped ease New

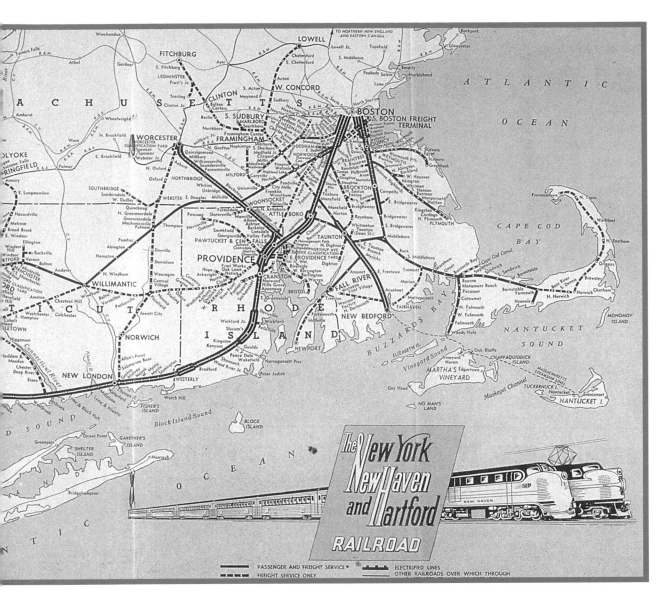

Jammed with commuters en route to Grand Central Terminal, a New Haven suburban M.U. (multiple-unit) train skims along the main line west of Greenwich, Connecticut, in June 1968. M.U. trains such as this plied the electrified routes on frequent schedules serving nearly all local stops. The unusual triangular catenary was a hallmark of the New Haven electrification. A modernized electrical distribution system has since replaced this interesting wirework. *Mike Schafer*

Haven's financial problems. The 1920s proved to be a brighter era for U.S. railroads, including the New Haven, and business prospered. During this decade, the mighty Pennsylvania acquired 25 percent interest in the New Haven, now a critical connection thanks to the Hell Gate Bridge route.

Alas, the Great Depression reversed the fortunes of nearly all railroads, and New Haven became one of the nearly one third of U.S. railroads to declare bankruptcy during the dark days of the 1930s. In some ways, the 1935 bankruptcy was good news for the New Haven, for the trusteeship, led by Howard Palmer, made haste in undoing some of the unwise moves of pre-World War I New Haven. Many of the rendundant lines in the company's bewildering array of routes were

abandoned and its subsidiary bus and steamship lines sold or abolished. New Haven became an early proponent of streamlined passenger trains, piggyback freight service, and diesel-electric locomotives. In 1934 New Haven debuted its *Comet* streamliner and began taking delivery of new semi-streamlined coaches. In 1938, NH introduced trailer-on-flatcar (TOFC) service between Boston and New York City.

New Haven had dabbled in diesels since 1931, and the road's trustees early on recognized the vastly improved economics of diesel over steam. New Haven continued to take delivery of diesel-electric locomotives—mostly yard engines—into World War II. The last group of steam locomotives was delivered in 1937, and in 1941 the railroad began acquiring a fleet of 60 dual-purpose (freight and passenger) diesel-electrics from Alco—locomotives that, along with new General Electric electric passenger units, would be instrumental in keeping war-period operations efficient.

Thanks to the Palmer management improvements, the New Haven weathered World War II rather well. The war itself maxed out the road's passenger operations and tripled freight traffic—together with infrastructure improvements the perfect formula for solvency. In 1947 the New Haven emerged from bankruptcy and Palmer was appointed president. Despite good intentions, Palmer's leadership was short-lived. In 1948, Boston financier Frederic Dumaine and his affiliates, including one Patrick B. McGinnis, leveraged control of the New Haven.

From here, the New Haven sank and never fully recovered. Following management principles that would become commonplace in American industry by the end of the twentieth century, the Dumaine regime went right for the bottom line by slashing costs, laying off legions of workers, and implementing a policy of deferred physical plant maintenance. Loyalists whose talent had lifted the railroad out of its 1935 bankruptcy were fired. The results were predictable. Employee morale and loyalty diminished while the railroad became the object of public animosity account of increasingly shabby service and the discontinuance of several passenger routes.

Nonetheless, an interesting twist occurred in 1951 when Dumaine died and his son, Frederic "Buck" Dumaine Jr., took over his father's position, but with a noticeably different management style. He improved employee morale, purchased new passenger equipment, restored service to abandoned routes, and completed dieselization.

Not surprising, Patrick McGinnis locked horns with the new Dumaine management and, through a proxy fight (and many campaign promises) in 1954, had Dumaine ousted. McGinnis became New Haven's newest leader in this period of revolving-door management. Probably the brightest thing to come out of the McGinnis era was New Haven's flashy new orange, red, and black paint scheme. Beyond that, the effects of the McGinnis administration were largely negative: greatly reduced (again) maintenance, reduction of electric operations, and a downgrading of passenger services—ironically in the face of a fleet of high-speed trains proposed by McGinnis. The railroad did post a profit in 1956, but it had come at high cost. Within two years of his rise to NH presidency, McGinnis was given his walking papers by NH directors.

New Haven's new leader, George Alpert, had new challenges. Not only did he have to undo McGinnis trail of destruction, but he had to face what nearly all major U.S. railroads were coming to grips with as the 1950s unfurled: increased competition in the form of public-sponsored highways, the expansion of the trucking industry on those highways, and the boom in auto and airline travel. Furthermore, New England in particular had undergone a drastic change from industrial might to a region of technological and service-based business, neither of which required any significant degree

Ten streamlined 4-6-4s built by Baldwin Locomotive Works were New Haven's final steam locomotive order in the late 1930s. One of the clean-lined Hudsons stands at the head end of a passenger train preparing to depart Boston's South Station on September 4, 1937, not long after the locomotive had been delivered. *Bob's Photo*

Big EP-4-class electric No. 362 seems to overwhelm its little local train westbound at Stamford, Connecticut, in the summer of 1958. The EP-4s were built in 1938 by GE. *Richard J. Solomon*

of freight transport. In 1961, with more than half of its passenger traffic gone, and a good deal of its freight, the New Haven again went bankrupt.

For most of the 1960s, the carrier lived a hand-to-mouth existence. As things grew more desperate, the trustees felt that merger with a stronger railroad was the only solution. On February 1, 1968, the Pennsylvania and New York Central merged to form Penn Central, and on January 1, 1969, the New Haven was thrust upon PC as a condition of the merger. In 1970, PC went bust and Northeastern railroading collapsed.

PASSENGER SERVICE

The New Haven offered the only direct rail route between New York and Boston, so it was no surprise that this became New Haven's showcase operation. The 229-mile Shore Line Route linking the two heavily populated urban areas also included Rhode Island's capital city, Providence. The line west of New Haven into New York was (and is) a corridor of densely populated cities and towns, many of them "bedroom" communities populated by people who work in "The City.'

For nearly its entire existence, the NYNH&H offered New York–Boston service throughout the day and night, serving both Grand Central Terminal

Two Alco PAs are eastbound at Providence with what may be the *Murray Hill* on May 16, 1957. The lead locomotive wears the so-called "McGinnis scheme" that is still very closely associated with the New Haven Railroad and can still be seen (sidebar, page 108). *William T. Clynes*

The New Haven Survives

The sight of what was once modern New Haven diesel power can still be experienced on the Railroad Museum of New England's 19-mile Naugatuck Railroad which operates on the former-NH Waterbury–Winsted, Connecticut, line. The General Electric U25B pulling this excursion train at Waterville, Connecticut, in October 1999 was the last locomotive purchased by the New Haven in 1965. *Scott Hartley*

A typical rail rider in Connecticut or metropolitan New York City might find it difficult to believe that the New York, New Haven & Hartford Railroad went out business three decades ago. In recent years, more than two dozen active locomotives have worn New Haven colors and are visible to thousands of passengers every day. The organization most responsible for this NH revival is Connecticut's Department of Transportation, which started painting its commuter locomotives in complete NH images in 1984. Ten veteran FL9 dual-mode electric/diesel-electric locomotives, all actually purchased by the New Haven between 1956 and 1960, are owned by CDOT and painted in NH colors. They are assigned to work on Metro-North commuter trains on CDOT's own lines in Connecticut as well as on M-N routes in New York. Beginning in 1990, CDOT instituted "Shore Line East" commuter service, operated by Amtrak between New Haven and New London. Eleven additional locomotives in four types (none of which was ever owned by the New Haven!) also were adorned in red, white, and black. Rounding out today's New Haven roster are several more locomotives wearing NH colors working on New England short lines or in museums. Still in regular service on the Railroad Museum of New England's 19-mile Naugatuck Railroad, based out of Thomaston, Connecticut, are immaculately restored Alco RS3 No. 529 and GE U25B No. 2525, the very last locomotive purchased by the New Haven, in 1965.

and Pennsylvania Station in Manhattan. A 1946 public timetable reveals a minimum of hourly departures from Boston to New York, from 7 A.M. until 9 P.M. The *Merchants Limited*, in its heyday an extra-fare all-parlor-car train, and the *Yankee Clipper* were the pride of the Shore Line Route. The names of other New York–Boston flyers reflected New Haven's very "Yankee" nature: the *Roger Williams*, the *Patriot*, the *Pilgrim*, the *Narragansett*, the *Minute Man*, the *Mayflower*, and the *Puritan*.

By way of a joint arrangement with the Pennsylvania Railroad, prompted by the 1917 opening of Hell Gate Bridge, New Haven also operated through trains between Boston and Washington, D.C., via Pennsylvania Station. Trains like the *Senator*, *Federal*, *Quaker*, and *Colonial* allowed NH passengers to travel through Manhattan to Philadelphia, Baltimore, and Washington.

The railroad's second-busiest intercity route was the line to Springfield, Massachusetts, which split from the Shore Line at New Haven. In addition to a number of independent New York–Springfield runs, nearly all New York–Boston trains featured connecting Springfield service at New Haven. The Springfield line also hosted through trains to Vermont and Canada, operated jointly with Boston & Maine and Central Vermont.

Catering to tourists, New Haven operated service onto Cape Cod, at one time all the way to the tip at Provincetown, Massachusetts. Seasonal trains—the *Day Cape Codder* and *Neptune*—operated from New York through Taunton, Massachusetts, to Buzzards Bay where the trains split for Hyannis and Woods Hole. Boat connections could be made at the latter for Martha's Vineyard and Nantucket. The *Cranberry* provided Boston–Hyannis service as did several local trains.

When it came to commuter service, New Haven offered an incredibly dense network of services tied to both New York and Boston. Suburban-type service out of Grand Central focused on the string of communities clinging to the Shore Line Route all the way from New Rochelle, New York (where the Grand Central and Penn Station lines joined), to New Haven as well as branches to New Canaan, Danbury, and Waterbury.

Suburban service at Boston was more sprawling and catered to the south suburban area, with numerous branches—most of them former Old Colony lines—reaching out to Plymouth, Braintree, Fall River, New Bedford, and other locales. Commuter service was also provided on the main line between Providence and Boston. In some respects, the New Haven Railroad was first and foremost a giant commuter-rail entity. The railroad operated commuter trains more than any other type of train, including freight.

A considerable amount of the old New Haven passenger service survives. Amtrak has operated a number of former-New Haven intercity trains since 1971. Until nearly the end of the twentieth century and the subsequent changes in Amtrak service between Washington, New York, and Boston involving new high-speed, all-electric *Acela* service, it was still possible to hop aboard the likes of the *Yankee Clipper* and fabled *Merchants Limited* for a trip along the beautiful former-NH Shore Line Route.

Today, NH New York-area suburban services are under the flag of the Connecticut Department of Transportation. In the Boston area, former-NH suburban services are thriving well under the auspices of the Massachusetts Bay Transportation Authority—the "T".

FREIGHT SERVICE

When New England was an industrial might, New Haven was well positioned to gather and forward freight traffic out of New England to connecting carriers—and likewise carry it in. New Haven's blanket of lines served countless factories, mills, warehouses, and other traffic sources throughout southern Massachusetts, Rhode Island, and Connecticut. Much of this traffic was funneled into Cedar Hill Yard—the heart of NH freight operations near New Haven—where it was reclassified into through trains to New York City and to Maybrook via the Poughkeepsie Bridge Route. Traffic to New York City went to the Harlem River Freight Terminal, to the Long Island Rail Road at Fresh Pond Junction, or to Bay Ridge for transfer by ferry to New Jersey.

The Maybrook line saw more than 50 freights a day during World War II, but settled down to eight scheduled freights each way in the 1950s; it was half that by 1969. South Boston was New Haven's main freight facility in metro Boston, and

8–10 freights in each direction along the Shore Line Route originated and terminated there. Through freights on the Springfield line were mostly night operations, as locals worked the line in daylight gathering traffic. NH and B&M shared freight facilities in Springfield.

Other notable freight routes included Cedar Hill–Holyoke, Massachusetts via the old Canal Line and the Boston & Albany (NYC) connection at Westfield, Massachusetts; Cedar Hill–Worcester via Groton, Connecticut; and Hartford–Boston via Willimantic, Plainfield, and Providence.

The New Haven was never very large to begin with, so the long, 900-mile-plus freight runs that made money for roads like the Erie and New York Central were unheard of on the NH where the longest freight run was only about 280 miles. New England's decline as an industrial might struck a fatal blow to the New Haven. What little freight traffic that remains on former-NH lines today is operated by B&M (under Guilford Transportation), CSX, and various new shortline operators including Providence & Worcester, the Housatonic Railroad, Connecticut Southern, Bay Colony, and a revived (but quite a bit smaller) Central New England.

Looking a bit worse for wear, a General Electric EP-5 electric breezes through Mamaroneck, New York, with the Washington–Boston *Colonial* in June 1968. Ten of these smartly styled rectifier locomotives were delivered in 1955 and tended to work the trains that served Pennsylvania Station. Their loud blowers (for cooling) earned these locomotives the nickname "Jets." The A. C. Gilbert Company, the New Haven-based manufacturer of S-gauge American Flyer electric toy trains, produced many models of New Haven locomotives and rolling stock, including the EP-5 electric. *Jim Boyd*

MAIN STREET OF THE NORTHWEST
Northern Pacific

On July 2, 1864, President Abraham Lincoln signed an Act of Congress creating the Northern Pacific Railroad Company, a railway chartered to build from the Great Lakes to Puget Sound on the West Coast. Its route followed the journey of the famed 1804–1806 Lewis and Clark expedition across the West. The twenty years which followed saw a continuous struggle to complete the road in the face of shaky financing, battles for control of the company, and national economic upheavals.

Groundbreaking on the eastern end began near Carlton, Minnesota, in 1870. Construction on its western end began on the banks of the Columbia River at Kalama, Washington Territory, that same year. From 1870 to 1873 crews pushed the railheads from Duluth, Minnesota, to Bismarck, Dakota Territory, in the east, and from Kalama to Tacoma, Washington Territory, in the west.

Directors hired Jay Cooke & Co., the great Civil War bond sellers, to promote the route. Jay Cooke spent so much time and money promoting the lushness of the line that it quickly became known as his "Banana Belt." Unfortunately, the bonds failed to sell. Cooke & Co. overextended itself in support of the NP and closed its doors in 1873.

ENTER HENRY VILLARD

The road languished unfinished for several years, until a group of Eastern businessmen reorganized it in 1878. Streamlining finances, its coffers were augmented with more than $40 million in bonds. This helped kick off a building boom which lasted for more than a decade.

Pushing its railheads again, construction moved west from Bismarck and east from the present-day Pasco, Washington, at the confluence of the Snake and Columbia rivers. This same period saw the rise of a man who was to play a key role in completing the line—Henry Villard.

Villard was a representative of the financial concerns that were speculating in American railroads. Prior to 1880, Villard intervened in Oregon on behalf of these interests in transportation systems.

PASSENGER TRAIN SCHEDULES

ALL SCHEDULES ARE SHOWN IN STANDARD TIME

Route of the Vista-Dome NORTH COAST LIMITED

Most came under the control of the holding company Villard formed, the Oregon & Transcontinental. The most important of the O&T's lines was the Oregon Railway & Navigation Company. The OR&N ran east from Portland along the south bank of the Columbia River to the fertile interior and eventually became part of the Union Pacific. Henry Villard's growing transportation empire in the Pacific Northwest had but one real competitor, the slowly-expanding Northern Pacific.

The NP was moving to complete its line to Puget Sound, an outcome which would mean the rise of Seattle and Tacoma over Oregon's premier city—Portland—and turmoil for Villard's empire. To prevent the NP from reaching tidewater at Tacoma, Villard formed what came to be known as the "Blind Pool," a fund of more than $8 million from his financial connections. Astoundingly, his backers were not told what the unprecedented sum was to be used for. In fact, it formed Villard's answer to NP's threat. He would simply buy control of it.

Villard secured control of the Northern Pacific by the fall of 1881, becoming the road's president in September. He then set about using the OR&N as the NP's route to Puget Sound (via Portland and a ferry across the Columbia River to Kalama), and connecting the OR&N with a direct route to the East by completing the NP.

During 1881 and 1882 the NP's construction crews made tremendous strides. From the east, the railheads were pushed nearly to the banks of the Yellowstone River at Glendive, Montana Territory, 690 miles from St. Paul. In the west, track gangs built from Wallula, near the confluence of the Columbia and Snake rivers, northeast to Spokane Falls. Simultaneously, crews in Spokane pushed across Lake Pend Oreille toward the Clark Fork River.

By December 1882, eastern crews reached the last crossing of the Yellowstone, on the outskirts of Livingston, Montana Territory, having come 115 miles in three months. Bozeman Tunnel, between Livingston and Bozeman, was begun in the first months of 1882, even before the railhead had reached Billings, 128 miles away. Working through

FACING PAGE: Ready for its trip into the chilly Minnesota night, the westbound *North Coast Limited* stands in fresh snow at the Great Northern Station in Minneapolis in 1969. The train had spent most of the afternoon and evening on the Burlington, which forwarded the train from Chicago to St. Paul. There, CB&Q locomotives were exchanged for a set of NP diesels clad in the road's elegant two-tone green livery, developed by noted industrial stylist Raymond Loewy. *Mike Schafer*

FACING PAGE, INSET. An elderly but classic wood caboose at Pasco, Washington, in 1969 displays NP's well-remembered slogan and distinctive monad logo. *Mike Schafer*

LEFT: The *North Coast Limited* was NP's premier train for over 70 years. The domed version of the train from 1954 was featured on the cover of the timetable issued in October 1963.

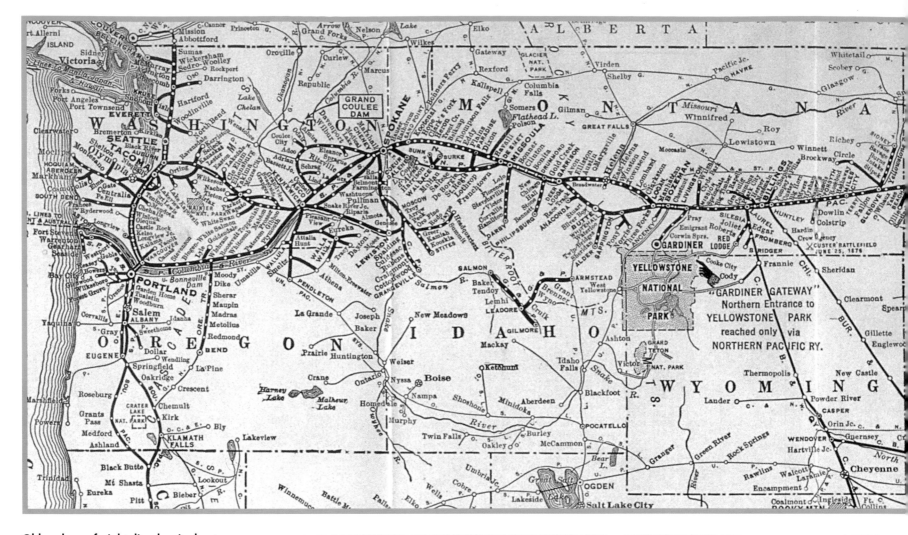

Old and new freight diesels mingle at NP's Northtown Yard facilities in the Twin Cities. At left, a venerable Electro-Motive GP9 from the 1950s shares a bit of the limelight (and sunlight) with one of the road's newest diesel models, a 2500-hp.General Electric U25C, which had just been delivered to the NP on this summer day in 1966. NP was one in a relatively modest group of U.S. railroads to employ completely separate freight and passenger paint schemes right up to the end of its existence. *Jim Boyd*

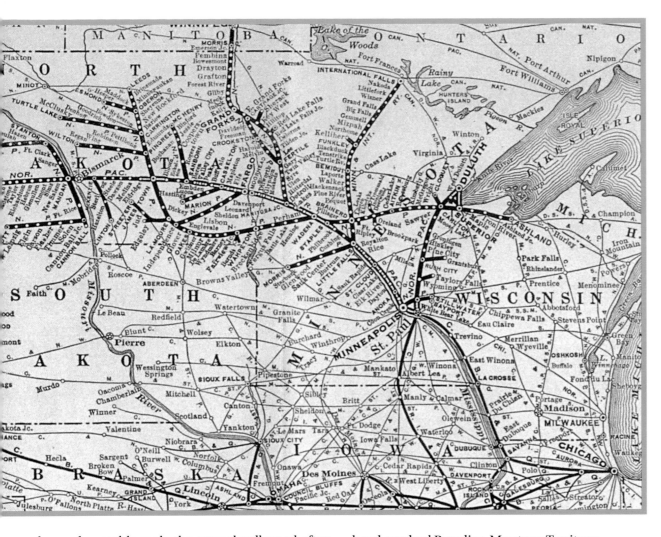

The map from a 1939 NP public passenger timetable went so far as to differentiate between single and double track. Note that the SP&S lines are drawn so as to appear to be a part of the NP—which in a sense they were, as NP co-owned the Spokane, Portland & Seattle with rival Great Northern.

clay and unstable rock, the tunnel collapsed after five months. When efforts were renewed, hydraulic mining methods were used, with the clay being washed away in a long flume. The railroad also built a temporary line over the summit of Bozeman Pass in the winter of 1882 to close the gap in the line. While crews were repairing Bozeman Tunnel, another crew was grading and boring the line to Mullan Tunnel on the segment between Helena and Missoula. Facing a completion date no sooner than the winter 1883, Villard ordered yet another temporary line to close the gap.

Crews on the west end put about 150 miles of track into service in 1881 and 1882. By the spring of 1882 workers had pushed into Montana proper, following the surveyors and working southeast along the Clark Fork River, aiming for Missoula. The work force of nearly 4,000 men, 2,600 of whom were Chinese, created boomtowns of saloons, restaurants, flophouses, and tents at the construction sites. In the spring of 1883 the rail-head reached Paradise, Montana Territory.

June 1883 saw the railhead at just under 40 miles west of Missoula, with two major accomplishments having been made, Marent and O'Keefe trestles, which consumed six months. By August, the gap between east and west had closed to 64 miles near Missoula. East of Missoula, work was slowed by a large amount of trestle construction, while in the west, crews were working their way down the 2.2 percent grades of Evaro Hill. The NP was averaging a mile and half of track a day.

Final ceremonies at Gold Creek, Montana Territory, were held on September 8, 1883. Though the NP had ordered 23 Pullman sleepers and 48 day coaches in anticipation of its grand opening, the group of visiting dignitaries proved so large that enough leased equipment for four passenger trains was necessary to transport guests to the spot. Villard, former President Ulysses S. Grant, Secretary of the Interior Henry Teller, the Fifth Infantry Band from Fort Keogh, as well as scores of

NP employed some massive steam power to move its freights through mountainous territory. The road first embraced giant steam power with a set of 2-10-0 Decapods that were acquired to haul trains over the steep, temporary main line over Bozeman Pass while Bozeman Tunnel was being built. In the modern steam era, NP acquired some real giants: 4-6-6-4 Challenger-type articulated steam locomotives, one of which barely fits the turntable at Missoula, Montana, in August 1949. *Jim Fredrickson*

Northern Pacific was the first railroad to use the 4-8-4 wheel arrangement, and in that honor this locomotive type became known as the "Northern" on nearly all the different railroads that eventually owned 4-8-4s. Northern 2686 is working up Cushing Hill on the main line between Little Falls and Staples, Minnesota, with an excursion train on June 30, 1957. *Barry A. Carlson*

Montanans, looked on as western and eastern crews finished the remaining 1,200 feet of track. The last spike and the sledge hammer had been connected to make a telegraphic click at offices in New York, St. Paul, and Portland, a sound that NP operators heard at 5:18 P.M. Shortly thereafter, the Army unit started a hundred gun salute. The Northern Pacific had come 1,198 miles from Lake Superior, 847 from Puget Sound. It was just a week short of Villard's second year as NP president.

NP's completion caused Villard to yield control of the road. His dramatic rise ended, as massive construction costs, coupled with the large dividends he had been paying his supporters to ensure their backing, now consumed his empire. On January 4, 1884, control passed to a new president, Robert Harris, and the construction work, so recently completed, soon began anew.

THE CASCADE BRANCH: A DIRECT ROUTE TO PUGET SOUND

In the middle 1880s, prompted by its charter stipulation of reaching Puget Sound directly and facing the threat of revocation of its great land grant if it did not, the Northern Pacific began pushing the completion of its Cascade Branch. This line was to follow the Yakima River through Yakima and Ellensburg, Washington Territory, pierce the Cascade Range via a tunnel, and descend to Puget Sound at Tacoma.

On July 1, 1884 grading began, with crews reaching Yakima by the end of the year. Construction during 1885 was slowed by several circumstances. Building through the rugged Yakima Canyon was difficult at best. Officials also struggled over whether to continue to lease the OR&N—indecision which delayed the work. Exorbitant rates asked by the OR&N, board members with large holdings in Tacoma real estate, and pressure from Congress would force the completion of the Cascade Branch.

In January 1886, Nelson Bennett won the contract to drive the tunnel under Stampede Pass. The tunnel itself was to be 9,850 feet long, 22 feet high, 16 feet wide, saving the NP from an additional 800-foot climb over the summit. Once again, to expedite work, the NP built a temporary bypass line while the tunnel was under construction. The "switchback," as it came to be known, utilized a brutal grade of 5.6 percent—a climb of almost 300 feet per mile. To overcome this grade, the NP purchased the two largest steam engines in the world at the time.

Enjoying a few moments of respite from their work at a gravel pit spur west of Detroit Lakes, Minnesota, a local train's crew waits for through traffic to clear before they venture back out on the main line. Their steel co-worker on this lazy July day in 1955 is NP 2-8-2 No. 1836. *Jim Shaughnessy*

Bennett wasted no time, purchasing as much equipment as possible for the job in New York City. He bought an electric light plant, narrow-gauge engines, air compressors and drills and sent all of it to the end of the line at Yakima. From there it was dragged 82 miles to the tunnel site. On February 13 his crews began work at the east portal, joined by a crew at the west portal on March 18. In a year 300 men had drilled 4,100 feet, making nearly 16 feet every day. On May 3, 1888, the two crews met inside the mountain, breaking through the last wall of rock that separated the east and west crews. By the end of the month Bennett had the bore fully opened and the NP was complete to Puget Sound.

RECEIVERSHIP, REORGANIZATION, RECOVERY

Between 1888 and 1893 the NP spread a vast system of branch lines across its territory to feed its main line. The road's debt soared past $100 million by 1890. Even with gross earnings of more than $22 million, scarcely $2 million was left to build for the future when expenses were stripped away. When uncertainties about monetary and tariff policies touched off a panic, the Northern Pacific Railroad fell into its second and final receivership on August 15, 1893. On March 16, 1896, the road emerged from reorganization as the Northern Pacific Rail*way*. It was now under the financial auspices of J. P. Morgan & Company, though Great Northern Railway chieftain James Jerome Hill had bought an interest in the road.

Around this time the NP adopted its distinctive monad trademark. In 1893 Chief Engineer

Edwin Harrison McHenry had visited the Korean exhibit at the Columbian Exposition in Chicago. The Korean flag included a red-and-blue "Ying-and-Yang" monad, a striking design which the NP adopted as its own.

In 1901 a fight once again broke out for the control of the NP. This time, a war of stock control was waged by the two most powerful railroad tycoons in the country—James J. Hill and Union Pacific's Edward Henry Harriman. The contest revolved around control not of the NP, but of the Chicago, Burlington & Quincy. Hill and Harriman had both been courting this powerful Midwestern system as a link to the rail hub of Chicago. Hill won the contest in 1899 when he paid Burlington President Charles E. Perkins' asking price of $200 a share; the GN and NP each got a 48.59 percent controlling interest of Burlington's common stock. When Harriman requested a minority interest only to be rebuked by Hill, he turned to a crafty plan—wield influence over the Burlington through control of the NP.

On May 3, 1901, Harriman kicked off what became known as the "Northern Pacific Corner."

NP's *Mainstreeter* was a secondary train which ran on a schedule that was slower than that of its big sister, the *North Coast Limited*. The *Mainstreeter* served more stops, handled considerable mail and express, and, between Logan and Garrison, Montana, diverted from the *NCL* route to serve Helena, the state capital. Secondary status notwithstanding, the train featured Pullman sleeping cars (including new "Slumbercoach" economy sleepers delivered in 1959), parlor-bar-lounge cars, and full dining service. The weather's a bit on the dreary side as the westbound *Mainstreeter* arrives from Chicago at Seattle's King Street Station in the spring of 1967. *Ron Lundstrom*

Through crafty and perhaps questionable stock transactions which themselves could fill a book, Harriman ended up controlling the NP by the end of May 6, 1901.

Harriman appointees were put on the boards of the Burlington and the NP to avoid litigation. To suppress another skirmish, Hill also set up a holding company for all the NP, GN, and CB&Q stock—the Northern Securities Company. Soon after, suits were brought by both the State of Minnesota and the federal government. The U.S. Supreme Court ordered Northern Securities to divest itself of the stock in 1904. Thus, one of the first attempts to merge the GN, NP, and Burlington failed. The parties tried again in the 1920s, to be told the merger could only proceed if the Burlington was spun off. Not wanting to part with a key element of the system, the Hill Lines dropped the subject.

INTO THE TWENTIETH CENTURY

The years from 1896 to World War I was a halcyon period for the road. A key bridge brought the NP directly into Portland and ended ferry service on the Columbia. Portions of its route were double-tracked in Washington, Montana, and elsewhere; grand stations were built, and the property greatly improved. In 1900 the road introduced the *North Coast Limited*, first-class passenger service between the Midwest and Northwest. Five years later GN and NP created the Spokane, Portland & Seattle Railway. Running between Spokane and Portland via Pasco, the superbly engineered SP&S proved its worth in the years ahead by allowing GN and NP to serve Portland.

By the early 1920s, NP had installed automatic block signals from the Great Lakes to the Pacific. The NP was also one of the first to develop the 4-8-4 Northern. These locomotives, delivered in 1926, featured a massive grate of 115 square feet, designed to burn low-grade coal from company-owned mines. Beginning in 1929, the NP again rostered the largest steam engine in the world, the massive 2-8-8-4 Yellowstone.

Though the Great Depression plunged traffic levels to one mainline freight each way a day, the NP pushed for improvement. In 1936 it became one of the first roads in the country to install welded rail. Throughout the Depression, the NP undertook improvement projects to accommodate its thirst for ever-larger motive power. In February 1944, it took delivery of some of the first FT freight diesels from the Electro-Motive Division of General Motors, which were used on its toughest routes during World War II. Though key segments of the railroad were quickly dieselized, the NP's last steam run did not happen until January, 1958.

After World War II, the NP consisted of 2,831 miles of main line, and 4,057 miles of branch line. It installed its first Centralized Traffic Control system in 1947. In the years which followed, NP installed first radio, then computers and microwave systems, to improve communications. The NP also opened a sprawling classification yard at Pasco in 1955, at the time one of the few hump yards in the nation. In 1968 the NP began unit coal-train service with Powder River coal. This was the start of a boom in low-sulfur Western coal which would dramatically change its descendants.

THE HILL LINES

In 1955 the merger dream was dusted off once again at a series of informal meetings between the GN's John M. Budd and the NP's Robert S. Macfarlane. Not until February 1961 did the roads take the matter to the Interstate Commerce Commission. Eight months later, hearings began in St. Paul. Against the opposition of various railroad crafts, communities along the line, and the Milwaukee Road, the Hill Lines touted four major benefits of merger to the public: faster service, improved car supply, more direct and wider routing choices, and improved funding. Few, if any, officers of the roads thought they could survive without merger.

In 1966, the ICC, in a surprise decision, blocked the merger. That same year, NP installed a new president, Louis W. Menk, whose overriding priority was merger. Menk concluded that the plan had failed to compromise with the unions, as well as the Milwaukee Road. To gain the ICC's approval, both were offered concessions. To placate railroad towns along the line, which were prone to being hotbeds of anti-merger sentiment,

promises were made to keep facilities open after the merger. The revised plan was approved by the ICC and M-Day was set for May 10, 1968. Then, at the last minute, the Supreme Court blocked the merger. The Justice Department had claimed that the ICC had not adequately contemplated the monopolistic nature of the merger. An additional two years of deliberation ensued.

The Supreme Court finally voted seven to zero in favor of the merger. The Burlington, GN, NP, and SP&S were merged into the Burlington Northern Railroad on March 3, 1970.

"MAIN STREET OF THE NORTHWEST"

The men, women, and companies involved in creating the Northern Pacific took incredible risks supporting it. When construction began and even when it had been completed, there was little populace or industry to support the new railroad. Most of its breadth ran through territories—not states—when it opened all the way through to Puget Sound; only Minnesota and Oregon had joined the Union. In the end, the Northern Pacific helped build up the country by bringing people to its route and linking them—and the fruits of their labor—to the rest of the nation. Over the course of a century, the road served every great city in the northern tier of states, becoming what the Northern Pacific's L. L. Perrin called the "Main Street of the Northwest."

Bedecked with Vista-Domes, the Chicago-bound *North Coast Limited* accelerates away from its stop at Livingston, Montana, as a westbound freight enters the yard in June 1959. Aside from serving as a crew-change point, Livingston was the gateway station to nearby Yellowstone Park. Buses of NP subsidiary Northern Pacific Transport shuttled passengers between Livingston and Gardiner, Montana, at the doorstep of the great national park. *Barry Carlson*

The Orange Blossom Special Going Through Orange Groves in Florida

THROUGH THE HEART
OF THE SOUTH

Seaboard
Air Line

on't let the name fool you. The Seaboard Air Line was in every respect a railroad. In the early days of railroading, "air line" depicted a route that was the shortest distance between two points. Seaboard was among the very few railroads that continued using the term well into the jet age.

Not that the Seaboard was necessarily overall shorter than arch rival Atlantic Coast Line, but the SAL did advertise itself as the shortest route to *some* points in the South, such as Atlanta. By the time the Seaboard was formally merged out of existence in 1967, it had evolved into a highly regarded railroad with exemplary passenger trains and high-speed freight service—a far cry from its troubled beginnings.

SAL's origins can be traced to the Portsmouth & Roanoke Rail Road, chartered in 1832–33 to build between its namesakes: Portsmouth, Virginia, and the Roanoke River at Weldon, Virginia, 78.6 miles. Beset by a convoluted series of problems, the P&R was reorganized as the Seaboard & Roanoke in 1846.

Meanwhile, another key SAL component road had been built. The Raleigh & Gaston Railroad was completed in 1840 between Raleigh and (old) Gaston, North Carolina, west of present-day Gaston near Weldon. Like the P&R, it failed financially and in 1845 became a ward of the state. The State upgraded the railroad and put it back on its feet. In 1853 the R&G closed the gap between it and the S&R at Weldon.

After the Civil War, the S&R did well and by 1871 had acquired control in the R&G—which itself had come to control a company that was known as the Raleigh & Augusta Air-Line Railroad. This company was building southwesterly from Raleigh and would reach Hamlet in 1877. By this time, one John M. Robinson had come to head all three companies, which collectively became known as the Seaboard Air Line System. Robinson was also president of the Richmond, Fredericksburg & Potomac—a railroad between Washington, D. C., and Richmond, Virginia, that long would be critical to north-south traffic on the East Coast.

Under Robinson, the Seaboard Air-Line System—its "leading" railroad still the S&R—expanded rapidly during the last two decades of the 1800s. The next acquisition of note during this period, in 1883, was the Carolina Central, which in 1887 completed a line from Rutherfordton, North Carolina, to the coastal port of Wilmington, North Carolina, via Charlotte and Hamlet—the latter now becoming a strategic hub on the Seaboard.

Now the Seaboard headed for Atlanta, which it reached through acquisition of the Georgia, Carolina & Northern, a road building southeast from Monroe, North Carolina, to Atlanta. To get the GC&N into Atlanta proper, the Seaboard built the Seaboard Air Line Belt Railroad, which possibly was the first railroad to legally feature the "Seaboard Air Line" name in its title. This newest entity put the Seaboard into Atlanta in 1892. Meanwhile, Seaboard had also begun building south from Hamlet toward Columbia, South Carolina, through its Palmetto Railroad subsidiary. The Palmetto reached Cheraw, South Carolina, 18 miles, and quit.

Prompted by an "invasion" of its territory around Norfolk by the Southern Railway late in the 1890s, the Seaboard decided it was time to get its own line north to Richmond (and the ever-strategic RF&P) to secure an all-rail route to northern points. Heretofore, much of the traffic between the North and the Seaboard at Portsmouth moved on ships owned by Robinson concerns. The Seaboard acquired the Richmond, Petersburg & Carolina, set to build north from Norlina, North Carolina (on the Raleigh & Gaston), to Richmond via Petersburg, Virginia. The RP&C put the Seaboard Air-Line System into Richmond in 1900.

At the end of the century, Seaboard control shifted from the Robinson clan to that of the Williams associates of banking firms. This group controlled the Georgia & Alabama and the Florida Central & Peninsular. The G&A ran east from Montgomery, Alabama, to Savannah, Georgia. The FC&P ran from Columbia to Tampa, Florida, via Savannah and Jacksonville as well as from Jacksonville west to Tallahassee, Florida. Williams

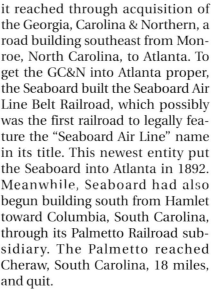

FACING PAGE: **The Seaboard Air Line was a hot piece of railroad between the North and South, with numerous high-speed passenger and freight movements throughout the day on mostly single-track main lines. At Norlina, North Carolina, in 1963, southbound train No. 75 out of Richmond with a new set of EMD GP30s exchanges cars with southbound train 83 out of Portsmouth, Virginia.** *Warren Calloway*

FACING PAGE, INSET: **Among the most common collectible railroad postcards are those issued by the Seaboard in the 1940s touting its Florida-bound passenger trains.** *Dave Oroszi collection*

LEFT: **A Seaboard timetable from 1964. Perhaps the railroad avoided using its full name, Seaboard Air Line, on the cover for fear of confusing a public now well versed in air travel!**

SEABOARD AIR LINE AT A GLANCE

Headquarters: Norfolk, VA

Route mileage circa 1950: 4,146

Locomotive fleet as of 1963:
Diesels: 531

Rolling stock as of 1963:
Freight cars: 27,560
Passenger cars: 446

Principal lines circa 1950:
Richmond, VA–Homestead, FL (Miami) via Columbia, SC, and Jacksonville and Auburndale, FL
Coleman–St. Petersburg, FL
Hamlet, NC–Savannah, GA
Norlina, NC–Norfolk
Hamlet–Birmingham, AL
Savanna, GA.–Montgomery, AL
Baldwin–Chattahoochee, FL
Baldwin–Gross, FL (cutoff around Jacksonville)
Waldo–Sulphur Springs, FL
Plant City–Fort Myers, FL
Durant–Venice, FL
Hull–Port Boca Grande, FL
Valrico–West Lake Wales, FL

Notable passenger trains (slash denotes multiple destinations):
Cotton Blossom (Washington–Atlanta)
Gulf Wind (Jacksonville–New Orleans)
New York–Florida Limited (New York–Miami/St. Petersburg)
Orange Blossom Special (New York–Miami)
Palmland (New York–Tampa/Boca Grande, FL)
Silver Meteor (New York–Miami/St. Petersburg/Venice/Fort Meyers)
Silver Comet (New York/Portsmouth–Birmingham)
Silver Star (New York–Miami/St. Petersburg/Venice/Boca Grande, FL)
Sunland (formerly the *Southern States Special*, *Sun Queen*, and *Camellia*, Washington, D.C./Portsmouth–Miami/Venice)
Suwanee River Special (Cincinnati–Florida points)

NOTE: North of Richmond, SAL passenger trains were handled by Richmond, Fredericksburg & Potomac and Pennsylvania Railroad. West of Chattahoochee, the *Gulf Wind* was handled by L&N

Heart of the Seaboard Air Line was Hamlet, North Carolina, where five main lines converged. Aside from being an important division point, the railroad maintained extensive shop facilities here and—judging by this billboard photographed in 1967—considerable pride. *Warren Calloway*

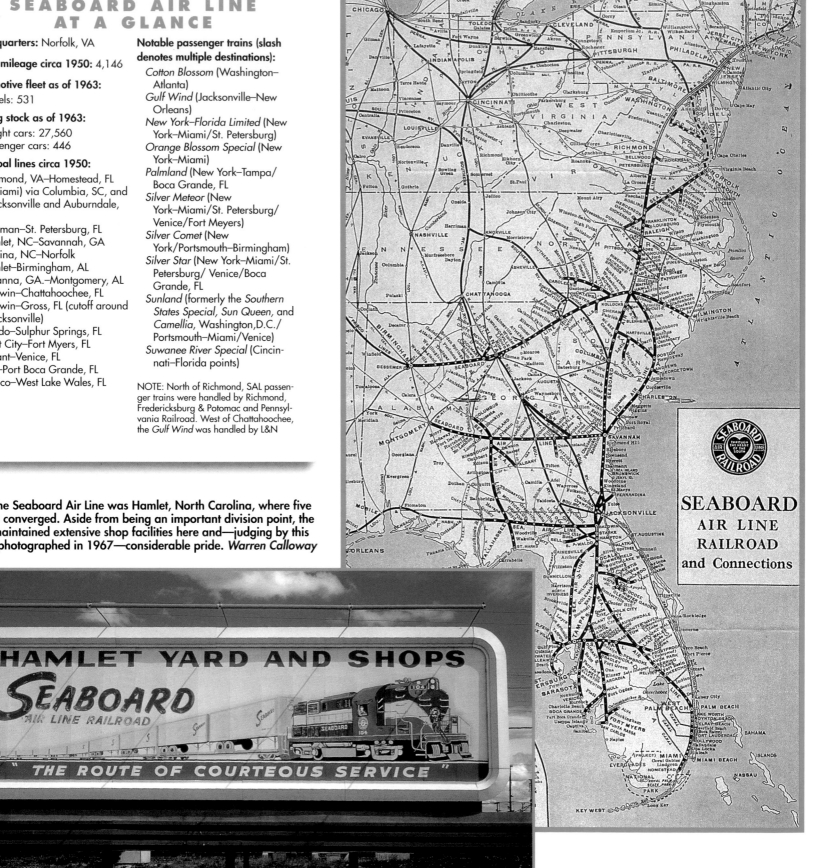

SEABOARD AIR LINE RAILROAD and Connections

HAMLET YARD AND SHOPS
SEABOARD AIR LINE RAILROAD
"THE ROUTE OF COURTEOUS SERVICE"

management was quick to close the 91-mile gap between the Palmetto at Cheraw and the FC&P at Columbia. By the end of 1901, the myriad of companies that had comprised the Seaboard Air-Line System, including the G&A and FC&P, were formally merged into the Seaboard Air Line Railway.

Now the SAL set out for Birmingham, Alabama, 167 miles west of Atlanta. By acquiring the East-West Railroad already under construction between the two cities and merging it with a new subsidiary known as the Atlanta & Birmingham Air Line, the Seaboard was able to extend its reach to Birmingham and nearby Bessemer in 1904.

As World War I got under way, the SAL completed a 263-mile low-grade freight main line between Hamlet and Savannah via Charleston, South Carolina, thereby avoiding the grades—and the impending influx of passenger trains—of the Columbia main line.

A look at the SAL map reveals a tangle of lines in western Florida, most of which were acquired during the World War I period to tap rich agricultural and phosphate traffic sources. The most important addition to the SAL in Florida, however, was the route to Miami—one of the last major main lines constructed in America. The extension was built by Seaboard subsidiaries Florida Western & Northern and the Seaboard-All Florida Railway, and train service to Florida's most famous city began in 1927.

While one would think that this critical line would boost SAL's fortunes, the railroad's expansions in Florida had perhaps been overly ambitious. That coupled to the stockmarket crash of 1929 and intense competition from Atlantic Coast Line, Florida East Coast (an ACL ally), and the Southern Railway put the 4,490-mile Seaboard into receivership in 1930—the first of many railroads that would fail during the Depression.

THE NEW SEABOARD

Several factors helped the Seaboard begin life anew following its fall from grace in 1930. Line "rationalization" cut many routes in Georgia and Florida from the SAL map but also reduced expenses. The rise of the paper and pulp industry in the Southeast greatly increased freight revenues. Government loans paved the way for modernization programs that provided the railroad with new equipment, including diesel-electric locomotives and Centralized Traffic Control.

Perhaps signifying an even greater forthcoming turnaround was the 1939 inaugural of

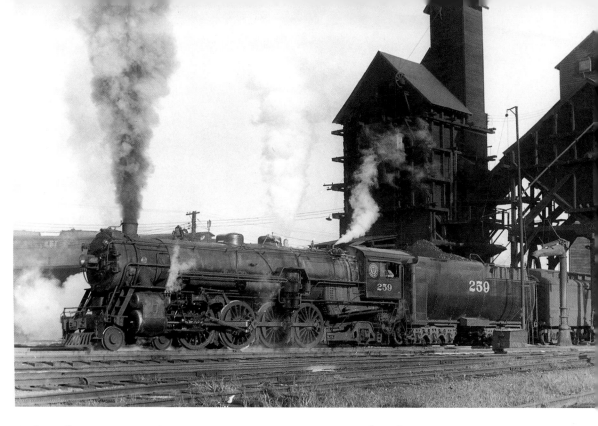

Seaboard's new New York–Florida streamliner, the *Silver Meteor*. The popularity of the *Meteor* as the first streamliner serving Florida would help revive the railroad financially. In terms of traffic, nothing had quite the positive effect, though, on the Seaboard (as well as nearly all other U.S. carriers) as World War II. Once the U.S. entered the fray, the amount of freight tonnage moved by the SAL rose dramatically. By 1943, SAL was hauling 33 million tons of freight, more than double that in 1939.

After World War II, the Seaboard ended its receivership and in 1946 was reorganized as the Seaboard Air Line Railroad. This was a new era for American railroads, though not necessarily a good one in the long run. But Seaboard was an exception to this rule, thanks to being positioned strongly throughout the "New South" that saw unprecedented boom after World War II.

Early dieselization—a program which had begun in the late 1930s and was completed in 1952—further improved the Seaboard's efficiency, as did the continued spread of CTC over SAL's mostly single-track system. (Rival Atlantic Coast Line boasted a 100-MPH double-track main line between Virginia and Florida, but SAL simply could not afford double tracking.) By 1965, some 1,700 route-miles was under the direction of CTC.

The Seaboard of the 1960s was a showcase railroad, with high-speed, high-quality passenger and freight service. By now, though, negotiations

Seaboard's 4-8-2 Mountains were, appropriately, classified by the railroad as its M class. The 259, shown at Raleigh in 1941, was an M-2 built in the mid-1920s by Baldwin. About ten years later, it and some of its siblings received larger tenders for sustained running.
Homer R. Hill

Seaboard's first road-freight diesels were purchased from General Motors' Electro-Motive Division. Forty-four FT sets were delivered during World War II and saw about 20 years of service. FT cab-booster set 4005, coupled to an EMD GP7 road-switcher and flying white flags (to indicate that they were pulling an "Extra" or non-scheduled train) are shown at Hamlet in 1961. *Wiley M. Bryan*

Seaboard's diesel roster was more eclectic than most, with locomotives representing nearly all the big diesel builders of the postwar era: Electro-Motive, Alco, General Electric, and Baldwin. Among the more unusual locomotives rostered by SAL were 14 behemoth "Centipede" diesels delivered by Baldwin from 1945 to 1948. The many "feet" of Centipede 4500 grips the rails with a reefer train at Southern Pines, North Carolina, circa 1946. *Baldwin, courtesy Warren Calloway*

had been under way since the 1950s with Atlantic Coast Line on merger possibilities. The main thrust of the merger would be improved performance through the elimination of redundant facilities—and nearly everywhere the ACL went, so did the SAL.

Together the two roads became the Seaboard Coast Line Railroad on July 1, 1967. Unlike the disastrous Pennsylvania-New York Central merger that would follow in 1968, the SCL union went smoothly. Subsequent mergers would render the SCL to history in the 1980s, and today surviving lines of the old Seaboard (several were shed after the SCL merger) are but a relatively small component of the huge CSX Transportation network.

SEABOARD'S PASSENGER TRAFFIC

Throughout its history, Seaboard served as an artery for passengers and freight moving between North and South. Once Florida had been transformed from a swampy wildland to exotic vacation destination, the Seaboard became a means of escape from harsh northern climes. Even before Seaboard reached Florida, it was carrying passengers to the Sunbelt. Shortly after the line to Atlanta was completed in 1892, SAL and its connecting railroads inaugurated a through train between New York and Atlanta, the *Atlanta and Washington Special*. When Seaboard finally got to West Palm Beach in 1925, it inaugurated what would long stand as one of its most posh trains, the fabled *Orange Blossom Special*. The winter-season train

was extended to Miami in 1927 and also featured a west coast section serving Tampa/St. Petersburg.

Aside from offering ultra luxurious travel, complete with barber and maid service and shower baths, the *OBS* claimed several other accomplishments. In 1934 it became one of the first trains in the U.S. to be completely air-conditioned. Then in 1938 it became the first conventional train in the Southeast to be dieselized.

Another early Seaboard seasonal "sunliner" was the *Suwanee River Special*, a Midwest–Florida train jointly operated with Southern Railway. The train was an early victim of the Depression, but it was revived in 1936 as the *Florida Sunbeam*.

The standard-bearer of Seaboard's New York–Florida runs was the *Southern States Special* (known as the *Sun Queen* after 1941, the *Camellia* in 1947, and finally as the *Sunland* beginning in 1948), principally a New York–St. Petersburg run

The *Silver Comet* is at Atlanta's Terminal Station in 1958 behind an Electro-Motive E7 and E8 still clad in Seaboard's famous older passenger livery, the so-called "citrus paint scheme" of dark green, yellow, and orange. *Howard Robins*

Triple EMD E7s blaze through snow-dusted North Carolina countryside at Milbrook in February 1963 with a rake of stainless-steel cars that comprise the *Silver Star*—running late account of weather-related problems. By this time, Seaboard had changed its passenger diesel scheme to light green (so light that it usually appeared as off-white to casual observers) with coral striping. *Wiley M. Bryan*

TOP: An Alco RS3 road-switcher has just coupled to the tail end of the *Silver Meteor*, which a few minutes earlier had arrived at SAL's Miami depot from New York on an August afternoon in 1965. Once all passengers have disembarked, the road-switcher will tote the consist to the yards for servicing. *Mike Schafer*

ABOVE: Among Seaboard's motive-power oddities were two motorcars, Nos. 2027 and 2028, built by Electro-Motive and St. Louis Car Company in 1936. The 2027, shown on an unidentified local run in 1948, was retired in 1957, but its sister was used to forward through cars off the *Silver* trains to branchline destinations into 1971. *F. E. Ardry Jr., courtesy Warren Calloway*

the *Cotton Blossom*, operated between Birmingham and Washington.

Seaboard's rather unremarked main line between Jacksonville and Tallahassee hosted through service to New Orleans in conjunction with Louisville & Nashville. The premier train was the *New Orleans–Florida Limited*, which in 1949 became the new *Gulf Wind* streamliner.

The train that created the most stir on the Seaboard (and raised the hackles of Atlantic Coast Line) was the *Silver Meteor*, the first streamliner ever to serve the lucrative New York–Florida market. Seaboard began the service with a single trainset: a 2000-hp. Electro-Motive E4 diesel and seven stainless-steel passenger cars built by the Budd Company. Having only a single set of equipment initially limited the number of departures from New York to once every third day. The train served both Miami and St. Petersburg, alternating between those two destinations with each trip out of New York. The train was a phenomenal success, and delivery of additional cars and locomotives by the end of 1939 allowed for daily service between New York and Miami.

The demand for passage on the *Meteor* never seemed to let up, and following World War II, Seaboard expanded its "Silver" fleet by adding more cars to the *Meteor*, running additional sections of the *Meteor*, and introducing a whole new train, the *Silver Star*. The Silver fleet also expanded to the Birmingham main line in the form of the new *Silver Comet* streamliner in 1947, replacing the *Cotton States Special*.

In addition to mainline passenger services, Seaboard operated a dizzying array of local and branchline trains on nearly all its routes at one time or another. Some of these runs were strictly local in nature, while others ferried through cars off the big trains to secondary terminals such as Venice, Sarasota, and Boca Grande, Florida.

Competition between Seaboard and ACL's *Champion* streamliners, the famed *Florida Special*, and other trains was fierce. But other, more formidable competitors loomed, especially following World War II: government-sponsored highway systems and a burgeoning airline industry. By the 1950s a national decline in rail passenger traffic was evident. As popular as Seaboard's trains had been, the railroad was not immune to the decline, and cutbacks and train consolidations became an accepted practice in the 1950s.

Fortunately, Seaboard's pro-passenger stance, high service standards, and a particularly devoted

but with a Miami section that split from the main train at Wildwood, Florida. The train carried a full complement of equipment for all classes of travel and catered largely to people bound for all manner of destinations in Florida. A more workhorse passenger train was the *New York–Florida Limited*, which catered largely to customers traveling to and from the Carolinas. This train became known as the *Palmland* in 1941.

On the main line to Atlanta and Birmingham, the notable runs were the *Cotton States Special* and the *Robert E. Lee*. The *Special* ran only between Birmingham and Hamlet, north of which the train's through cars to and from Washington and New York were handled by the *Southern States Special*. The *Robert E. Lee*, which in 1947 became

clientele in the New York–Florida market not only saved Seaboard's passenger network from the complete ruin that had struck many other carriers by the mid-1960s, but allowed it to remain largely intact beyond Seaboard's existence. A look at a current Amtrak timetable reveals two familiar names: the *Silver Star* and the *Silver Meteor*. In those trains, a bit of the Seaboard Air Line lives on.

FREIGHT SERVICE ON THE SEABOARD

Seaboard's strategic position in the Southeast allowed it to carry a wide variety of freight, but it was probably best known for carrying perishable fruit and produce between Florida and Georgia and the North. Despite the high profile of hauling perishables, though, Seaboard hauled more mineral traffic than anything. As of about 1950, about half of Seaboard's freight traffic was mineral-based, mostly phosphate, used for fertilizer and in the manufacture of matches and ammunition. Cement, iron ore, clay, and aggregates also fell under the mineral category.

Next were manufactured products, most of which originated in the North. Such general merchandise accounted for nearly 30 percent of the freight moved by SAL at mid-century. Forest products, which accounted for about 15 percent of the traffic, included pulpwood, paper, and pine tree stumps, used to make pine oil and turpentine.

The remaining 5 percent or so of the traffic was agricultural, including grain and cotton products and the perishables. Even though perishables accounted for only about half of the agricultural traffic, the revenues from perishable traffic were of enough importance that SAL held an interest in Fruit Growers Express, a consortium that operated a fleet of refrigerator cars (reefers) and piggyback trailers for perishable commodities.

In the 1950s, the trailer-on-flatcar (TOFC or "piggyback") concept, first championed on a large scale by the Pennsylvania Railroad, began to catch on, and in 1959 Seaboard introduced piggyback service. The innovation was a hit with Seaboard customers, and soon the railroad was operating a whole fleet of TOFC trains.

Seaboard was one of a relatively small number of railroads that named its principal freight trains. Among the best known was its *Merchandiser* between Richmond and Miami, one of the few freights that held first-class operational status, putting it on par with passenger trains in terms of priority handling. A northbound counterpart was the *Marketer*, with a section out of Miami and one out of Tampa joining at Baldwin, Florida. Other named freights included the *Tar Heel* (Richmond–Bostic, North Carolina, the latter a connection with the Clinchfield Railroad); the *Capital* (Richmond–Birmingham); the *Iron Master* (Birmingham–Atlanta); the *Clipper* and the *Alaga* (Montgomery–Savannah); and the *Pioneer* (Montgomery–Jacksonville).

In the 1960s, Seaboard championed its high-speed piggyback service, the best train of the TOFC fleet being the *Razorback*. This hot trailer train—for years the fastest freight train in North America—originated on the Pennsylvania Railroad at Kearny, New Jersey, and ran through to Hialeah Yard, Miami, over 1,000 miles, in less than 30 hours. Seaboard's memorable *Razorback* marketing featured a mean-looking razorback (an aggressive hog indigenous to the South) with wheels instead of hocks.

During Seaboard's last full year of independence, 1966, it carried 66 million tons of freight—more than double that during World War II and the most ever in the railroad's sparkling history.

The modern Seaboard as it appeared shortly before its merger with Atlantic Coast Line. In 1966, Seaboard introduced an eye-catching new freight paint scheme that replaced the dark Pullman Green with a lime color. Three new EMD GP40s—the locomotives that first wore the revised livery—glow in their new garb while making time with piggyback train TT23 at Raleigh, North Carolina. *Warren Calloway*

Southern Railway

"The Southern Serves the South." That simple statement encircling a stylized "SR" was much more than slogan—it was a statement of considerable truth. For 88 years the Southern Railway System was a major transportation force in its namesake region. Until the Southern's familiar image disappeared into Norfolk Southern, it was one of the most highly regarded railroad companies in the nation.

From the very beginning, Southern was an assemblage of various lines. Some of the oldest antecedent companies traced their history to 1830, the very earliest days of flanged wheels and strap-iron rails. As a corporation, Southern Railway was created on July 1, 1894, when Samuel Spencer presided over the consolidation of the Richmond & Danville and the East Tennessee, Virginia & Georgia.

The Richmond & Danville was chartered in 1847 with a main line between those two Virginia points opened in 1856. After the Civil War, the R&D launched into a period of expansion, leasing the North Carolina Railroad in 1871, which then operated a line from Goldsboro to Charlotte. After the acquisition of several smaller roads, the R&D (better known as the Piedmont Air Line) formed the Washington-to-Atlanta spine of what would eventually become the Southern.

The East Tennessee, Virginia & Georgia, also known as the Kennesaw Route, was organized in 1869 as a consolidation of the East Tennessee & Virginia, and the East Tennessee & Georgia. The former opened a line from Dalton, Georgia, on the Western & Atlantic (of "Andrews Raid" fame) and Loudon, Tennessee. By 1859, the line had reached Knoxville to the east and Chattanooga to the west. Earlier, the East Tennessee & Virginia had completed a 131-mile line from Bristol, Virginia/Tennessee (where it connected with the Virginia & Tennessee, later Norfolk & Western) to Knoxville. These routes formed the nucleus of the central portion of what would become the Southern System.

An attempt to consolidate the R&D and the ETV&G had occurred as early as 1887, but legal and financial circumstances prevented the merger.

At this point, famed financier J. P. Morgan stepped in to reorganize and consolidate the various components into the Southern Railway Company.

Quickly, the Southern expanded its empire through the acquisition of other roads. A year after its creation, entrance into Florida was gained through control of the Georgia, Southern & Florida. Several short lines were acquired in the years just prior to the turn of the last century, notably several lines in the Carolinas, and the Louisville, Evansville & St. Louis to the west.

Important acquisitions in the early part of the century included the Virginia & Southwestern Railway, which became Southern's coal-hauling Appalachia Division in 1916. Another key acquisition was the eventual control of the Queen & Crescent Route, which included the Cincinnati, New Orleans & Texas Pacific between Cincinnati and Chattanooga, the Alabama Great Southern to Birmingham and Meridian, Mississippi, and the New Orleans & Northeastern beyond to New Orleans and Shreveport, Louisiana. These three lines became part of the Southern in 1917.

Later acquisitions included the coal-rich Interstate Railroad in western Virginia, added in 1961, and the Central of Georgia, the Georgia & Florida, and the Savannah & Atlanta, all added in 1963. The *original* Norfolk Southern was added in 1974.

In all, some 125 individual companies were combined to form the Southern Railway System. The various corporate entities often continued to exist, and Southern rolling stock was frequently sublettered for companies such as "CNO&TP," "AGS," "INT," or even "CTC" (for the diminutive Chattanooga Traction Company).

In its ultimate configuration, the Southern's main artery was its Washington, D.C.–Atlanta line, a double-track route which carried its finest passenger trains and priority freight traffic between the East and the South. This line made key connections along the way, such as at Lynchburg, Virginia, where several interline passenger trains were passed back and forth with the Norfolk & Western. Danville, Virginia; Greensboro, Salisbury

FACING PAGE: Southern's famous 2-8-2 Mikado No. 4501 is pleasing onlookers at Oakdale, Tennessee, during an excursion run as the *Royal Palm* makes its station stop on a gray day in late fall 1968. *Mike Schafer*

INSET: Southern collectibles, including a dinner menu from the *Southern Crescent* streamliner of the 1970s and a demitasse cup and saucer. *Andover Junction Publications*

LEFT: For many years, Southern public passenger timetables featured variations of this colorful artist's rendering of a Southern passenger train heading through lush Southeastern scenery. *Kevin Holland collection*

(Spencer), and Charlotte, North Carolina; and Spartanburg and Greenville, South Carolina were key locations along the line to Atlanta. Continuing westward, the line split from the Chattanooga main at Austell, then continued to the steel-making city of Birmingham. From that point, the main followed the Queen & Crescent Route via Meridian all the way to New Orleans. Near that city, the NO&NE crossed Lake Pontchartrain, which at one time featured a 21.5-mile trestle.

The Cincinnati–Chattanooga segment of the former Queen & Crescent Route eventually became Southern's most densely trafficked line. Financed by the City of Cincinnati to compete with its downriver competitor city, Louisville, the Cincinnati Southern (which was operated by the CNO&TP) was once marked by numerous tunnels. Its center section, from Wilmore, Kentucky, to Oakdale, Tennessee, was known as the "Rat Hole," nicknamed for the abundance of tight "smoke

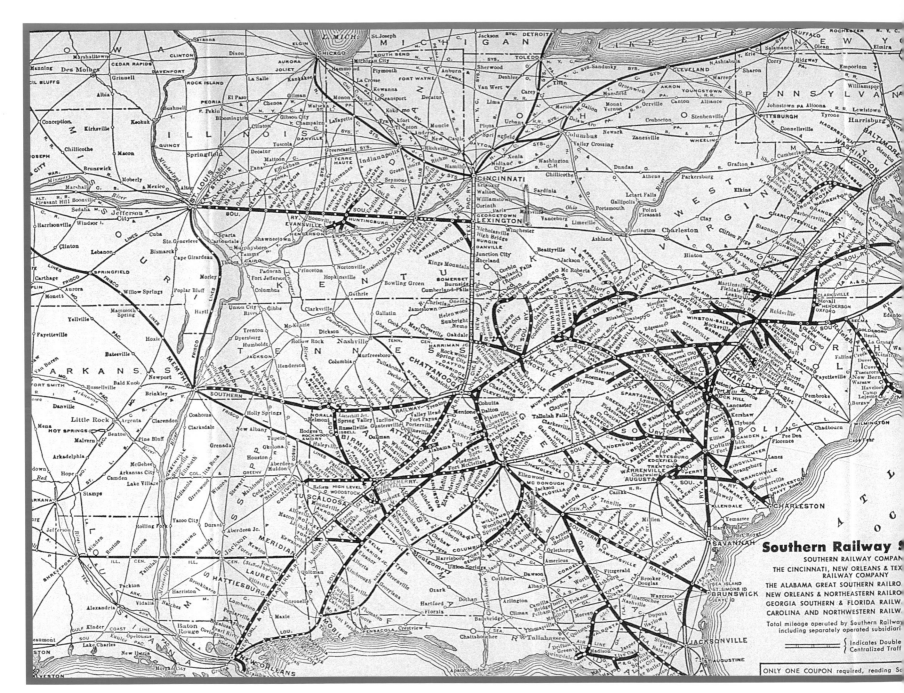

This map from a 1962 Southern public passenger timetable shows the extent of the railroad just before it expanded through the acquisition of the Central of Georgia, Savannah & Atlanta, and Georgia & Florida the following year.
Kevin Holland collection

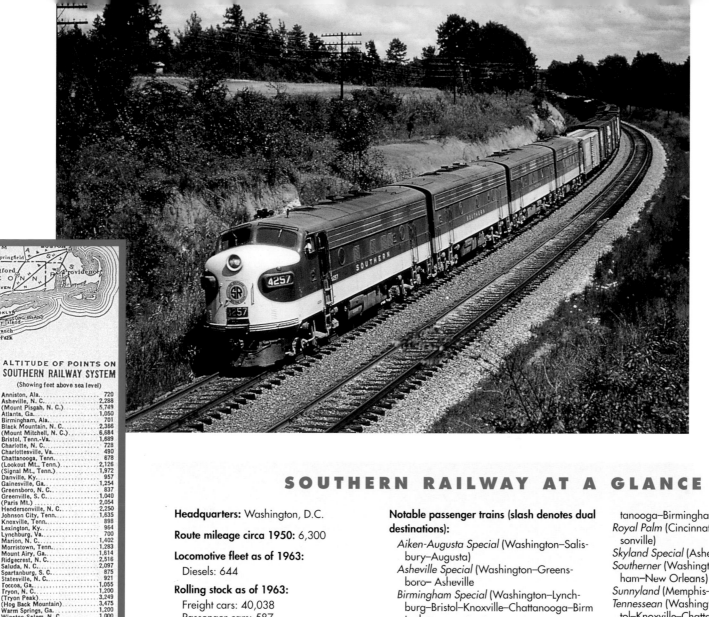

A four-unit set of Electro-Motive F-units barrels through Austell, Georgia, with northbound freight No. 54 during the summer of 1960. Southern's influence on Southeast transportation was widely felt, for the railroad had a comprehensive network of trackage in the Carolinas, Georgia, and Alabama. *Ron Flanary collection*

ALTITUDE OF POINTS ON SOUTHERN RAILWAY SYSTEM

(Showing feet above sea level)

Anniston, Ala.	720
Asheville, N. C.	2,288
(Mount Pisgah, N. C.)	5,749
Atlanta, Ga.	1,050
Birmingham, Ala.	701
Black Mountain, N. C.	2,366
(Mount Mitchell, N. C.)	6,684
Bristol, Tenn.-Va.	1,689
Charlotte, N. C.	728
Charlottesville, Va.	490
Chattanooga, Tenn.	678
(Lookout Mt., Tenn.)	2,126
(Signal Mt., Tenn.)	1,972
Danville, Ky.	957
Gainesville, Ga.	1,254
Greensboro, N. C.	837
Greenville, S. C.	1,040
(Paris Mt.)	2,054
Hendersonville, N. C.	2,250
Johnson City, Tenn.	1,635
Knoxville, Tenn.	898
Lexington, Ky.	964
Lynchburg, Va.	700
Marion, N. C.	1,402
Morristown, Tenn.	1,283
Mount Airy, Ga.	1,614
Ridgecrest, N. C.	2,516
Saluda, N. C.	2,097
Spartanburg, S. C.	875
Statesville, N. C.	921
Toccoa, Ga.	1,055
Tryon, N. C.	1,200
(Tryon Peak)	3,249
(Hog Back Mountain)	3,475
Warm Springs, Ga.	1,200
Winston-Salem, N. C.	1,000

SOUTHERN RAILWAY AT A GLANCE

Headquarters: Washington, D.C.

Route mileage circa 1950: 6,300

Locomotive fleet as of 1963:
Diesels: 644

Rolling stock as of 1963:
Freight cars: 40,038
Passenger cars: 587

Principal lines circa 1950 (includes subsidiaries):

Washington, D.C.–Charlotte, NC–Atlanta, GA–Birmingham, AL—New Orleans, LA
Cincinnati, OH–Chattanooga, TN—Birmingham
Danville, KY–St. Louis, MO
Chattanooga–Memphis, TN
Chattanooga–Morristown–Knoxville–Bristol, TN
Chattanooga–Atlanta–Valdosta, FL–Jacksonville, FL
Valdosta–Palatka, FL
Salisbury–Asheville, NC–Morristown, TN
Asheville–Spartanburg–Charleston, SC
Charlotte–Jacksonville
Danville–West Point, VA
Greensboro, NC–Norfolk, VA
Rome, GA.–Mobile, AL

Notable passenger trains (slash denotes dual destinations):

Aiken-Augusta Special (Washington–Salisbury–Augusta)
Asheville Special (Washington–Greensboro– Asheville
Birmingham Special (Washington–Lynchburg–Bristol–Knoxville–Chattanooga–Birmingham
Carolina Special (Cincinnati–Knoxville–Asheville–Greensboro/Charleston)
Crescent (New York–Washington–Atlanta–Montgomery–New Orleans)
Florida Sunbeam (Cincinnati–Atlanta––Florida points)
Kansas City–Florida Special (Kansas City–Birmingham–Atlanta–Brunswick/Florida points
Peach Queen (Washington–Atlanta)
Pelican (New York–Lynchburg–Bristol–Knoxville–Chattanooga–Birmingham–New Orleans
Piedmont Limited (Washington–Atlanta–Montgomery–New Orleans)
Ponce de Leon (Cincinnati–Atlanta–Jacksonville)
Queen & Crescent (Cincinnati–Chattanooga–Birmingham–New Orleans)
Royal Palm (Cincinnati–Chattanooga–Jacksonville)
Skyland Special (Asheville–Jacksonville)
Southerner (Washington–Atlanta–Birmingham–New Orleans)
Sunnyland (Memphis–Birmingham–Atlanta)
Tennessean (Washington–Lynchburg–Bristol–Knoxville–Chattanooga–Memphis)
Washington–Atlanta–New Orleans Express (Washington–Atlanta–Montgomery–New Orleans)

PASSENGER NOTES:
SR trains operating east of Washington were handled by PRR
SR trains operating via Bristol were handled by N&W between Lynchburg and Bristol
SR trains operating to and from New Orleans via Montgomery were handled by the A&WP, WRofA, and L&N west of Atlanta
SR trains between Memphis and Birmingham
The *Kansas City–Florida Special* was handled by Frisco west of Birmingham
The Memphis–Birmingham segment of the *Sunnyland* was handled by Frisco
The *Florida Sunbeam* was handled by Seaboard Air Line south of Jacksonville

Three steam locomotives—two at the head end and one at the rear of the train (out of photo)—are necessary to move train 9, the *Skyland Special*, up Saluda Mountain on September 16, 1948. To this day, Saluda is the steepest mainline grade on any U.S. railroad. *F. E. Ardrey*

holes"—tunnels. Despite the heavy traffic, the CNO&TP remained an operational problem until major line changes and other upgrades tamed the route in 1963. As with the Washington–Atlanta main, the CNO&TP saw much of its double track removed in favor of ten-mile stretches of single, then double main, all dispatched by Centralized Traffic Control (CTC) in the late 1950s and early 1960s. An important feeder to the CNO&TP was the St. Louis Division, via Louisville.

The Chattanooga–Atlanta main connected the lines from Bristol, Knoxville, and Asheville to the east, and Memphis to the west, with the railroad's operational center at Atlanta (the company's administrative offices were located in Washington). An interesting, but operationally difficult feature of the line between Asheville and Spartanburg was Saluda Mountain. There, the line descended from the town of Saluda some 2.7 miles to Melrose, a nerve-wracking descent of 4.7 percent. Saluda was a challenge for both upgrade trains to Asheville (which to this day must be separated into three parts for the ascent), and eastbound trains to Spartanburg. Safety tracks were installed just below Saluda, and again at Melrose, along with timing circuits to ensure the safe descent of these trains. With dieselization and improved braking, the upper safety track was removed after the end of steam. Saluda still ranks as the steepest mainline railroad grade in the U.S.

Headliner of Southern's passenger fleet was the Washington–New Orleans *Crescent*. This flagship train had been inaugurated in 1891 by the Richmond & Danville as the *Washington & Southwestern Vestibuled Limited*. After formation of the Southern in 1894, the "Vestibule" continued to grow in popularity. Earlier, connecting service via the Atlanta & West Point (Atlanta–West Point, Alabama), the Western Railway of Alabama (West Point–Montgomery), and the L&N beyond to New Orleans was initiated. This was also the route of infamous mail train "Old 97," whose derailment in Danville, Virginia, in 1903 inspired the familiar ballad "The Wreck of Old 97." By 1925, the train was re-equipped and renamed the *Crescent Limited*, a true all-Pullman extra-fare train. The following year Southern's grand Class Ps4 Pacific-type locomotives began handling the *Crescent Limited*. By 1938 the name became simply the *Crescent*. It was dieselized in 1941 and streamlined in 1949. The *Crescent* also carried the through coast-to-coast sleepers of the "Washington-Sunset Route" in conjunction with the Southern Pacific west of New Orleans to Los Angles. The companion train on this same route was the more plebian *Piedmont Limited*.

The streamlined *Southerner* was inaugurated in 1941 on an all-Southern routing between Washington and New Orleans. This fine train served Birmingham, and initially was an all-coach service. Later, Pullman sleeping-car service was added. The *Southerner* was always regarded by the company to be on a par with the *Crescent* in terms of importance and eventually superseded it when the *Crescent* was downgraded in the 1960s.

The interline service between New York, Washington, and Chattanooga and points south via Bristol was also an important passenger corridor. Norfolk & Western handled the Southern's trains between Lynchburg (Monroe) and Bristol, serving Roanoke and other southwestern Virginia locations along the route. The key trains included the *Washington-Chattanooga-New Orleans Limited*, which thankfully was renamed the *Pelican* in the 1940s. The *Birmingham Special* operated over the same route as far south as its namesake city. The old heavyweight *Memphis Special* between Washington and Memphis was replaced by the streamliner *Tennessean* in 1941, same year the *Southerner* began operation.

The western portions of the system were not without fine service, and the CNO&TP route hosted the *Royal Palm* between Cincinnati and Florida (via Macon, Georgia) and the heavyweight *Ponce de Leon*. The seasonal *Florida Sunbeam*, operated jointly with Seaboard Air Line, provided daily winter season service on the route. Briefly, the *New Royal Palm* continued this tradition until the days of the seasonal trains between the Midwest and Florida came to an end.

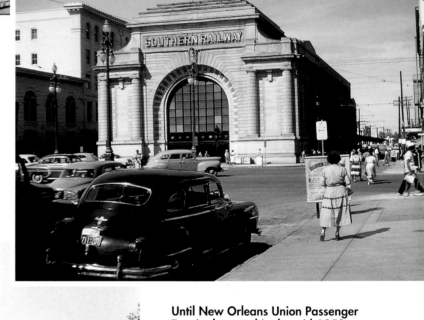

ABOVE: Ps4-class Pacific No. 6482 is at Reidsville, North Carolina, in March 1952 with train 11, a local run between Danville, Virginia, and Knoxville, Tennessee. Southern was a colorful exception to a world of all-black steam locomotives, painting several of its steam passenger locomotives in Virginia Green. *Ron Flanary collection*

Until New Orleans Union Passenger Terminal opened in the mid-1950s, Southern maintained its own depot—known as Terminal Station—in the Crescent City. Street traffic bustles outside the stately building early in the 1950s. *Dave Ingles collection*

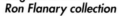

Carrying its new postwar rolling stock, the eastbound *Southerner* slips through Weems, Alabama, junction with the Central of Georgia a few miles east of Birmingham on March 28, 1948. The overpass beyond the Weems train-order station belongs to rival Seaboard's route to Birmingham. *F. E. Ardrey Jr.*

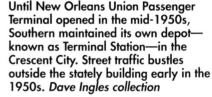

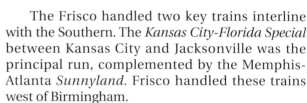

Not all of Southern's routes were heavy-duty main lines populated with husky steam locomotives or high-horsepower diesels. The short stretch of line connecting Southern's CNO&TP main line at Lexington, Kentucky, with the Danville–St. Louis main featured spindly Young's High Bridge at Tyrone, Kentucky. Bridge weight restrictions limited motive power in later years to a single switcher. This Electro-Motive SW1 has halted briefly for the photographer during its cautious trip 195 feet above the serene waters of the Kentucky River in the summer of 1977. *Mike Schafer*

Southern's early diesel scheme featured green and light gray with gold trim and lettering, as shown on this new road-switcher from Alco in 1948. *Ron Flanary collection*

Three Electro-Motive cab units—an E and two Fs—wearing the black-and-light gray livery idle at Bristol, Virginia, with the westbound *Birmingham Special* in November 1968. *Jim Boyd*

The Frisco handled two key trains interline with the Southern. The *Kansas City-Florida Special* between Kansas City and Jacksonville was the principal run, complemented by the Memphis-Atlanta *Sunnyland*. Frisco handled these trains west of Birmingham.

In the Carolinas, the *Carolina Special* was an exceptional coach-and-Pullman train in its day. The train originated at Cincinnati, and at Asheville split into two trains, one for Goldsboro, North Carolina, and the other for Charleston, South Carolina. Other important trains on the routes into and out of Asheville from the east included the *Asheville Special* and the *Skyland Special*, the latter to and from Florida points.

Back on the main line, the *Aiken-Augusta Special* and the utilitarian *Peach Queen* were just two of a number of lesser lights and a plethora of locals and secondary runs that filled out the large selection of passenger services throughout the Southern system.

SOUTHERN STEAM: CLASS TO THE END

Southern's steam locomotive fleet was an eclectic lot. During the heyday of steam, the high-water mark of freight power was the Ms4-class 2-8-2s. These engines were of the "Heavy Mikado" design of the USRA (United States Railroad Administration) era of World War I. Augmented by smaller and lighter 2-8-2s, these engines powered most of the mainline freights over much of the system. Other freight power included several classes of

2-8-0, or Consolidation-type locomotives, two classes of Santa Fe (2-10-2) engines, and even a few articulateds. The last-named engines included both simple and compound 2-8-8-2s. The Santa Fes spent most of their lives in the mountains of Tennessee and North Carolina, while the articulateds worked both the Appalachia Division in southwestern Virginia, the mountainous lines east of Asheville (particularly the Saluda grade route), and some mainline work in Georgia and Alabama.

Several classes of Pacifics and two classes of Mountains handled most passenger trains. The crown jewels in Southern's roundhouse, though, were the Ps4-class Pacifics. Built by American Locomotive Company in 1926, this group of locomotives arrived in a striking livery of Virginia Green with gold leaf trim. Locomotive historians point to the Ps4s as the finest examples of conventional steam locomotives in this country, in terms of lines and overall good looks. After the end of steam, Southern fittingly retired No. 1401 of this class and donated her to the Smithsonian in 1962.

DIESELS ARRIVE

Dieselization arrived on the Southern in 1939, when the road received six railcars from St. Louis Car Company. These die-sel-electric cars were powered by Fairbanks-Morse opposed-piston engines. Trailing each power car was a rebuilt coach and/or baggage car. Shortly thereafter, the railroad began purchasing diesel-electric switchers, first from Electro-Motive and later from Alco.

When General Motors' fledgling Electro Motive Corporation fielded its first over-the-road freight diesel—the four-unit FT cab-unit set numbered 103—in 1940, Southern's CNO&TP between Cincinnati and Chattanooga became a major proving ground for this revolutionary form of motive power. In tests, Southern found that the dark green quartet of demonstrator units could handle 4,000 tons over the grueling Rat Hole district. This bested an Ms4-class Mikado, which could only wrestle 1,750 tons over the same route. To add insult to injury, the diesels could do the trick in one less hour running time. Southern had purchased its last new steam

THE TAVERN CAR This gay and delightful rendezvous is one of the high notes in the symphony of beauty and comfort characteristic of the entire train. A festive atmosphere is achieved in the modernistic treatment in green, gold and red and in the semi-circular bar with its modern fixtures.

In full confidence that your highest expectations will be more than fulfilled and that you will marvel at the low cost for so much beauty, so much comfort and pleasure, we invite you to ride The Tennessean at the first opportunity and become acquainted with this Streamliner that is making railroad history.

FRANK L. JENKINS, PASSENGER TRAFFIC MANAGER, WASHINGTON, D. C.

SOUTHERN RAILWAY SYSTEM

The launching of the *Tennessean* and *Southerner* streamliners in 1941 was accompanied by colorful advertising that focused on the modern trains. This ad featured an interior view of chic travelers enjoying the smart lounge accommodations of the *Tennessean*. *Joe Welsh collection.*

The streamlined consist of the *Tennessean* has been bolstered with several heavyweight cars in this view of the train at Monroe, Virginia, circa 1948. Twin E7s power the New York–Memphis train. *Standard Oil Company, Bill Schafer collection*

Southern's Steam Program

One of SR's goodwill steam ambassadors, 2-8-2 No. 4501, pauses at Columbus, Georgia, on subsidiary Central of Georgia during a 1972 excursion. *Mike Schafer*

One interesting aspect of Southern's later years was its famed steam program. A modest number of North American railroads have featured restored steam operations during the last half of the twentieth century, but—except for Union Pacific—few have approached the magnitude and longevity of Southern's steam program.

Through the efforts of Southern's Paul Merriman and the Tennessee Valley Railway Museum in Chattanooga, Southern's original Mikado, Ms-class No. 4501, was reacquired from shortline Kentucky & Tennessee in 1964. After a two-year rebuilding, the engine embarked on an odyssey to Louisville and southern Indiana, and then south and eastward to Richmond to take part in the 1966 convention of the National Railway Historical Society (NRHS). Under the leadership of new SR President Graham Claytor (an avowed steam fan), Southern then launched an ambitious program of steam excursions that would last nearly 30 years.

Claytor augmented the 4501 with two other former SR steam locomotives, Consolidations 630 and 722. The two nearly identical engines were still in service in 1967 on Tennessee shortline East Tennessee & Western North Carolina. The shortline received two ex-Central of Georgia Alcos RS3s in trade, and the pair of 2-8-0s had their Southern numbers restored, and then steamed back into mainline service.

Future years would see the program expand further, with other engines joining or replacing Southern's original trio. Savannah & Atlanta 4-6-2 No. 750 was borrowed from the Atlanta Chapter–NRHS and often ran with the 630 or 722. Ex-Texas & Pacific oil-burning 2-10-4 No. 610 was leased in 1976, and even a former Canadian Pacific "Royal" Hudson, No. 2839, worked under lease in 1979. A former Chesapeake & Ohio Kanawah-class 2-8-4, No. 2716, worked briefly in 1982, until firebox problems sidelined her.

The steam program took on a decidedly N&W look after 1983. In that year, Claytor's younger brother, Robert (who was at the helm of the N&W), was instrumental in returning streamlined J-class No. 611 to service. Joined in 1987 by A-class 2-6-6-4 1218, these engines provided most of the power for the program for the remaining years of the program. Southern became Norfolk Southern in 1990, absorbing N&W in the process, and after the Claytors had left the railroad scene, NS abruptly and unceremoniously ended the steam program.
Throughout the life of the steam program, a tremendous amount of positive public relations had been generated by these steam-powered goodwill ambassadors.

locomotive in 1928, so the road was ripe for early dieselization. Slowed only slightly by production restrictions imposed by World War II, the FT demonstrator became a harbinger of things to come. Southern purchased two four-unit FT sets, including the 103 (which was refurbished by Electro-Motive and repainted to the road's green and light gray paint scheme with gold lettering).

If diesels were good for freight, they were definitely great for passenger service. Coincidentally with the inauguration of two new streamlined passenger runs, Southern received new E6 passenger units from EMC in 1941. The new units were assigned to the Washington–New Orleans *Southerner* and the Monroe–Memphis leg of the *Tennessean* (a streamlined steam locomotive handled the Washington–Monroe portion) .

Additional E6s were added, and even Alco pitched in with DL109/110 sets to take over some of the heavier passenger runs through the mountains. Postwar acquisitions included newer E7 and E8 units to dispatch the final passenger steam by the end of 1952. By that time, only 180 steam locomotives were still in service.

Electro-Motive F3 and F7 units arrived in large numbers in the late 1940s and early 1950s, along with GP7 (and later GP9) and Alco RS3 road-switchers. Dieselization was officially complete on June 17, 1953, when Ms4 6330 arrived at Chattanooga's Citico Yard with a freight from Oakdale.

Later motive-power acquisitions included a small number of Fairbanks-Morse units, and many more Electro-Motive units. Five of F-M's hulking six-axle Train Master diesels were purchased in 1955, bringing on the era of heavier power. EMD delivered 48 2,400-hp. turbocharged SD24s in 1959. During the decade of the 1960s, second-generation EMD diesel power such as GP30s, GP35s, and a variety of SD units were acquired, relegating much of the older units to scrap. A wave of new GP38s (and later GP38–2s) helped to finish off the last of the old F-units. Southern's last freight-service Fs ran in 1974 (although a few passenger service FP7s ran several more years). General Electric also made inroads beginning in 1968 with a small order of U30Cs. Many more GE units were to follow.

SHOWCASE SOUTHERN

Many key personalities were instrumental in Southern's rise to the upper echelons of the industry. From the beginning, Samuel Spencer was a dominant force during the road's early days of expansion. Sadly, Spencer was killed when a following train plowed into the rear of his office car at Lawyer's Station, Virginia, in 1906.

Fairfax Harrison presided during the USRA days, the 1920s, and the darkest days of the Depression. It was he who decided to paint the Ps4 Pacifics green and gold. Ernest Norris, his successor, guided the company into dieselization. Southern's marginal financial condition in the late 1930s was a major factor in the company's early and eager embrace of diesels. Norris knew Southern's steam fleet looked great, but the system roundhouses were full of worn-out locomotives ripe for replacement.

After World War II, successor Harry deButts sensed the Southern was at the precipice of greatness, and prepared the railroad for the long-delayed emergence of the South as a region of economic growth. Mr. deButts' key assistant, D.W. Brosnan, was his hand-picked successor.

Brosnan became Southern's president in 1960, a post he held until 1967. Until that time, he drove the Southern into the future like a jockey whipping a racehorse toward the finish line. He "daylighted" (removed tunnels) the Rat Hole, brought several key regional roads into the fold, pioneered the use of radio-controlled mid-train locomotive helpers, designed and built (in company shops) a revolutionary fleet of mechanized track equipment, and put the Southern at the forefront of computerization. Innovations like systemwide microwave and centralized hotbox detectors helped bring more efficiencies to the railroad. His huge, new "Big John" grain hoppers drew him into a protracted rate battle with the Interstate Commerce Commission. Brosnan won, of course, and a new era in transportation competitiveness was born.

The Southern entered the 1970s under the more gentile guidance of Graham Claytor. Besides launching the steam program, Claytor initially kept the Southern out of Amtrak in 1971 (the irony being that Claytor would eventually wind up as Amtrak's president). His renamed *Southern Crescent*'s E8s regained their regal green and gold paint in 1972, which they kept until SR turned the train over to Amtrak in 1979. First Stanley Crane (who went on to resurrect Conrail), and then Harold Hall closed out Southern's corporate independence as the road's chief executive.

In its final form, the Southern was a 10,250-mile system serving a 13-state region, from the nation's capital at Washington to Jacksonville, Florida, and from East St. Louis, Illinois, to New Orleans. The Southern owned some 75,000 freight cars in 1981 and 1,459 locomotives. The freight mix was highly diversified, with major traffic in coal, chemicals, pulp and paper products, agricultural and food products, automobiles, lumber and wood products, stone, clay, glass, and concrete products. Particularly in its last 30 years, the Southern was a major moneymaker. In 1981, its revenues were almost $1.8 billion, with net revenue of over $212 million.

Southern was not immune from the merger fever that followed the Staggers Act of 1980 (which effectively deregulated the industry). In June 1980, merger talks with the equally profitable and coal-dominated Norfolk & Western began. Earlier, Chessie System had merged with Seaboard Coast Line Industries (which included such major roads as the Louisville & Nashville and Seaboard Coast Line) to form CSX. In response, Southern's strategy to maintain its competitive position was to join with N&W. The ICC approved the merger on March 25, 1982, and the railroad was formally launched on June 1 of that same year. A proud name in American railroading was replaced by the Thoroughbred symbol of the new Norfolk Southern. The new NS inherited a well-maintained, well operated, efficient, and highly profitable and historically distinguished transportation system. True to its slogan, the Southern continued to "Serve the South," right until the very end of its corporate existence.

The 90 "Silverside" gondolas trailing the four Electro-Motive SD40–2s on the point of the first section of westbound train 91 lean through the curve over Bum Hollow trestle in East Stone Gap, Virginia, on April 26, 1985. The Appalachia Division was a major generator of coal traffic for the Southern. Once reloaded with bituminous coal, this train will make the return cycle to an electrical generating plant in North Carolina. *Ron Flanary*

The splendor of autumn in the Appalachians is aptly felt in this view between Marion and Asheville, North Carolina, of a westbound freight at Ridgecrest in October 1978. The Southern's climb over Blue Ridge Summit between Asheville and Marion makes this one of the railroad's most scenic lines, one that features numerous tunnels and loops. *Dale Jacobson*

FOLLOW THE FLAG

Wabash

"**W**abashing the high cars" was steam-era slang for running a freight train fast and hard. Few railroads were as celebrated in legend and lore as the Wabash. Nearly everyone can recite the first few lines of the folksong "Wabash Cannon Ball," which begins, "From the great Atlantic Ocean to the wide Pacific shore. . .". Never mind that they are completely inaccurate in terms of describing the width and breadth of the real Wabash; no one ever let facts get in the way of a good legend. But the Wabash earned its legendary status legitimately, from its lines that laced the Midwestern heartland to its pivotal role in the schemes of rail baron Jay Gould, to its penchant for running fast trains.

THREE SEEDS

The Wabash had three beginnings between 1837 and 1853 and was united as one railroad under financier Jay Gould in 1879. The Wabash had its genesis in 1834 when Illinois Governor Joseph Duncan persuaded the legislature to authorize and fund a railroad along the "Northern Crossing" trail between the Indiana state line (and nearby Wabash River) at Danville and the Mississippi River at Quincy. Grading commenced in November 1837, and on November 8, 1838, the 4-2-0 *Rogers* steamed the first eight miles of strap-iron rail from Meredosia, on the Illinois River, east toward Morgan City. Only the fourth locomotive produced by Rogers, Ketchum & Grosvenor of Paterson, New Jersey, it was the first steam locomotive to operate in Illinois. The railroad's second locomotive, the *Illinois*, was lost at sea while en route from Baldwin in Philadelphia to New Orleans in 1839. The state-operated Northern Cross Railroad reached Springfield in 1842 and stalled there until it was sold for $21,000 to Nicholas H. Ridgely in 1847, who changed the name to the Sangamon & Morgan Railroad. By 1851 the line had been rebuilt with new iron "T" rail. In 1853 the name changed again to the Great Western Railroad of Illinois and resumed eastward construction, reaching Danville in December 1856.

Meanwhile, the eastern lines that would give the Wabash its name were begun in 1853 with two railroads that were chartered to reach westward from the Lake Erie port of Toledo, Ohio. The Toledo & Illinois was to build from Toledo to the Ohio/Indiana state line, with the Lake Erie, Wabash & St. Louis continuing westward to Attica, Indiana, where it could connect with the Great Western of Illinois. Construction was rapid, and by 1856 the two lines were united as the Toledo, Wabash & Western Railway, which shortly thereafter acquired the Great Western to produce a single railroad stretching 476 miles from Toledo to Quincy with an additional branch to Keokuk, Iowa, also on the mighty Mississippi.

In early 1867 the TW&W began building its important second main line, heading south from Decatur 110 miles to Illinoistown (East St. Louis), which was completed in 1870. A year later the TW&W had built a line westward from the original line at Naples, Illinois, and bridged the Mississippi to reach Hannibal, Missouri. The railroad continued to expand, acquiring connecting lines, but the business depression of 1875 forced it into receivership. In 1877 the TW&W was reorganized as the Wabash Railway Company, operating 678 miles of track.

Back in 1851, investors in St. Louis had been reaching north-westward toward Iowa with their North Missouri Railroad, which was built to the broad "Missouri standard gauge" of 5 feet, 6 inches. In 1859 the new railroad encountered the barrier of the Missouri River less than 20 miles away at St. Charles, Missouri. Cargo had to be unloaded and barged across the river and reloaded into freight cars. The NM continued building and arrived at the Iowa state line at Coatesville, Missouri, in 1858. The Civil War interrupted the railroad's further expansion, as it became the target of Confederate raiders.

Following the war in 1867, the NM converted to real standard gauge and began constructing northward into Ottumwa, Iowa, and westward from Moberly, Missouri, toward Kansas City. The shop town of Moberly was created by the railroad

FACING PAGE: **Train time at Decatur, Illinois, March 14, 1962: The combined** *Blue Bird-Wabash Cannon Ball* **has arrived from St. Louis and has just been separated into two trains. At far left stands the** *Blue Bird* **section as an Electro-Motive E8 backs on to take the train on to Chicago. The middle locomotive set of Alco PAs is on the** *Wabash Cannon Ball* **section. The Fairbanks-Morse Train Master at far right had come up on the combined train, but will remain in Decatur after the** *Blue Bird* **and** *Cannon Ball* **depart for Chicago and Detroit, respectively.** *R. R. Wallin*

FACING PAGE, INSET: **Wabash's banner logo is one of the most well-known of America's classic railroads. Here it adorns a new Electro-Motive GP35 at Wabash's Landers Yard in Chicago.** *Mike Schafer*

LEFT: **The Wabash passenger timetable from 1951 featured the often-used heart symbol to emphasize Wabash's transportation role in America's heartland.** *Kevin Holland collection*

WABASH AT A GLANCE

Headquarters: St. Louis, MO

Route mileage circa 1950: 2,393

Locomotive fleet as of 1963:
Diesels: 319

Rolling stock as of 1963:
Freight cars: 14,240
Passenger cars: 126

Principal routes circa 1950:

Buffalo, NY–Detroit, MI.–Fort Wayne, IN–Decatur, IL–Springfield, IL–Moberly, MO.–Kansas City, MO

Chicago–Decatur–St. Louis (utilized Buffalo–K.C. line Bement–Decatur)

St. Louis–Moberly, MO–Des Moines, IA

Brunswick, MO–Council Bluffs, IA

Toledo, OH–Chicago Bluffs, IL–Keokuk, IA

Notable passenger trains (slash denotes dual destinations):

Banner Blue (Chicago–St. Louis)
Blue Bird (Chicago–St. Louis)
City of Kansas City (St. Louis–Kansas City)
City of St. Louis (St. Louis–Denver–Cheyenne–Los Angeles)
Des Moines Limited (St. Louis–Des Moines)
Detroit Arrow (Chicago–Detroit)
Detroit Limited (St. Louis–Detroit)
Kansas City Express (St. Louis–Kansas City)
Midnight Limited (St. Louis–Kansas City)
Omaha Limited (St. Louis–Omaha)

Pacific Coast Special (St. Louis–Pacific Coast points)
Red Bird (Chicago–Detroit)
St. Louis Limited (Detroit–St. Louis)
St. Louis Limited (Des Moines/Omaha– St. Louis)
St. Louis Special (Kansas City–St. Louis)
The Midnight (Chicago–St. Louis)
"Wabash Cannon Ball" (St. Louis–Detroit)

NOTES: Chicago–Detroit service in conjunction with PRR Chicago–Fort Wayne; Union Pacific handled through trains operating west of Kansas City

This Wabash map from the late 1950s illustrates the strategic advantage the railroad had in its Buffalo–Kansas City main line, which bypassed the congestion long associated with the Midwest's two great rail centers of Chicago and St. Louis. West of Detroit, this main line still offers this asset as a critical, high-speed artery for the Norfolk Southern system.

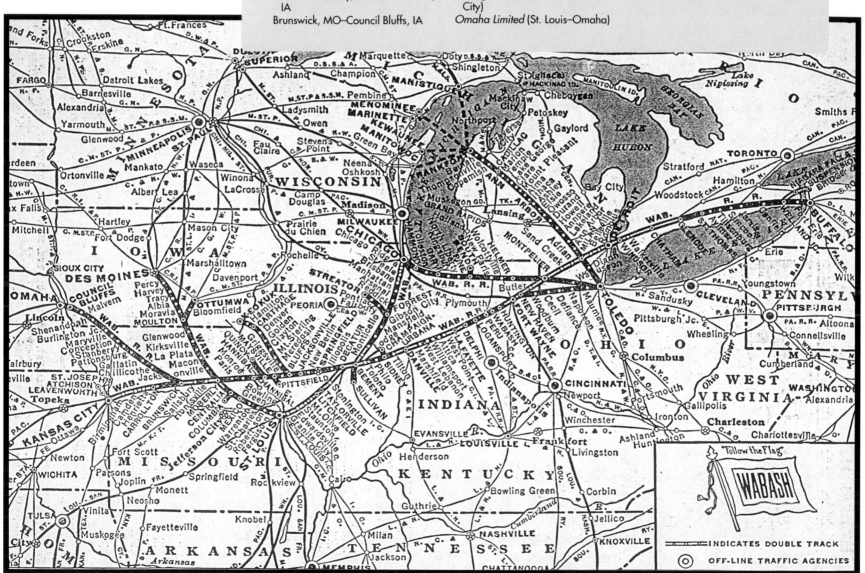

at its junction point. The Missouri River was conquered with a massive bridge at St. Charles in 1871, and trains could then run directly from St. Louis to Ottumwa and Kansas City. But all this expansion stressed the railroad financially to the breaking point, and in 1872 it was reorganized as the St. Louis, Kansas City & Northern.

The new StLKC&N pressed the extension of its west line in an effort to connect with the transcontinental Union Pacific at Omaha, Nebraska. The Omaha line, which split off the Kansas City line at Brunswick, Missouri, was completed into Council Bluffs, Iowa, in October 1879.

LINED WITH GOULD

The Union Pacific at this time was under the control of Jay Gould, a ruthless financier and stock manipulator who saw railroads as fertile ground for all sorts of financial skullduggery. With dreams of a true transcontinental empire "from the great Atlantic Ocean to the wide Pacific shore," Gould saw the StLKC&N from Council Bluffs to St. Louis and the Wabash from St. Louis to Toledo as the perfect centerpiece for this grand scheme. On November 10, 1879, Gould united the two railroads as the Wabash, St. Louis & Pacific and began

an aggressive campaign of buying up connecting regional lines.

The process of extending the Wabash to Chicago had begun before Gould when in 1877 the Wabash had acquired the Chicago & Paducah, which was building a line between Effingham and Streator, Illinois, crossing the Wabash at Bement. Breaking off the Streator line at Strawn, the Chicago & Strawn Railway was incorporated to complete the 90 miles north to Chicago, and in 1880 an ownership agreement was reached with the Chicago & Western Indiana to provide trackage rights and terminal facilities in Chicago itself. At about this same time the railroad was directing its attention toward Detroit by building a 110-mile line eastward from Butler, Indiana, which was completed in 1881. Carferries on the Detroit River between Detroit and Windsor, Ontario, would give the Wabash, St. Louis & Pacific access to considerable traffic out of eastern Canada.

The 1880s were a decade of corporate chaos as Gould fought rate wars with neighbors like the Burlington and the Rock Island and gobbled up lines like the Cairo & Vincennes. Just before his empire's collapse in 1884, Gould's "Wabash" boasted 3,549 miles of railroad, united under his famous

In a scene that brims with the quaint side of Wabash, tri-weekly mixed train No. 52 between Gary, Indiana, and Montpelier, Ohio, calls at Lakeville, Indiana, 56.7 miles into its 145-mile run over the "Pumpkin Vine" in August 1954. This line, which connected with a branch to Toledo at Montpelier— junction with the Detroit–Decatur main— was built as a shortcut to Chicago out of Canada, Detroit, and Toledo. After the 1964 Wabash-Nickel Plate-Norfolk & Western merger, the Pumpkin Vine became superfluous and most of it was abandoned. *Bill Eley collection*

red, white, blue and gold "banner" flag herald, which was copyrighted in 1884. The Wabash also went bankrupt in 1884, and Gould tried his ultimate gambit by having himself appointed as the receiver. But his house of cards fell apart, and the Wabash began to fragment as rivals and on-line investors began to pick at the corpse.

In 1888 a Purchasing Commission of investors and shippers managed to pull the critical segments of the railroad back together and reorganize it as the Wabash Railroad Company on May 27, 1889, though it remained under Gould control. By 1890 business was back enough to justify the construction of a new line from Montpelier, Ohio, directly into Chicago to handle the increasing traffic out of Detroit and Canada. To shorten the route between Detroit and Kansas City and Council Bluffs, the Wabash in 1894 worked out an agreement with the Missouri-Kansas-Texas (Katy) to use its line from Hannibal to Moberly, Missouri, for a route 50 miles shorter than via St. Louis.

INTO THE TWENTIETH CENTURY

In 1898 Charles M. Hayes was the president of Canada's Grand Trunk Railway, but he had begun his career on the Wabash, working his way up to president before moving to the GTR. Hayes regarded the Wabash as a friendly connection and worked out a trackage-rights deal that would permit the Wabash to operate over the Grand Trunk between Windsor (across the river from Detroit) and Fort Erie, Ontario (across the Suspension Bridge from Buffalo, New York). Because of the differences between U.S. and Canadian government regulations, the Wabash tended to keep a dedicated fleet of locomotives on the Canadian side.

Though a high-speed route in other ways, there was a bottleneck of sorts in the Buffalo–Kansas City main line, and it was called the Detroit River. Competitor New York Central System had a tunnel under the river to link Detroit (just out of view to the left in this scene at Windsor, Ontario) with Canada, but Wabash and successor Norfolk & Western had to rely on tug-propelled barges to ferry freight cars across the watery gap. *Mike McBride*

Wabash served "the heart of America," and Decatur—at crossroads of the Buffalo–Kansas City and Chicago–St. Louis routes—was the heart of the Wabash. Dominating this central Illinois city was a yard and shop complex, partially visible in this 1962 view of the westbound *Wabash Cannon Ball* behind an Alco PA approaching the Decatur station. The view looks eastward from the interlocking tower guarding the Wabash-Pennsylvania Railroad-Illinois Central crossing. *Dave Ingles*

Decatur Shops could handle all manner of shopwork, from car repairs to heavy overhauls on even the largest of Wabash power, such as hulking 4-8-4 No. 2900, built by Baldwin at the onset of the Depression. Wabash needed brute power like this to expedite Red Ball freights. These were considered "dual-purpose" locomotives and therefore also saw service on high-speed passenger trains. *Railfan & Railroad* collection

The Wabash improved its operations in 1902 by building a line from Butler to New Haven, Indiana, to route all the Decatur–Detroit traffic via Fort Wayne and Peru and selling the older Butler-Logansport line to the Pennsylvania Railroad.

Even though Jay Gould had died in 1892, the Wabash continued to be subjected to his influence. His son, George Jay Gould, revived the father's dream of an empire in 1904 by linking the Wabash at Toledo with the Wheeling & Lake Erie in an attempt to reach the East Coast via the Western Maryland. Encouraged by steel-maker Andrew Carnegie, George Gould invested heavily in the spectacular and expensively engineered Wabash Pittsburgh Terminal Railway to reach downtown Pittsburgh. Vehemently opposed by the Pennsy, which considered Pittsburgh its exclusive domain, Gould was forced into bankruptcy in 1911, and the Wabash withdrew back to Toledo, leaving behind the W&LE and the Wabash Pittsburgh Terminal, which in 1916 would become the Pittsburgh & West Virginia. As a result of Gould's expensive Pittsburgh venture, the Wabash Railroad was sold at foreclosure and was reorganized on October 22, 1915, as the Wabash Railway.

World War I saw the Wabash come under the jurisdiction of the U. S. Railroad Administration on December 26, 1917, along with the rest of America's railroads. The government operated the railroad during the war emergency until early 1920. Probably the most enduring evidence of the USRA on the Wabash was a fleet of 20 handsome government-designed 2-8-2 freight locomotives delivered in 1918.

Following the war, the Wabash found itself in the heart of Detroit's rapidly developing automobile industry with a direct connection to the Omaha and Kansas City gateways that avoided the traffic congestion and interchange delays at Chicago and St. Louis. Westbound automobile traffic could be balanced by eastbound fresh produce from California, and both types of traffic thrived on speed and swift delivery. A hefty business in automobile parts developed with Chrysler, and especially from Ford's massive River Rouge plant in Dearborn to outlying assembly plants like the one

BELOW: Wabash had an eclectic diesel roster, having purchased locomotives from nearly every principal builder of diesels. Even short-lived (as a diesel builder) Lima was represented. This Lima switcher heads up the Columbia–Centralia, Missouri, mixed train (freight will also be picked up during its run) at Columbia circa 1960. This train made two round trips daily on the 22-mile Columbia branch, connecting with the *City of Kansas City* and *City of St. Louis* at Centralia. *George C. Drake,* Railfan & Railroad *collection*

LOWER RIGHT: The only road diesels that Wabash purchased from General Electric were a fleet of 15 GE U25B locomotives, delivered in 1962. These were considered the first second-generation diesels bought by the Wabash to begin replacement of its earliest road diesels. With its cyclops-like single front windshield, "U-boat" 501 is at East St. Louis. *Jim Boyd*

in Kansas City. Studebaker also became valued customer when in 1926 the Wabash bought the 11-mile New Jersey, Indiana & Illinois between Pine (on the Montpelier–Chicago line) and South Bend, Indiana, where Studebaker had its plant.

To guarantee its share of the produce business, the Wabash acquired one-third interest in the American Refrigerator Transit Company, and trainloads of yellow ART ice-cooled refrigerator cars rolled off the Santa Fe every day at Kansas City, bound for points east on the Wabash. The same expedited service was given automobile and merchandise traffic that the Wabash referred to as "Red Ball" freight. Its reputation for sheer hustle was to become legendary.

In another effort to bypass the congestion of Chicago, in 1925 the Wabash acquired stock control of the 292-mile Ann Arbor Railroad in Michigan. The Ann Arbor connected Toledo with Frankfort, on Lake Michigan. A fleet of huge, rugged, all-weather ferryboats carried freight cars across the lake to connections with the Green Bay & Western at Kewaunee and the Chicago & North Western and Soo Line at Manitowoc. Although under firm Wabash control, the Ann Arbor kept its separate corporate identity and locomotive fleet.

Having taken on the Ann Arbor, the Wabash began looking eastward with the idea of extending itself into New York City and other points in the Northeast. Teaming up with the Delaware & Hudson, the Wabash acquired control of the Lehigh Valley Railroad in 1926, which prompted the Pennsylvania Railroad to make a move to defend its territory. The resourceful Pennsy quickly bought up majority stock control of the Wabash and LV by 1932 and scared off the D&H.

The Great Depression dealt the Wabash a severe blow as manufacturing slumped and farm prices plummeted. By 1933 the Wabash was once again in receivership. As the country pulled itself out of the Depression, the Wabash Railway was reorganized on January 1, 1942, as the Wabash Railroad Company, though it was still under PRR ownership. The wartime boom quickly put the hustle back into the Wabash.

WABASH STEAM

The Wabash steamed into the war effort with an interesting mix of old and new motive power. Its biggest fast freight locomotives were 25 husky 70-inch-drivered 4-8-4s built by Baldwin in 1930 that shared duties with 25 very similar and only slightly smaller 4-8-2s. The railroad's only other big freight engines were 25 powerful but slow 2-10-2s built in 1917, many of which were sold to other railroads during the war.

The freight workhorses of the Wabash were numerous classes of 2-8-2s whose birth dates ranged from 1912 to 1925. A handful of smaller and older engines like 2-6-0s, 2-6-2s and 2-8-0s handled branchline and light freight duties. About 50 modest 0-6-0s and 45 rugged USRA-design 0-8-0s covered most yard switching duties.

The Wabash had developed a solid passenger business before the Depression with coach trains on daytime runs and sleeping-car trains plying the night. By 1900, the Civil War-era 4-4-0s had given way to fast 4-4-2s and 4-6-0s. Amazingly, the Wabash bought its last new steam passenger locomotives in 1912 in the form of 16 medium 4-6-2s. It expanded this fleet of Pacifics between 1916 and 1926, however, by rebuilding 23 of its 2-6-2s in the Decatur Shops into 4-6-2s.

During World War II, passenger traffic was booming, and the 4-8-2s could not be spared for passenger service, so the Wabash turned again to Decatur Shops for a solution. Beginning in 1943, Decatur converted five 2-8-2s into 80-inch-drivered 4-6-4s, complete with streamlined white side skirts and blue boiler jackets. These were followed by two more 4-6-4s rebuilt from conventional heavy Mikados. The 706, completed in 1947, was the Wabash's last "new" steam locomotive.

PASSENGER SERVICE

Wabash passenger trains had a solid reputation that lasted as long as the railroad. Flag-bearers of the Chicago–St. Louis route were the *Banner Blue Limited* and the *Midnight Limited*. In 1938 the Wabash inaugurated another fast new daytime passenger train between St. Louis and Chicago; the *Blue Bird* received the same blue and gold livery previously reserved for sister train *Banner Blue*. The railroad even ran a modest commuter service out of Chicago to Orland Park that still operates through Chicago's Metra commuter-rail agency.

Wabash's longest intra-line run was the *Central States Limited* between Buffalo and Kansas

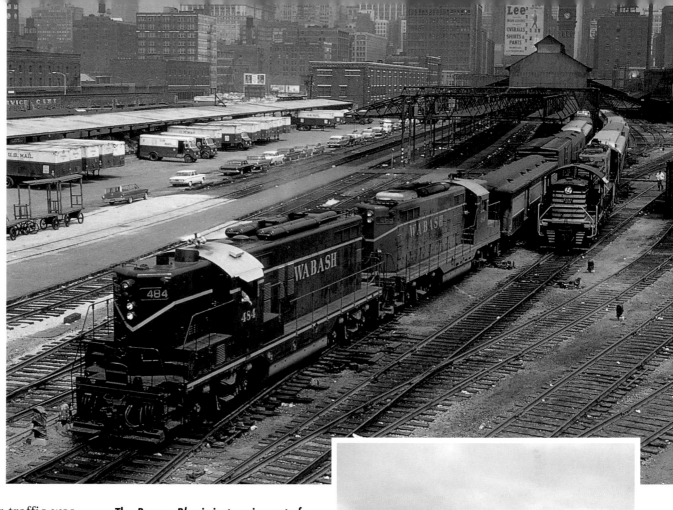

The *Banner Blue* is just easing out of Chicago's Dearborn Station at the start of its run to St. Louis behind a set of passenger-version GP9s on the morning of July 24, 1962. The Alco road-switcher at right belongs to the Chicago & Western Indiana Railroad, which owned and operated Dearborn and on which the Wabash had trackage rights to reach downtown. The C&WI is about to pull the Wabash commuter train out of the depot and to the yards. *Dave Ingles*

Vista-Dome parlor observation car 1601 was built by the Budd Company in 1950 for the *Blue Bird*. As the 1950s progressed, Wabash redistributed much of its new streamlined equipment to all the mainline runs. This reshuffling found the handsome *Blue Bird* car on the *Banner Blue* more often than on the *Blue Bird*, as this mid-1960s scene at Decatur reveals. *Mike McBride*

City. Day schedules as well as overnight service was provided between Detroit and Kansas City with trains like the *St. Louis Limited* and the *Detroit Special.* On the St. Louis–Kansas City line, the feature train was the *Pacific Coast Limited*, which operated through to West Coast points in conjunction with the Union Pacific. The *Kansas City Express* and *St. Louis Special* provided day service between St. Louis and Kansas City while the *Midnight Limited* provided overnight service.

One of the more interesting passenger runs was the joint Wabash-Pennsylvania service between Chicago and Detroit via Fort Wayne. The *Detroit Arrow, Chicago Arrow,* and the *Red Bird* used swift PRR and Wabash 4-4-2s to cover the 295 miles between the two cities in five hours flat.

The Wabash didn't join the streamliner movement until after World War II. In 1946, in conjunction with the UP, the streamliner *City of St. Louis* was launched between St. Louis and Cheyenne,

Wyoming, and later Los Angeles. In 1947, Wabash introduced its own new streamliner, the *City of Kansas City*, between St. Louis and Kansas City.

The Wabash really made a publicity splash, however, when it introduced the newly streamlined *Blue Bird* on February 26, 1950. The six-car Budd-built consist—featuring four Vista-Dome cars—made a daily round trip between St. Louis and Chicago behind an Electro-Motive E-unit clad in Wabash's classic blue, gray, and white scheme.

DIESEL-ERA WABASH

Diesels had come quietly to the Wabash in the form of a high-hood Alco 660-hp. diesel switcher and three Electro-Motive SW1s in April 1939. By the end of the war, the Wabash rostered 26 black diesel switchers from Alco, Baldwin, General Electric, and EMD. Many more would follow.

The first road diesels were two pairs of EMD E7 units acquired in August 1946 for the new *City of St.*

Louis streamliner. They were painted in a stunning blue, gray, and white livery designed by the EMD Styling Section. Another E7 arrived in 1947 for the new *City of Kansas City* streamliner. Four Alco 2000-hp. PA1 passenger units were acquired in 1949 for the St. Louis–Detroit trains.

In February 1949 the Wabash began an all-out commitment to freight diesels with five A-B-A sets of Alco FA1 1500-hp. cab units and nine A-B-A sets of EMD F7s. Diesels continued to arrive—including motive power from newcomer Fairbanks-Morse—and by the end of 1953 the railroad was completely dieselized, with one notable exception. The Bluffs-Keokuk branch, which included the very first piece of Northern Cross trackage, retained a small fleet of 2-6-0 Moguls because the Illinois River bridge at Meredosia could not support a road diesel. The site of the Wabash's first steam operation also became the refuge for its last. Mogul 573 made its final run on January 28, 1955, and was then donated to the National Museum of Transportation in St. Louis.

Second-generation diesels began arriving from Electro-Motive, GE, and even Alco early in the 1960s, although the eye-catching blue, gray,

and white livery was replaced by solid blue with yellow striping. During this time the Pennsylvania Railroad was beginning negotiations with the New York Central to create the Penn Central, and it knew that it would not be permitted to retain its ownership of the Wabash. The Norfolk & Western and Nickel Plate had been talking merger since 1958, and the Pennsy encouraged them to include the Wabash in the deal. As a result, on October 16, 1964, the Ann Arbor was spun off to the Detroit, Toledo & Ironton, and the Wabash became part of the Lake Region of the Norfolk & Western.

But the legendary *Wabash Cannon Ball* would not be silenced. In 1949, the Wabash had named Detroit–St. Louis day trains the *Wabash Cannon Ball*. It was the first time that name had been applied to a real train. The new N&W continued to run the train, and when it tried to discontinue the famous name in the mid-1960s and then the train itself in the late 1960s, the public outcry was so loud that the train managed to survive right up to the start of Amtrak in 1971. Had the train not carried such a famous name, it would have probably been dropped five years earlier. Don't ever underestimate the survivability of a legend.

In a scene that's classic Wabash, a pair of F7s roll through Forrest, Illinois, on the Decatur–Chicago main line with a Decatur-bound freight in June 1957. The water plug at far right stands as a reminder to Wabash's great steam era. The track in foreground is the Toledo, Peoria & Western main line. Were one to stand at this location today, the TP&W line would be visible, but little remains of Wabash's once-fast Chicago-Decatur main line at this point, much of it having been abandoned. In 1964, Wabash became one of the first in a series of fast-falling flags as merger mania swept America. *M. L. Powell*

THE FEATHER RIVER ROUTE

Western Pacific

In the late 1800s, the Central Pacific Railroad's stranglehold on California's economy was so infamous and far-reaching that it even inspired a novel, Frank Norris' scathing classic *The Octopus*. The nickname stuck, to the certain displeasure of Leland Stanford, Charles Crocker, Mark Hopkins, and Collis P. Huntington—the "Big Four" who lorded over the Central Pacific kingdom. Had these men wanted attention from the literary world, they would no doubt have reached a tentacle into their deep pockets and bought a more flattering depiction. The Big Four used money, coercion, and political influence to increase their power and debilitate the competition. In 1869, when an upstart Scottish immigrant and surveyor named Arthur Keddie sought financing for his dream of a trans-Sierra railroad through the Feather River Canyon, Huntington thought simple mockery would be enough to sink Keddie's scheme. "No man will ever be fool enough to build a railroad through the Feather River Canyon," Huntington scoffed. Keddie, however, would not be so easily deterred.

Throughout Western Pacific's 72-year history, numerous incidents suggested that perhaps Huntington was right. The railroad's continuing existence both in the corporate world and on the landscape itself was often extremely tenuous. WP managed to survive bankruptcy in 1916 and 1935, and rebuffed hostile takeover attempts from Southern Pacific and Santa Fe in the 1960s.

FALSE STARTS AND OTHER SETBACKS

Like many other American railroads, the 930-mile WP main line from Oakland, California, to Salt Lake City, Utah, came together from an assortment of smaller, underfinanced, local ventures which were themselves preceded by numerous false starts. Soon after construction began in 1869 on Keddie's Oroville & Virginia City Railroad, the Big Four pressured investors to stop financing the project and persuaded Congressmen to deny land grants. With no money and no land, the O&VC quickly collapsed. Twenty years later a

ROUTE OF THE **CALIFORNIA ZEPHYR**

WESTERN PACIFIC FEATHER RIVER ROUTE

TIME TABLE

ASTA

OCTOBER 29, 1961

group of California merchants, joined by the unwavering Arthur Keddie, attempted an end run around the Central Pacific monopoly by forming the San Francisco & Great Salt Lake Railroad. Though twenty years had passed since Keddie's first attempt, the company met the same obstacle—C. P. Huntington—and the same fate: failure.

To build a railroad through the Feather River Canyon, a man was needed who could compete with the Big Four on their own terms: wealth and deviousness. The man was George Gould, son of railroad baron Jay Gould and inheritor of his father's rail empire. To prevent his adversaries from learning of his scheme, Gould and his millions remained behind the scenes. His people established two innocent-sounding shortline railroads, the Indian Valley and the Butte & Plumas, and a mining company as a front for purchasing the railroads.

Though Gould kept his fellow tycoons in the dark, he discovered to his surprise that a man named Arthur Keddie had recently incorporated the Stockton & Beckwith Pass Railroad along the very route Gould sought for his own railroad. The millionaire joined forces with the dreamer, and incorporated the Western Pacific Railway on March 3, 1903. And despite enormous resistance from the more powerful transcontinental railroads and from Mother Nature herself, Gould made Keddie's dream a reality, 40 long years after it first began to take shape. On November 1, 1909, the pounding of a gold spike echoed through the Feather River Canyon at the new station site of Keddie, marking the completion of the Western Pacific.

WP'S SIERRA CROSSING

The six years between incorporation and completion saw WP forces in the Sierra facing the same incredible obstacles and dangers Central Pacific's men had encountered 20 years earlier. Suspended in baskets against sheer granite cliffs, Chinese immigrants had carved and blasted CP's Overland Route toward Donner Pass. The steep walls of the Feather River Canyon forced WP's surveyors to use the same perilous method simply to

FACING PAGE: **If there was one location on the Western Pacific that might be the railroad's "charismatic epicenter," Keddie, California, at the upper end of the Feather River Canyon just might be the place. Here, WP's "High Line" took off northward for Bieber, California, and the connection with Great Northern. A complete wye perched on the mountainside, partially on trestles and with tunnelwork, made Keddie a particularly scenic location. In this 1981 view from the highway past Keddie, a westbound freight crosses Keddie Wye's often-photographed bridgework over Spanish Creek. *Jim Boyd***

FACING PAGE, INSET: **A rustic reminder of WP's steam era, a wood reefer weathers the years at Carbona, California, in 1976. *Ted Benson***

LEFT: **Although the Feather River Canyon comprised a relatively short portion of WP's Oakland–Salt Lake City main line, its scenic beauty was integral to the charisma of the Western Pacific—"The Feather River Route," as this 1961 timetable proclaimed.**

GP9 No. 703 at Stockton presents a clean, new face in December 1976 following the application of the Western Pacific's new green-and-orange livery, a reflection of the railroad's operation during the Al Perlman era. *Ted Benson*

stake out the line. The dark cloud Huntington cast on Keddie's dream hung like a curse over the WP. In return for sharing its canyon with a railroad, the Feather River took a dozen lives. Fifty years later, in the winter of 1955–56, crews managed to dig the railroad out from a landslide near Rock Creek just in time for another slide to come down in the same spot. The cliffs were so unstable, the only solution was a new 3,000-foot tunnel, built at a cost of $2 million. As recently as 1997 Union Pacific, which took over WP in 1982 and spent millions upgrading the line, seriously considered abandoning the Canyon Subdivision after floods and landslides damaged 100 miles of track.

Instead, UP spent approximately $30 million to rebuild the Feather River route. Why would UP make such an enormous commitment? After all, UP had recently acquired Southern Pacific and thus owned the shorter ex-Central Pacific line over Donner Pass. Perhaps Huntington's ridicule merely concealed his envy for the remarkable jewel Keddie had discovered. For although WP's route into the San Francisco Bay Area is longer than SP's, the WP crosses the Sierra at 5,000-foot Beckwourth Pass, a remarkable 2,000 feet lower than Donner Pass. So while SP's rotary snowplows battled against a seasonal average of 200 inches of snowfall, WP had a far easier time keeping its line open, provided there weren't too many rock slides! A second valuable feature of the Feather River Route is its comparatively easy climb over the mountains. The steepness, or grade, of a mountain pass determines its usefulness as a potential rail route. A steeper grade requires more powerful locomotives, more fuel, shorter trains, and slower speeds. Three percent is considered the maximum practical grade for a railroad, though several shorter and less-traveled passes around the country approach four percent. An eastbound train leaving the Sacramento Valley for Donner Summit faces 80 grueling miles of grades ranging from 1.0 to 2.3 percent. Grades on the WP never exceed one percent, thanks to Keddie's surveying skill and long tunnels under mountain ridges at Chilcoot and Spring Garden. Just west of Spring Garden the line maintains its easy grade by crossing over itself at Williams Loop, a lesser-known counterpart to the famous Tehachapi Loop in Southern California.

WP IN THE TWENTIETH CENTURY

Despite the desirability of WP's route, business was painfully slow to materialize. WP purchased 112 steam locomotives to handle the anticipated traffic and promoted itself as best it could. But with no branch lines and few customers along the route, WP was headed toward its first bankruptcy. When it re-emerged in 1916, new president Charles Levey wisely expanded WP's influence, a process which would continue for 15 years. WP built a branch line to San Jose, purchased a line into Reno, Nevada, and took control of electric interurban lines Tidewater Southern and Sacramento Northern (sidebar).

In defiance of the Great Depression, WP completed its boldest and most important expansion in 1931: a remote and rugged 113-mile main line running north from Keddie to a connection with the Great Northern at Bieber, California. This Inside Gateway, also known as the Northern California Extension or simply the High Line, allowed GN, Western Pacific, and Santa Fe to compete with SP hauling freight between the Pacific Northwest and Southern California. But the circuitous route never seriously threatened SP's dominance, and four years later WP was bankrupt again. The High Line did, however, give the WP its most distinctive and immediately recognizable feature: The line joined the east-west main line high above Spanish

Train 17, the westbound *California Zephyr,* slithers up the Feather River Canyon at the height of the summer travel season in 1969. Huge boulders and rock piles belie the region's serenity—they have long been WP's nemesis in the 116-mile long canyon. Raging snow on Donner Pass to the south has stopped the CZ's one-time rival *City of San Francisco,* but rock slides and washouts have delayed (and on one occasion, derailed) the *Zephyr* in the spectacular Feather River Canyon. *Mike Schafer*

Creek, forming the dramatic, V-shaped trestle known as Keddie Wye.

Ironically, it was the tragedy of World War II which first brought prosperity to the WP. Freight and passenger business increased exponentially, and WP found itself in the unusual position of railroad innovator. Centralized Traffic Control was put into service through the canyon, and in 1942 WP became the second railroad in the nation, after the Santa Fe, to purchase diesel road-freight locomotives. This period of economic success and astute management lasted beyond the war years, when in the late 1940s, Western Pacific decided to take full advantage of another characteristic of the Feather River Route: its sublime beauty. WP replaced its mainstay standard steam train, the *Exposition Flyer*, with a streamlined, diesel-powered stainless-steel streamliner featuring five Vista-Dome cars. Like the *Exposition Flyer*, this new train—the famous *California Zephyr*—was a joint effort of the Chicago, Burlington & Quincy, the Denver & Rio Grande Western, and the WP. The train made full use of its five dome cars, its schedule between Chicago and Oakland timed to offer passengers daylight views of the Feather River Canyon and the Rocky Mountains.

The westbound *Feather River Express* is making its station stop at Sacramento in the 1940s. This local train provided day service between Oakland and Portola, the east end of the Feather River Canyon. In essence, the *California Zephyr* was placed on this train's time slot in both directions five years later between Oakland and Portola. *WP, Railfan & Railroad collection*

The westbound *Exposition Flyer* is in the middle of its afternoon stop at Winnemucca, Nevada, not long before the train was replaced with the new *California Zephyr* (as is evident, the *CZ*'s new diesels have already arrived and have been pressed into service). The train has spent most of the day crossing the deserts of Utah and Nevada after leaving Salt Lake City. The *CZ* would operate on a considerably different schedule, serving Winnemucca in the night hours. *Railfan & Railroad collection*

Burlington, Rio Grande, and Western Pacific provided seamless transport for passengers aboard their *California Zephyr*. All three roads owned cars in the *CZ* pool; all three supplied service crews on a rotation basis (for example., WP dining-car crews periodically worked through to Chicago). The train itself ran through from Chicago to Oakland with no changes required of passengers. Only engine changes occurred, at Denver and Salt Lake City, and usually they were accomplished quickly. Late on a July night in 1969 at Salt Lake City, Rio Grande (whose locomotives are visible at right) has handed the *CZ* off to WP for the remainder of the trip to California. *Mike Schafer*

For a time, the CZ had a companion train known as the *Zephyrette*. The service was provided by WP Budd-built Rail Diesel Cars, which covered the Oakland–Salt Lake City route at times more or less opposite of big sister *CZ*. Here, eastbound and westbound *Zephyrettes* meet not long before midnight at Merlin, California, in the Feather River Canyon. *Budd Company*

Though the *CZ* quickly lived up to its billing as "the most talked-about train in the country," the following decades saw fewer and fewer people talking about rail travel. Train No. 17, the westbound *CZ*, made its final journey on March 22, 1970, 21 years, almost to the day, after its inaugural run. On the WP as on so many other American railroads, the passenger trains which once symbolized the railroad's prosperity were now battered tokens of a battle lost to the airplane and the automobile. Yet, as of the year 2000, the *California Zephyr* still lived in the public mind as such a powerful emblem of luxurious travel that Amtrak adopted the name for its Chicago-Oakland service, even though the new *CZ* was now using the Overland Route!

Though the Western Pacific is best known for the *CZ* and the Feather River Canyon, it was a freight hauler before and after the *Zephyr*, and a railroad of great variety both east and west of the Canyon. Far from the cool spray of the Feather River, in the remote and arid landscape of western Utah and eastern Nevada, massive 4-6-6-4 steam locomotives hauled freight trains on WP's Eastern Division. While the western half of the WP has long been popular with railroad photographers, these coal-burning giants were seldom seen since WP ran only oil-fired locomotives west of Winnemucca, Nevada. WP purchased over 200 steam locomotives between 1909 and 1943, and retired the last of them in 1953. Today only five survive in museums around California.

West of the Central Valley, the 1 percent grades of Altamont Pass were the final obstacle for westbound trains on the WP main line. Upon arrival at the Port of Oakland, some of WP's freight cars floated across the bay to San Francisco on WP's fleet of tugs and car barges. As if surmounting the Sierra Nevada Range had not been trouble enough for the young WP, reaching the Oakland waterfront was a battle of a different sort. Southern Pacific was fiercely protective of what it believed were its exclusive rights to the port. In the middle of the night on January 5, 1906, WP track gangs hastily hammered together a track to the waterfront. SP's

Three of WP's four celebrated restored F-units that had survived into the late 1970s wind over Altamont Pass and SP's Altamont line (under bridge) between Oakland and Stockton, California, in May 1978. Leading the four-unit locomotive set that includes a road-switcher is F7A 913, which received a special orange-and-silver scheme that harkened to the *California Zephyr* era. *Ted Benson*

attorneys were livid, but WP successfully defended its rights in court, and Oakland had two railroads serving its waterfront. In 1957 WP spent $1 million on a modern self-propelled car ferry, the *Las Plumas*, which became a familiar sight on the bay with its sleek design and large orange feather. But 70 years after WP's forces stormed the beach on the Oakland mud flats, the prized access to San Francisco Bay had become a money-losing anachronism, as WP's isolated web of spur tracks in San Francisco served fewer and fewer customers. The *Las Plumas* was retired 20 years after its first voyage.

Though the 1960s had been lean years for the WP, the railroad entered a new era in 1970 under the leadership of Alfred Perlman and R. G. Flannery. Making the kinds of decisions which please investors and break the hearts of train enthusiasts—like eliminating the *California Zephyr*—Perlman initiated a decade of profitability, remarkable given WP's unstable history. But nostalgia and corporate shrewdness need not always be at odds. In 1977, WP was still operating four vintage F7 locomotives. To the delight of WP's fans, the railroad decided it would be cheaper to rebuild the "covered wagons" than to replace them after having encountered some mishaps. Three returned to service in WP's new standard green-and-orange livery, but the real celebrity was No. 913, which emerged in a modified version of the silver-and-orange *Zephyr* look, complete with the classic feather herald on the nose.

In 1979, WP unveiled a new corporate logo—a simplified, boxy version of the feather—and a "new image" paint scheme for the locomotives. Unfortunately, a new image is often the last effort of a company on the wane, and so it was on the Western Pacific. Deregulation had made it very difficult for smaller railroads to remain competitive. On December 22, 1982, WP became an early victim of the process which has led to four enormous corporations—UP, Burlington Northern Santa Fe, Norfolk Southern, and CSX—dominating the American railroad landscape. The F7s are long gone, and UP's Armour Yellow has replaced WP's orange and green.

To its credit, Union Pacific elevated the Feather River Route and its branch lines to world-class standards. The number of trains increased dramatically, and new heavier rail in the canyon allowed the trains to travel at higher speeds.

A similar good fate came to the High Line following its purchase by BNSF in 1997. BNSF's

WP's Interurban Subsidiaries

As WP's steam locomotives gave way to diesels, and jet airliners ended the reign of transcontinental passenger trains, the automobile had its greatest impact upon electric interurban lines. Still, a decade after the last WP steam engine chugged across the rugged deserts of the Eastern Division, electric steeple-cab locomotives continued shuffling cars on WP's subsidiary Sacramento Northern.

Built primarily to provide local passenger service between communities in a region, interurban railways flourished during the first three decades of the twentieth century. Interurbans were considered rivals by parallel steam railroads, but Western Pacific acquired control of two electric lines of note as a means of tapping additional traffic sources—the SN and Tidewater Southern.

Until SN discontinued passenger service in 1941, this fascinating railway offered the longest interurban ride in the country—nearly 200 miles. Boarding one of SN's interurban cars at the Transbay Terminal in San Francisco, a passenger would cross the Bay Bridge to Oakland, then wind through the dry grass and eucalyptus trees of the Oakland Hills down into the San Ramon Valley. At Pittsburg, California, the carferry *Ramon* carried the cars across the Sacramento River. Beyond, SN trains sped across the delta lands on trestles and levees toward its namesake city, then northward through the fertile Sacramento Valley to Chico.

When SN began scrapping its steeple-cab electrics in the 1950s, it acquired its own roster of diesel locomotives, painted in WP colors but lettered for Sacramento Northern. Gradually, several long segments of track were abandoned and SN became a collection of spurs reached via trackage rights on other railroads. One section, between Marysville and Yuba City, remained electrified until 1965.

Western Pacific's other electric railroad, the Tidewater Southern, evolved more successfully into the age of diesel-powered freight service. WP took control of the 46-mile route in 1917, gaining a connection at Stockton to the towns of Modesto and Turlock. Passenger service on the Tidewater fell victim to the Great Depression in 1932, but the wineries and fruit-packing sheds of the San Joaquin Valley nurtured the railroad into the current era.

Where interurban passenger trains had once rumbled through the streets, diesel-powered freights now ply the asphalt. In July 1969, a Sacramento Northern switcher wearing the colors of parent WP invades the streets of Yuba City. Until four years earlier, this route had been electrified. *Mike Schafer*

Though most closely associated with the Feather River Canyon, a large majority of WP's 924-mile Oakland–Salt Lake City main line crossed desert lands. An eastbound freight in March 1981 leaves the Sierra Range behind as it heads into Nevada at Flanigan. Mixed UP and WP locomotives are a portend of things to come; the following year, UP will merge WP into its system. *Brian Jennison*

Proudly sporting the feather emblem, a bright red WP caboose trails an intermodal train near Clio, California, in the fall of 1982. In all too short a time, not only will the WP have disappeared, but so will cabooses. *Mike Schafer*

upgrade of the route will allow it to claim its share of the lucrative container business between California and the Port of Seattle; perhaps the Inside Gateway was simply 70 years ahead of its time. In the 1960s and 1970s, GN's green-and-orange locomotives would occasionally journey south of Bieber and into the Feather River Canyon in the consist of WP trains. Then GN merged into the Burlington Northern, which in turn merged into the Burlington Northern Santa Fe. Today BNSF's dazzling green-and-orange locomotives, inspired by the historic GN livery, are regular visitors to UP's Canyon Subdivision on their way to and from the High Line at Keddie. Some things *don't* change.

Though UP has eliminated most traces of the Western Pacific, the landscape and its challenges remain. Hi-rail vehicles still precede trains through the canyon when landslides are likely, as they did on the Western Pacific. BNSF keeps a rotary snowplow parked at Westwood on the High Line, out of respect for the snows which can quickly bury the railroad. And train crews have inherited from their predecessors a terminology, understated yet definitive, which downplays the dangers and honors the uniqueness of the awesome Sierra landscape. The line over Donner Pass is still known as "The Hill," and the Feather River Route is simply "The Canyon."

Aglow in evening sun, Bieber-bound F-units and GP9s grind up the High Line a few miles north of Keddie in July 1969. This "Inside Gateway" route allowed Great Northern and WP to compete with the mighty Southern Pacific between Northern California and the Pacific Northwest. *Mike Schafer*

Index